# Advance Praise for *TIME POWER*

"Brian Tracy's principles on time productivity work! Using them, I have built a multi-million dollar business, dramatically reduced the hours I work per week, taken more time off, and enjoy more quality time with my wife and boys on a daily basis. In studying successful people for over 22 years, I have learned that there is one differentiating factor they have arrived at, and it's this: There is a difference between being busy and being productive.

**—Todd Duncan, author of *High Trust Selling***

"You have one life to live; read this book if you want to accomplish twice as much. Forget watching the clock. This book will make your competitors watch *you*."

**—Peter Montoya, President, Peter Montoya Inc.**

"Time is everything, because we only have 24 hours in a day. How you use it determines your success. For anyone who wants to do more in less time and accomplish bigger and better results, this is a must read."

**—Mitch Huhem,
President, Millionaires in Training, Inc. (MIT)**

"When it comes to managing your time, your priorities, and your life, Brian Tracy knows his stuff. Do what Brian Tracy advises you to do in *Time Power* and you are guaranteed to increase your income and your quality of life . . . significantly."

**—Bill Bachrach, CSP, author of *Values-Based Selling***

"*Time Power* is a must read for streamlining your entire life, so you get more of what you want. Make better decisions, execute with focus, and perform with excellence!"

**—Tony Jeary, "Mr. Presentation"™,
author of *Life Is a Series of Presentations***

# CHAPTER ONE

# The Psychology of Time Management

*"The mind is the limit. As long as the mind can envision the fact that you can do something, you can do it—as long as you believe 100 percent."*

—ARNOLD SCHWARZENEGGER

T he Law of Correspondence says that your outer life tends to be a mirror image of your inner life. Everywhere you look, there you are. Everywhere you look, you see yourself reflected back. You do not see the world as it is, but as you are— inside. If you want to change what is going on in the world around you—your relationships, results, and rewards—you have to change what is going on in the world *inside* you. Fortunately, this is the only part of your life over which you have complete control.

## The Starting Point of Success

The starting point of excelling in time management is *desire*. Almost everyone feels that their time management skills could imagine a happy, fulfilled person whose life is in a state of disorganization and disarray. The best discovery I made was that, when you develop the disciplines of time management, you simultaneously develop many of the other habits that lead to high achievement, wealth, and success in every part of your life.

The starting point of developing good time management skills is for you to realize that time management is really *life* management. It is the way you take care of your most precious gift. As Benjamin Franklin once said, *"Do you love life? Then do not squander time, for that's the stuff that life is made of."*

As you learn to master your time, you simultaneously master your life and take complete control over your future.

## A Handbook for High Performance

This book is designed to give you every tool that you will ever need to become excellent in time management in your career and personal life. As you read, think about how you could apply these ideas immediately. Underline key points and make notes. Implement the action exercises at the end of each chapter. Be prepared to read and review this book more than once if you wish to memorize and internalize these ideas permanently. Spaced repetition is essential to learning.

Once you master these skills, you will be ready for a lifetime of increased personal efficiency and high achievement. You will become a new person, with a new way of looking at life. You will get more done in less time than you ever thought possible. You will take complete control over your life.

*"When every physical and mental resource is focused, one's power to solve a problem multiplies tremendously."*

—NORMAN VINCENT PEALE

that give us pleasure and make us feel good about ourselves and our lives.

In the final analysis, we all want to be happy. We spend most of our lives searching for the combination of lifestyle ingredients, relationships, work, money, sports, hobbies, and other activities that will give us the deep-down feeling of happiness and well-being we seek. This book on time management is designed to give you hundreds of valuable ideas you can use immediately to organize your life and activities so that you can have more of the things that you want and need to achieve your own happiness.

## Time Management Is a Tool

Time management can be viewed as a *tool* with which you can build a great life, marked by high achievement and a tremendous feeling of satisfaction and accomplishment. Time management can be looked upon as a *vehicle* that can carry you from wherever you are to wherever you want to go. Time management can be seen as a set of *personal disciplines* that, once mastered, will enable you to be, have, and do anything you want or need to achieve whatever successes in life give you the greatest pleasure and happiness.

This book is the result of more than twenty years of research and teaching in the area of personal effectiveness, and it is based on my twenty-five years of experience in sales, marketing, management, and consulting in more than 500 corporations.

## The Common Denominator of Success

The more I studied success and successful people, the more obvious it became to me that they all had one thing in common. They all placed a very high value on their time, and they continually worked at becoming better organized and more efficient.

I eventually came to the conclusion that no success is possible without excellent time management skills. You cannot even

# Getting More Done Faster

*"Success is focusing the full power of all you are on what you have a burning desire to achieve."*

—WILFERD A. PETERSON

T hank you for reading this book. I know how busy you are, and even reading a book on time management is something that you seldom have the time to do. I promise you that in the pages ahead you will learn more practical and immediately usable ideas, methods, strategies, and techniques for getting more done faster than you ever have before. When you learn and apply these powerful, practical techniques, you will dramatically improve the quality of your life in every area.

Throughout the ages, the greatest minds of all time have dedicated themselves to answering the question, "How shall we live in order to be happy?" Sigmund Freud, the father of modern psychology, wrote that the primary motivation of human beings is the *pleasure principle,* the constant striving toward the things

# Contents

*To my great friends, colleagues, and partners—Duane Hendrickson, Steve Black, Gary Troy, Sherry Jackson, Mitch Huhem, and Drew Owens—all top business professionals who have helped me so much over the years: I thank you for everything. Your support and assistance have been indispensable to me.*

This publication is designed to provide accurate and authoritative
information in regard to the subject matter covered. It is sold with
the understanding that the publisher is not engaged in rendering
legal, accounting, or other professional service. If legal advice or
other expert assistance is required, the services of a competent
professional person should be sought.

Library of Congress Cataloging-in-Publication Data

Tracy, Brian.
    Time power : a proven system for getting more done in less time than
you ever thought possible / Brian Tracy.
      p.   cm.
    ISBN 0-8144-7247-8
    1. Time management.   I. Title.

HD69.T54T73   2004
650.1'1—dc22

                             2003025550

Printing number

10  9  8  7  6  5  4  3

# TIME POWER

## A Proven System for Getting More Done in Less Time Than You Ever Thought Possible

Brian Tracy

**AMACOM**

**American Management Association**

New York • Atlanta • Brussels • Chicago • Mexico City • San Francisco
Shanghai • Tokyo • Toronto • Washington, D.C.

be vastly better than they are. People resolve, over and over again, to get serious about time management by focusing, setting better priorities, and overcoming procrastination. They intend to get serious about time management sometime, but unfortunately, "the road to hell is paved with good intentions."

The key to motivation is "motive." For you to develop sufficient desire to develop Time Power, you must be intensely motivated by the benefits you feel you will enjoy. You must want the results badly enough to overcome the natural inertia that keeps you doing things the same old way. Here are four good reasons for practicing what you learn in this book. You can:

1. Gain two extra hours each day.

2. Improve your productivity and performance.

3. Increase your sense of control.

4. Have more time for your family.

## Gaining Two Extra Hours Each Day

You will gain at least two additional productive hours per day by practicing what you learn in this book. Just think of it! What could you do or accomplish if you had the gift of two extra working hours each day? What projects could you start and complete? What books could you write and publish? What subjects could you learn and master? What could you accomplish with two extra hours if you were able to focus and concentrate on completing high-value tasks?

Two extra hours per day, multiplied by five days per week, equals ten extra hours a week. Ten extra hours a week multiplied by fifty weeks a year would give you 500 extra productive hours each year. And 500 hours translates into more than twelve forty-hour weeks, or the equivalent of three extra months of productive working time each year.

By gaining two productive hours each day, you can transform

your personal and working life. You can achieve all your goals, vastly increase your income over the next two to three years, and eventually achieve financial independence, if not become rich.

## Improving Your Productivity and Performance

Your productivity, performance, and income will increase by at least 25 percent over the next year. Two more productive hours, out of the eight hours that you spend at work each day, is the equivalent of at least a 25 percent increase.

What you are earning today is what you are being paid today as a result of what you are producing today. If you increase your productivity by 25 percent or more, you must eventually earn and be paid 25 percent more. And if your current boss won't pay you for improved performance, some other boss will come along and gladly give you more money for your ability to produce greater results.

## Increasing Your Sense of Control

You will have more energy and less stress as you practice these ideas. When you leverage the power of time, you will have a greater sense of control over your work and your personal life. You will feel like the master of your own destiny, and a power in your own life. You will feel more positive and powerful in every part of your life.

Over the years, psychologists have done extensive research in the area of what is called "locus of control." They have discovered that you feel positive about yourself and your life to the degree to which you feel in charge of your life; you have an "internal" locus of control. With an internal locus of control, you feel that your life is in your own hands. You make your own decisions, and you are responsible for your own actions and outcomes. You are the primary creative force in your own life.

Psychologists have also found that if you have an "external" locus of control, in that you feel that you are controlled by people and circumstances outside of yourself, such as your boss, your bills, your family, your health, or some other factor, you will feel negative, angry, and often depressed. You will feel frustrated and unable to change. You will develop what is called "learned helplessness" and see yourself more as a "creature of circumstances" rather than a "creator of circumstances." When you have an external locus of control, you feel that you are a prisoner of external forces. You often see yourself as a victim.

### *Take Control of Your Time and Your Life*
One of the keys to developing a stronger internal locus of control is to manage your time and your life better. The more skilled you become at managing your time, the happier and more confident you will feel. You will have a stronger sense of personal power. You will feel in charge of your own destiny. You will have a greater sense of well-being. You will be more positive and personable.

### Having More Time for Your Family
You will have more time for your family and your personal life as you get your time and your life under control. You will have more time for your friends, for relaxation, for personal and professional development, and for anything else you want to do.

When you become the master of your own time, and recapture two extra hours per day, you can use that extra time to run a marathon, complete a college degree, write a book, build a business, and create an outstanding life. With two extra hours a day, you can put your life and career onto the fast track and begin moving ahead at a more rapid rate than you ever thought possible.

## The Three Mental Barriers to Time Power

If everyone agrees that excellent time management is a desirable skill, why is it that so few people can be described as "well organized, effective, and efficient"? Over the years, I have found that many people have ideas about time management that are simply not true. But if you *believe* something to be true, it becomes true for you. Your beliefs cause you to see yourself and the world, and your relationship to time management, in a particular way. If you have negative beliefs in any area, these beliefs will affect your thinking and actions, and will eventually become your reality. You are not what you think you are, but what you *think*, you are.

## Barrier 1: Worries About Decreasing Your Naturalness and Spontaneity

The first myth, or negative belief, of time management is that if you are too well organized, you become cold, calculating, and unemotional. Some people feel that they will lose their spontaneity and freedom if they are extremely effective and efficient. They will become unable to "go with the flow," to express themselves openly and honestly. People think that managing your time well makes you too rigid and inflexible.

This turns out not to be true at all. Many people hide behind this false idea and use it as an excuse for not disciplining themselves the way they know they should. The fact is that people who are disorganized are not spontaneous; they are merely confused, and often frantic. Often they suffer a good deal of stress. It turns out that the better organized you are, the more time and opportunity you have to be truly relaxed, truly spontaneous, and truly happy. You have a much greater internal locus of control.

The key is structuring and organizing everything that you possibly can: Thinking ahead; planning for contingencies; preparing thoroughly; and focusing on specific results. Only then can you be completely relaxed and spontaneous when the situation changes. The better organized you are in the factors that are under your control, the greater freedom and flexibility you have to quickly make changes whenever they are necessary.

## Barrier 2: Negative Mental Programming

The second mental barrier to developing excellent time management skills is negative programming, which is often picked up
from your parents, but also from other influential people as you
are growing up. If your parents or others told you that you were
a messy person, or that you were always late, or that you never
finished anything you started, chances are that as an adult, you
may still be operating unconsciously to obey these earlier commands.

The most common excuse used for this type of behavior is:
"That's just the way I am," or "I have always been that way."
The fact is that no one is born messy and disorganized, or neat
and efficient. Time management and personal efficiency skills
are disciplines that we learn and develop with practice and repetition. If we have developed bad time management habits, we
can *unlearn* them. We can replace them with good habits over
time.

## Barrier 3: Self-Limiting Beliefs

The third mental barrier to good time management skills is a
negative self-concept, or what are called "self-limiting beliefs."
Many people believe that they don't have the ability to be good
at time management. They often believe that it is an inborn part
of their background or heritage. But there is no gene or chromo-
some for poor time management, or good time management, for
that matter. Nobody is born with a genetic deficiency in personal
organization. Your personal behaviors are very much under your
own control.

Here is an example to prove that most of what you do is
determined by your level of motivation and desire in that area.
Imagine that someone were to offer you a million dollars to manage your time superbly for the next thirty days. Imagine that an
efficiency expert was going to follow you around with a clip-
board and a video camera for one month. After thirty days, if you

had used your time efficiently and well, working on your highest priorities all day, every day, you would receive a prize of one million dollars. How efficient would you be over the next thirty days?

The fact is that, with sufficient motivation (one million dollars!), you would be one of the most efficient, effective, best-organized, and focused people in the world. The best news is that after one full month of practicing the very best time management skills you know, you would have developed habits of high productivity and top performance that would last you the rest of your life.

## You Are Free to Choose

Time management behaviors are very much a matter of choice. You choose to be efficient or you choose to be disorganized. You choose to focus and concentrate on your highest-value tasks, or you choose to spend your time on activities that contribute little value to your life. And you are always free to choose.

The starting point of overcoming your previous programming and eliminating the mental blocks to time management is for you to make a clear, unequivocal decision to become absolutely excellent at the way you use your time, minute by minute and hour by hour. You must decide, right here and now, that you are going to become an expert in time management. Your aim should be to manage your time so well that people look up to you and use you as a role model for their own work habits.

### Program Yourself for Effectiveness and Efficiency

There are several mental techniques that you can use to program yourself for peak performance.

#### Use Positive Self-Talk

The first of these methods for programming your subconscious mind is positive self-talk, or the use of *positive affirmations*.

These are commands that you pass from your conscious mind to your subconscious mind. Affirmations are statements that you either say out loud or say to yourself with the emotion and enthusiasm that drives the words into your subconscious mind as new operating instructions. Here are some examples of affirmative commands that you can use to improve your time management skills.

Begin by repeating over and over to yourself, "I am excellent at time management! I am excellent at time management!" Any command repeated again and again in a spirit of faith, acceptance, and belief will eventually be accepted by your subconscious mind. Your subconscious mind will then organize your words, actions, and feelings to be consistent with these new commands.

You can continually repeat, "I am always punctual for my appointments! I am always punctual for my appointments!" You can create your own mental commands, such as "I am well organized!" or "I concentrate easily on my highest payoff tasks!" My favorite time management affirmation is to repeat continually, "I use my time well. I use my time well. I use my time well." Used consistently, positive affirmations will start to influence your external behaviors.

### Visualize Yourself as Highly Efficient
The second technique that you can use to program your subconscious mind is *visualization*. Your subconscious mind is most immediately influenced by mental pictures. In self-image psychology, the person you *see* is the person you will *be*. Begin to see yourself as someone who is well organized, efficient, and effective. Recall and recreate memories and pictures of yourself when you were performing at your best. Think of a time when you were working efficiently and effectively and getting through an enormous amount of work. Play this picture of yourself over and over again on the screen of your mind.

In athletic training, this is called "mental rehearsal." This requires practicing and rehearsing actions in your mind before you actually engage in the physical activity. The more relaxed you are when you visualize yourself performing at your best, the more rapidly this command is accepted by your subconscious mind and becomes a part of your thinking and behavior later on.

THE PRACTICE OF MENTAL REHEARSAL

The method is simple. First, sit or lie in a quiet place where you can be completely alone in the silence. Then imagine yourself going through an important upcoming experience, such as a meeting, a presentation, a negotiation, or even a date. As you sit or lie completely relaxed, create a picture of the coming event and see it unfolding perfectly in every respect. See yourself as calm, positive, happy, and in complete control. See the other people doing and saying exactly what you would want them to do if the situation was perfect. Then, breathe deeply, relax, and just let it go, as if you had sent off an order and the delivery is guaranteed, exactly as you pictured it.

The best time to practice mental rehearsal is at night in bed, just before you fall asleep. The last thing you should do before you doze off is to imagine yourself performing at your best the following day. You will be amazed at how often the upcoming event or experience happens exactly as you visualized it.

In becoming excellent at time management, it's important to practice mental rehearsal by continually seeing yourself as you would be if you were one of the best-organized and most efficient people you could imagine. Eventually these pictures will "lock in." When they do, you will find yourself easily and automatically using your time efficiently in everything you do.

### Act the Part

The third mental technique you can use to program your subconscious mind for efficiency and effectiveness is to act the part of a highly efficient person. Imagine that you have been selected for a role in a movie or stage play. In this role, you are to act the part of a person who is extremely well organized in every re-spect. As you go through your daily life, imagine you are an actor who is playing this part, who is already very good at time man-agement. Act as if you are already using your time efficiently and well.

Pretend that you are an expert in personal efficiency. Fake it until you make it. When you pretend that you are an excellent time manager, eventually your actions, which are under your di-rect control, will foster a mind-set, or the belief in your subcon-scious mind, that is consistent with it.

### *Benchmark Against the Best*
The fourth mental technique you can use for becoming a highly efficient person is called "modeling." Modeling requires you to pattern yourself after someone you know who uses his time well. Think of someone you admire for good time management skills. Use that person as your standard or your model. Imagine what he would do in any given situation, and then do it yourself.

Many of the most effective men and women in America reached their positions by modeling themselves in their earlier years after someone who was already extremely effective, some-one they admired and respected for qualities they wanted to de-velop in themselves. Because of the Law of Correspondence, you always tend to become on the inside what you most admire in other people.

### *Become a Teacher*
The fifth technique for programming your subconscious mind is to imagine that you are going to be teaching a course in time management one year from today. This technique comes from discoveries in the field of accelerated learning. What the experts have found is that if you think about how you would *teach* new material at the same time you are *learning* the new material, you seem to absorb it and internalize it far faster than if you just thought about learning it and using it for yourself.

As you take in these new ideas on time management, think of how you would teach them to someone else. Think of someone in your life who could benefit from practicing what you are learning. Just as you become what you think about, you also become what you teach. Just thinking about teaching something to someone else increases the speed at which you learn it yourself. And you always think about teaching those things that you most want or need to learn for yourself.

One of the fastest ways to learn new ideas and techniques permanently is to share them with other people immediately after you learn them. Each time you come across a good idea in this book, take a few moments to share it with someone nearby, either at home or at work. The concentration you require to explain the new principle in your own words to another person seems to drive the information deeper into your subconscious mind where it becomes a permanent part of your long-term memory.

### Be a Role Model for Others

The sixth technique you can use to program your subconscious mind is to imagine that others are looking up to you as an example of excellence in time management. Imagine that you are setting the standard in your company or your organization. Imagine that everyone is looking to you for guidance on how they should plan and organize their own time. If others were watching you, what would you do differently each day? How would you behave in your daily work? How would you organize your time if you felt that everyone was looking up at you to set the standard, to be the role model?

When you see yourself as a model, an example of excellent performance, you will always do better and accomplish more than if you just thought of yourself as personally trying to be more efficient. The more you think about yourself as an excellent time manager, the more excellent you become. The more you see yourself as a role model for others, the better you become in organizing your own time and life.

# Your Self-Esteem Determines Your Life

Perhaps the most important part of the psychology of time management, and the role that your self-concept has in determining your performance and behavior, is the impact of your *self-esteem* in determining everything that happens to you.

Most psychologists agree that self-esteem is the critical determinant of a healthy personality. The best definition of self-esteem is "how much you like yourself." When you like and respect yourself, you always perform and behave better than if you do not. The more you like yourself, the more confidence you have. Self-esteem is the key to peak performance.

Your self-esteem is so important to your emotional health that almost everything you do is aimed at either increasing your feelings of self-esteem and personal value, or protecting it from being diminished by other people or circumstances. Self-esteem is the founding principle of success and happiness. It is vital for you to feel fully alive.

## The Key to Peak Performance

The flip side of self-esteem is called *self-efficacy*. This is defined as how effective you feel you are at doing or accomplishing a task or job. When you feel that you are really good at something, you experience positive feelings of self-efficacy.

One of the greatest discoveries in psychology was the uncovering of the connection between self-esteem and self-efficacy. Now we know that the more you like yourself, the better you do at almost anything you attempt. And the better you do at something, the more you like yourself. Self-esteem and self-efficacy feed on and reinforce each other. This finding is what makes time management so important for every part of your life. The better you use your time, the more you get done and the higher is your sense of self-efficacy. As a result, you like yourself more, do even higher-quality work, and get even more done. Your whole life improves.

## Three Self-Esteem Builders
There are three additional factors that affect your self-esteem that have to do with time management. These are:

1. Determining your values

2. Striving for mastery

3. Knowing what you want

### *Determining Your Values*
Living your life in a manner consistent with your deepest values is essential in order for you to enjoy high self-esteem. People who are clear on what they believe in and value, and who refuse to compromise their values, like and respect themselves far more than people who are unclear about what matters to them.

This immediately brings up the question, "How much do you value your life?" People who truly value their lives are people who highly value themselves. People who value themselves highly use their time well. They know that their time is their life.

The Law of Reversibility says that feelings and actions interact on each other. If you feel a certain way, you will act in a manner consistent with what you're feeling. However, the reverse is also true. If you act in a certain way, your actions will create within you the feelings that are consistent with them. This means that when you act as if your time was extremely valuable, the action causes you to feel like a more valuable and important person. By managing your time well, you actually increase your self-esteem and, by extension, you become better at whatever you are doing.

The very act of living your life consistent with your values, and using your time effectively and well, improves your self-image, builds your self-esteem and self-confidence, and increases your self-respect.

### *Striving for Mastery*

The second factor that affects your self-esteem is your sense of being in control of your life and work—your feeling of mastery in whatever you do.

Everything that you learn about time management, and then apply in your work, causes you to feel more in control of yourself and your life. As a result, you feel more effective and efficient. You feel more productive and powerful. Every increase in your feeling of effectiveness and productivity increases your self-esteem and improves your sense of personal well-being.

### *Knowing What You Want*

The third factor that directly affects your self-esteem involves your current goals and the activities that you take to achieve those goals. The more your goals and your activities are congruent with your values, the better you feel. When you are working at something that you believe in, and that is consistent with your natural talents and abilities, you like yourself more and you do your work better. We will talk about goals in greater depth in the Chapter 2.

## Three Steps to Performance Improvement

These, then, are the three keys to the psychology of time management. First, you determine your values, and then you resolve to live your life consistent with those values. Second, you dedicate yourself to mastery, to becoming absolutely excellent at what you do. Third, you make sure that your goals and activities are congruent with your true values and convictions.

When you do these three things, and manage your time well in the pursuit of value-based goals, you feel terrific about yourself all day long. You will have more energy and enthusiasm.

You will be more confident and committed. You will be more competent and creative. You will become more persistent and determined.

When you manage your time well, you will get more done, and what you accomplish will be of a higher quality. You will enjoy higher levels of self-esteem and self-respect. You will have a greater sense of personal pride. Practicing good time management techniques will even have a positive effect on your personality and your relationships.

The quality of your life is largely determined by the quality of your time management. The better and more effective you are at managing the minutes and hours of your day, which are the building blocks of your life, the more you will like and respect yourself, and the better will be every aspect of your inner and outer life.

## Twelve Proven Principles for Peak Performance

Here are twelve proven principles you can practice every day to get more out of yourself and improve your results in everything you do.

*Principle 1. Time management enables you to increase the value of your contribution.* Self-esteem comes from the knowledge that you are putting more into your life and work than you are taking out, that you are contributing more to your work than you are getting back. The greater the contribution you feel that you are making to your company and to your family, the greater will be your self-esteem. Good time management enables you to greatly improve your ability to contribute more and more value to whatever you are doing.

*Principle 2. Your rewards, both tangible and intangible, will always be equal to the value of your service to other people.*

The more you put in, the more you get out. Through the Law of Sowing and Reaping, time management allows you to sow more and better, and therefore to reap more and better in every area of your life. If you want to increase the quality and quantity of your rewards, you need only seek ways to increase the value of your service. This is very much under your control.

*Principle 3. Good time management requires that you see yourself as a "factory."* A factory has three phases of production. First of all, it has inputs of raw materials, time, labor, money, and resources. These are the "factors of production" that are necessary to create the end-product.

Second, inside the factory there are activities that take place. These are the production activities or work that are necessary to produce the product or service. The efficiency of operations within the factory determines the productivity of the factory and the productivity of each person involved in the production process.

Third, what emerges from the factory are the outputs or production of the factory. The value of the factory is determined by the quality and quantity of its outputs relative to its inputs. The central purpose of the management of the factory is to increase the quality and quantity of outputs.

One main difference between highly effective people and people who seem to produce very little is that top performers always focus on outputs or results. Average performers focus on inputs. Top performers focus on accomplishments; medium or low performers focus on activities.

Good time management requires that you continually ask yourself: What outputs are expected of me? What am I expected to produce? Why, exactly, am I on the payroll?

The more you focus on the required outputs of your position, the better and more effective you will become. As a result, you will create greater value and make a more important contribution. You will become more productive and, therefore, more valuable to yourself and to your company.

*Principle 4. Everything you accomplish, or fail to accomplish, depends on your ability to use your time to its best advantage.* Your levels of achievement and performance, in every area, are determined by your ability to think through and to apply the very best time management techniques available to you. You can only increase the quality and quantity of your results by increasing your ability to use your time effectively.

*Principle 5. Time is the scarcest resource of accomplishment.* In America today, the biggest problem most people have is "time poverty." People may have money and material success, but they don't have enough time to enjoy them. We are short of time in almost every area of our lives.

Time is inelastic; it cannot be stretched. Time is indispensable; all work and accomplishment requires it. Time is irreplaceable; there is no substitute for it. And time is perishable; it cannot be saved, preserved, or stored. Once it is gone, it is gone forever.

*Principle 6. The practice of time management skills allows you to develop judgment, foresight, self-reliance, and self-discipline.* These are the qualities of leadership and character. It is time management that enables you to get things done, and your ability to accomplish the tasks that are assigned to you is the chief measure of your value to your company, and to your world.

*Principle 7. A focus on time management forces you to be intensely results-oriented.* Results orientation is the key quality of successful men and women. Your ability to focus single-mindedly on the most important results required of you is the fastest and surest way to get paid more, promoted faster, and to eventually achieve financial independence.

*Principle 8. Time management enables you to work smarter, not just harder.* Many people who are failures actually work harder than successful people. But they produce less in the hours they work because of poor personal and time management skills.

*Principle 9. Good time management is a source of energy, enthusiasm, and a positive mental attitude.* The more productive you become, the more positive you feel about yourself. As you see yourself accomplishing large quantities of work, you actually experience a continuous inflow of additional energy that enables you to accomplish even more.

*Principle 10. You grow as a person in direct proportion to the demands that you place on yourself.* The self-discipline of time management builds character, confidence, and an unshakable belief in yourself and your abilities.

*Principle 11. Lasting motivation only comes from a feeling of achievement and accomplishment.* The more you get done, the better you feel about yourself, and the more eager you become to do even more.

*Principle 12. Now, this minute, is all the time you have.* If you manage yourself minute by minute, the hours and days will take care of themselves. The more tightly you manage your time, the more you are guaranteed that it will translate into a great life that's hallmarked by purpose, power, control, and worthwhile accomplishments.

## The Seven Practices of Time Power

There are seven methods that you can use to help develop the habits of time management. The more you think about and practice these methods, the more rapidly you will program yourself to be efficient, effective, and highly productive.

First, remember that *your self-image determines your performance.* You always perform on the outside in a manner consistent with the picture you have of yourself on the inside. Practice visualizing and imagining yourself as you want to be, not as you may have been in the past.

You can actually change your self-image permanently by repeatedly visualizing yourself as someone who is highly efficient and effective. See yourself as absolutely excellent in time and personal management skills. Play this picture over and over again in your mind's eye until it is accepted as a new set of commands by your subconscious. At that point, effective time management will become easy and automatic for you.

Second, remember that *it takes about twenty-one days of practice and repetition to form a new habit pattern.* It has taken you your entire lifetime to become the person you are today, with the time management habits you have at this moment. It takes time and commitment to change, and for your subconscious mind to accept the new commands, pictures, and affirmations as your new operating instructions for your personal behavior. Be patient with yourself. Don't expect to change everything at once.

Third, *promise yourself that you are going to become excellent at time management.* Promise yourself that you are going to be punctual, and that you are going to concentrate on your most important tasks. Then, promise others that you are going to be more effective and efficient in the future.

When you tell others, and promise others, that you are going to become better at the way you use your time, it makes it easier for you to make a firm commitment to yourself to follow through on these behaviors. When you know that other people are watching to see if you will do what you said you would, you tend to be far more disciplined and firm with yourself.

Fourth, in developing the habits of time management, *start in just one area where poor time management is holding you back.* Don't try to change everything at once. Change just one habit or activity where you know that improvement could be very helpful to you. As you discipline yourself to improve in a single area, you will find yourself becoming more productive in other areas at the same time.

Fifth, *launch your new time management habit strongly.* Never allow an exception once you have decided that you are going to become excellent in a particular behavior. If you decide to be punctual for every appointment, discipline yourself to be early every single time until the new habit of punctuality becomes a permanent part of your behavior. If you decide to start early and concentrate on your most valuable tasks, discipline yourself to do this every single day for at least three weeks until it becomes easy and natural for you to start early on your highest priority. Never let yourself off the hook. Never make excuses or rationalizations for slacking off. Resolve to repeat the new behavior every time until the new habit is firmly entrenched.

Sixth, *use the "trial and success" method* rather than the "trial and error" method. The trial and success method requires that you learn how to succeed by failing, and then by learning from your mistakes.

Analyze your reasons for poor time management. Stand back and look at the areas in your life where your time is the most poorly managed and ask yourself, "Why do I behave this way in this area?"

Ask yourself, "What are the obstacles to my operating more efficiently in this area?" Take some time to reflect on your current behaviors. This will give you the awareness to make the changes that you need to make to be the efficient and effective person that you are capable of becoming.

Seventh, and perhaps the most important of all, is for you to absolutely *believe that you can and will become outstanding at time management.*

The Law of Belief says that "Your beliefs become your realities." The more intensely you believe that you can and will become excellent at time management, the more rapidly this belief becomes your reality. If you hold to your belief long enough and hard enough, it will eventually materialize as new behaviors with regard to time.

The good news is that time management is a skill, like typing or riding a bike. Like any other skill, it is learnable with practice and repetition. You have the ability, right now, to develop the habits of excellent time management in every area of your life. It is simply a matter of getting started, then persisting until your new time management habits are permanent.

Time management is your key to personal effectiveness, self-esteem, self-respect, and greater personal productivity and happiness. With time management, you can overcome any obstacle and achieve any goal. With excellent time management skills, you can take complete control over your life and your future. Time management is your key to unlimited success.

*"You are searching for the magic key that will unlock the door to the source of power; and yet you have the key in your own hands, and you may make use of it the moment you learn to control your thoughts."*

—NAPOLEON HILL

## Action Exercises

1. Select one area where better time management skills can help you to be more effective and get more done. Resolve to go to work on yourself in that area immediately.

2. Think back on a time when you were performing at your best. Recall and replay the picture of this experience in your mind whenever you approach a new task.

3. Talk to yourself positively all the time. Repeat affirmations such as, "I use my time efficiently and well!"

4. Imagine that everyone around you is looking up to you as the role model of personal efficiency, and that they are going to organize their days the way you organize yours. Act accordingly.

5. Think about teaching a course in time management to your friends and colleagues. What would be the most important things you would want to teach them?

6. Determine the areas of your work that give you the most satisfaction, and make plans to become even more productive in those areas.

7. Resolve today that you are going to work and practice until you become one of the most efficient, effective, and productive people in your field. Take action immediately on your resolution.

CHAPTER TWO

# Mastering Time Through Goals and Objectives

*"You too can determine what you want. You can decide on your major objectives, targets, aims, and destination."*

—W. CLEMENT STONE

The most important word in personal effectiveness is the word *clarity*. The starting point of *Time Power* is for you to develop absolute clarity about your goals and objectives. The most common time waster and biggest obstacle to success in life is losing sight of what you are trying to accomplish, or forgetting what you set out to do. In *The Devil's Dictionary,* author Ambrose Bierce wrote, "Fanaticism is redoubling your efforts after your aim has been forgotten." Many people are working hard every day, but they have no clear idea of their real goals and objectives.

Time management, more than anything else, requires you to plan and organize your time in such a way that you accomplish your most important goals as quickly as possible. Organizing your goals and objectives clearly, and by priority, and then working with single-minded focus on the most important things you can possibly do to achieve them, is the key to using your time effectively and well.

## Join the Top 3 Percent

As it happens, fewer than 3 percent of people have clear, written goals, and they are usually the most successful in every field. Less than one percent of people rewrite and review their goals on a regular basis. In an article I wrote for a national publication in 1990, the publisher highlighted the words, "If you do not have goals for yourself, you are doomed forever to work for someone else."

That is just as true today as it was then.

In your career, you can work to achieve your own goals, or you can work to achieve the goals of another person or company. The very best situation occurs when you are achieving the goals of your company or organization while you are achieving your own personal goals. But in every case, you are always working to achieve goals of one kind or another.

## The Master Skill of Success

Goal setting is the master skill of success. Your ability to clearly and systematically create goals, and to make plans for their accomplishment, will help you to achieve success and happiness more than any other skill you can develop.

Goal setting is not complicated. It begins with a pad of paper, a pen, and you. Writing your goals down changes your life, sometimes in dramatic and unexpected ways. As motivational speaker Zig Ziglar says, "Written goals transform you from a *wandering generality* into a *meaningful specific*."

The very act of committing your goals to paper programs them into your subconscious. Your subconscious mind, in combination with your *superconscious* mind, then goes to work on your goals twenty-four hours a day, even while you are sleeping. You begin to attract people and circumstances into your life in harmony with your goals. You get ideas and insights that can help you. You come across articles and books with solutions to your problems. You begin to experience a flow of energy and excitement that drives you forward.

Until you have practiced goal setting on a regular basis, you may be skeptical about its power to change your life. But after you have tried it, along the lines I'll discuss here, you will be convinced. Your whole life will change.

## Increase Your Achievement Rate Exponentially

In February 2003, *USA Today* ran an article discussing New Year's resolutions. One year before, the newspaper had interviewed people about their resolutions for 2002. It divided the respondents into two categories: those who had written down their resolutions and those who had just thought about them.

One year later, only 4 percent of the people who had made resolutions, but not written them down, had made any changes. But 46 percent of those who had written down their resolutions had followed through on them. This is a difference of 1,100 percent in the rate of success and achievement explainable by the simple act of writing the resolution down on paper.

## Essential Goal-Setting Principles

There are several essential principles of goal setting that dramatically affect the speed at which you achieve your goals. These are principles that you can return to and practice repeatedly for the rest of your career.

## Principle 1: Dream Big Dreams!

Only big dreams have the power to motivate and inspire you toward the fulfillment of your full potential. Only big dreams liberate your imagination and energy, and give you the drive to overcome the obstacles and difficulties that you will experience on the path to your goal. Only big dreams can keep you excited and working enthusiastically every day toward their accomplishment.

When you set goals, practice *idealization*. Imagine that you have no limitations on what you can do, have, or be. Imagine your goal as if it were perfect in every respect when you set it in the first place. Don't allow yourself to think of all the reasons why it may not be possible for you to achieve this goal at this time. Put those mental roadblocks and excuses aside. Set your goal as though you could achieve anything you want, as long as you are perfectly clear about what it is.

## Principle 2: Write Your Goals in the Present Tense

Your goals must be in writing, in the present tense, as though they already exist. Your subconscious only accepts commands that are worded in the present tense, such as, "I weigh 150 pounds," or "I earn $100,000 per year," or "I live in a beautiful, 3,500-square-foot, custom-designed home." Each of these goals begins with the word "I" and is followed by an action verb. This is the fastest and most direct way to activate your subconscious mind and harness your superconscious powers.

Positive, present-tense goals program your subconscious and build faith and conviction that your goal is realizable. The more often you read and repeat your goal, the deeper you program it into your mind, and the sooner you begin to become absolutely convinced that you will attain this goal, exactly when the timing is right for you.

### Rewrite Your Goals Daily

My favorite technique for programming my goals deep into my subconscious mind is to rewrite my goals in the present tense each day in a spiral notebook. I learned this technique many years ago. I was absolutely astonished at the speed at which my life began to improve when I began to rewrite my goals each day.

The best time to rewrite your goals is first thing in the morning, before you start your day. This exercise only takes about five minutes, but writing out your goals activates all your mental powers so that throughout the day, you will be more sensitive and aware to possibilities and opportunities to achieve those goals.

### Affirm Your Goals Regularly

There is a wonderful technique for goal attainment called the Standard Affirmation Technique. To use this method, you get a stack of three- by five-inch index cards and write out your goals in the present tense, one per card, in large letters.

Each day, and throughout the day, take out your stack of goal cards and review them, one at a time. As you read each goal, concentrate on the words on the card as though you were trying to photograph them with the lenses of your eyes. Think about one or more things you could do to achieve that goal. Then go on to the next card.

When you combine the two methods, writing and rewriting your goals daily in a notebook, and regularly reviewing them on index cards, you begin to believe that these goals are achievable. You eventually convince yourself at a deep subconscious level that the attainment of these goals is *inevitable*. As you become more and more confident that your goals will soon become realities, you begin to move faster toward them, and they start to move faster toward you. You activate more of your mental powers. When you practice either one or both of these methods for thirty days, you will be astonished at the changes that will take place in your life.

## Principle 3: Keep Your Goals in Balance

Your goals must be in balance and cover the three most important areas of your life. They must be in harmony with each other, not contradictory. Just as a wheel must be perfectly balanced to rotate smoothly, your life must be in balance as well for you to feel happy and effective.

### *What Do You Really Want?*

The first types of goals you need are business, career, and financial goals. These are the tangible, measurable things that you want to achieve as the result of your efforts at work. These are the "what" that you want to accomplish in life. With these tangible goals, you must be absolutely clear about how much you want to earn, and in what time period you want to earn it. You must be clear about how much you want to save, invest, and accumulate, and when you want to acquire these amounts. Remember, you can't hit a target that you can't see.

### *Why Do You Want to Achieve Your Goals?*

The second types of goals you need are your personal, family, and health goals. In reality, these are the most important goals of all in determining your happiness and well-being. These are called the "why" goals because they are the reasons you want to achieve your business, career, and financial goals. They are your true aim and purpose in life.

Many people become so involved with their work and careers, and their financial goals, that they lose sight of the reasons why they wanted financial success in the first place. They get their priorities mixed up. As a result, their lives get out of balance. They start to feel stressed and driven. Sometimes they become angry and frustrated. No matter how hard they work to achieve business and financial goals, they don't seem to enjoy any more peace, happiness, and satisfaction in life. They need to get their goals back in the right order of priority and realize that achieving work and financial goals are the means to the end of enjoying family and relationship goals. They are not the ends in themselves.

### How Do You Achieve Your Goals?

The third types of goals you require are your personal and professional growth and development goals. These are the "how" goals. Learning and practicing new skills and behaviors are how you achieve the "what" in order to enjoy the "why." By working on yourself, you become the kind of person who is capable of achieving your business, career, and financial goals. As a result, you can achieve and enjoy your personal, family, and health goals faster and easier. By working on all three types of goals simultaneously, you keep your life in balance and continue moving onward and upward.

## Principle 4: Know Your Major Definite Purpose

You must decide what your "major definite purpose" is. This is the one goal in your life that is more important than any other. This is the one goal that, if accomplished, will allow you to attain more of your other goals.

The selection of a major definite purpose for your life is the starting point of great success. This decision enables you to focus and concentrate your mental and physical energies on a single point, the one that can have the greatest positive impact on your life at this time. Deciding upon your major definite purpose, at each stage of your life, is one of the major responsibilities of adulthood.

# How to Decide What You Really Want

There are several questions that you can ask yourself to help you determine your major definite purpose. These questions force you to think through who you are and what you really want to do with your life.

• *What would you do differently, or how would you change your life, if you won a million dollars in the lottery tomorrow?* If you became an instant millionaire, tax free, what would you do differently in your life from what you are doing today? What would you start doing that you are not doing right now? What would you stop doing? What would you do more or less of? Where would you go? Who would you see? What is the first change that you would make if you had a million dollars in cash in your hands right now?

Asking this question of yourself helps you to clarify what you really want in life. Most people hold themselves back and sell themselves short because they feel that they are limited or trapped financially. Because of this feeling of limitation, they never sit down and think through what it is they really want. They develop self-limiting beliefs. They begin to see themselves as victims. According to Dr. Martin Seligman of the University of Pennsylvania, they develop "learned helplessness." They feel that they are helpless and unable to change their situations because of their lack of money.

But when you ask yourself what you would do if you had a million dollars, you are really asking what you would do if you had *no fears of failure*. You are forcing yourself to decide how you would live your life if you had all the money that you really wanted. By imagining yourself free of financial worries, your mind clears and you see what you really want to be, have, and do in the months and years ahead.

• *If you could write your own biography, what would it say?* Project yourself forward to the end of your life, and imagine writing your own biography. If you could design your life in advance, and write your own story, what would you want to happen in your life? What kind of a person do you want to become? What sort of things do you want to achieve? Imagine that you could write the script of your own life, and if you were not happy with the script, you could tear it up and write a new one.

Imagine that you could write your own eulogy, to be read to your friends and relatives at your funeral. What would you want it to say? What would you want people to think about you after you pass away? How do you want to be remembered by the most important people in your life?

When you ask these questions, and imagine writing your own life story, or your own obituary, you free up your mind to see what is really important to you. You develop a "long-term perspective" and begin to become clear about what you *really* want to accomplish with your life.

• *What one great goal would you dare to set for yourself if you knew you could not fail?* If you were absolutely guaranteed of success in any goal, short-term or long-term, big or small, what one goal would you commit yourself to accomplishing?

Your mind is remarkable. Something amazing happens between your head and your hand. The very fact that you can write out a goal clearly on paper means that you have the ability to achieve it somehow. Your desire is the only real limit on your potential. The only question is, "How badly do you want it?"

Your ability to identify the one great goal that you would dare to commit yourself to if you were guaranteed of success is very often the best single indicator of your major definite purpose. This is the one goal you are meant to accomplish and that can have the most positive impact on your life.

• *What do you really love to do, at home or at work?* What gives you your greatest feeling of importance? What accomplishments give you your greatest sense of achievement and satisfaction? If you could only do one thing all day long, what one task or activity would it be?

Psychologists have discovered that the activities that give you your greatest feelings of self-esteem are usually the tasks or activities that you are ideally suited to do as a life's work. You will always love to do the things that you are most likely to have the natural talents and abilities to do extremely well. Organizing your life and activities around your special talents and abilities is the key to peak performance and high achievement. When you find the job or position where your special skills meet the needs of the situation, you will make more progress in the next two years than you may have made in ten years working at something else.

• *What are your three most important goals in life right now?* Use the Quick List method. Take a pen in hand and give yourself thirty seconds to quickly write down your response to this question. When you write down your three most important goals in this fashion, your answer will be as accurate as if you had thirty minutes or three hours. Your subconscious discards all secondary goals. Your important aims or purposes will pop to the surface of your mind and appear on the paper in front of you.

You can then ask, "What are my three most pressing worries or concerns in life right now?" Give yourself thirty seconds to write down your answer.

Once you have answers to both questions, you will have a snapshot of your current life. These responses will tell you a lot about yourself. First, your three goals will almost always be a financial goal, a health goal, and a relationship goal. Second, your three goals will almost always be the solutions to your three main worries and concerns. In most cases, your three goals are the flip side of the coin of your three worries. You can resolve your problems by achieving your goals.

## Analyze Your Life

Try this Quick List exercise in each key area of your life. Quickly write down your three most important business, family, health, and financial goals. You can give this exercise to members of your family or your coworkers as well. Give them thirty seconds to write down the three most important goals in their life.

Your three problems or worries represent your past, or where you are coming from or what you are moving away from. Your three goals represent your future, and what you are moving toward, both consciously and unconsciously. When you ask yourself these questions regularly, you will enjoy ever-greater clarity about who you are and what you really want. You will get more and more ideas to achieve your goals and solve your problems.

• *What specific steps will you have to take to achieve your most important goals?* A goal that is not accompanied by a detailed, organized list of actions that must be taken to accomplish it is like trying to build a house without a blueprint. The more detailed your plans of action, the more likely you are to achieve your goals, and in a shorter period of time.

## Imagine No Limitations

Here is a simple but powerful exercise to identify your goals and organize your life. Take out a sheet of paper. Write down everything you would like to accomplish in your business and personal life over the next five years. Imagine that you have no limitations of time, money, talent, people, resources, or abilities. When you write out your goals, imagine that whatever you write down is possible for you, as long as the goal is clear.

You can conduct this exercise as a brainstorming session with the members of your staff or with other key people. In your business, you can write down everything you would like to accomplish over the next five years regarding sales, growth, profitability, people, products, services, processes, and market share.

You can conduct this exercise with your spouse at home. Sit down together and write out everything that you would like to be, have, or do in your lives together over the next five years, or even longer.

In the Bible it says, "Let there be light." The more time you take to write out every possible goal that you would like to achieve sometime in the future, the greater light you will have in your life. You will be far more knowledgeable and aware of what it is you really want to accomplish in the months and years ahead.

As you write down your goals, think about the things you have always wanted to do in the past but may have given up on because of constraints of time, money, marriage, or other factors. When you write, let your imagination run freely. Concentrate on writing out as many goals as possible, without worrying about whether they are achievable, logical, or reasonable. Just get them down on paper.

## Organize Your Goals by Priority

Once you have written out your list of goals for the foreseeable future, go back over the list and organize it by priority. Put an A, B, or C in front of each of the goals. An "A" goal is something that is especially important to you. It is a goal that you would really like to achieve and would make you tremendously happy if you were to attain it.

A "B" goal is something that you would like to achieve and would enjoy acquiring if you were successful. It is important to you, but it is not quite as important as an "A" goal.

A "C" goal is something that would be nice to accomplish, or nice to have or do, but it is not as important as an "A" or "B" goal.

It is only when you write your goals down and compare them against each other that you develop absolute clarity about their relative importance to you.

## Select Your Most Important Goals

Transfer all of your "A" goals onto a separate sheet of paper. Review these goals and organize them by writing "A-1," "A-2," "A-3," and so on next to them.

Select from your "A" list the most important of all goals, the one goal that could have the greatest positive impact on your life if you were to achieve it. Ask yourself, "If I could achieve any goal on this list, which one goal would give me more happiness, satisfaction, and rewards than any other?" This becomes your A-1 goal.

Work through the "A" list by asking yourself this question: "If I could only accomplish one more goal on this list, which one goal would it be?" This becomes your A-2 goal. Then ask this question again and again, until you have organized all of your "A" goals by priority.

Finally, take your A-1 goal, the most important goal of all, and write it down at the top of a new page. This goal becomes your major definite purpose for the foreseeable future.

## Make Detailed Plans of Action

The next step is to make a list of every single action that you can think of that you can take to achieve your most important goal. You should come up with at least ten or twenty different things you could do to accomplish this goal. When you have written down everything that you can think of, you then organize this list of activities by writing an "A," "B," or "C" in front of each of the items. Ask yourself: "If I could only do one thing on this list, which one action would help me to achieve this goal more than any other?" Finally, go back and you write A-1, A-2, A-3, until your list of activities is organized into a plan of action, from beginning to end.

You can repeat this exercise with each of your "A" goals. Write the goal in the present tense at the top of a sheet of paper and then discipline yourself to generate ten to twenty specific, concrete actions that you can take to achieve that goal. Organize each of these lists by priority, using the A-B-C method. This entire exercise will only take you between one and two hours, perhaps on a Sunday afternoon. But once you have accomplished it, you will have a list of clear goals, organized in order of priority, combined with a series of action steps also organized by priority.

With this set of goals and plans, you will have moved yourself into the top 3 percent of people in our society. You will have taken control of your future. You will have grasped the steering wheel of your own life and turned it in a different direction.

What will happen to you as the result of this exercise will absolutely amaze you. Try it and see.

# Turbocharging Your Goal-Achieving Ability

There are five techniques that you can practice to accelerate the speed at which you achieve your goals. These methods will "turbocharge" your energies and abilities and allow you to accomplish more in a shorter period of time than you ever thought possible. These techniques are to:

1. Visualize your goal as a reality

2. Positively affirm your goal as accomplished

3. Accept complete responsibility for results

4. Step out in faith

5. Do something daily

### Visualize Your Goal as a Reality

Create a clear mental picture of your goal as if it has already been realized. Imagine your goal as though you were already enjoying the finished result. Close your eyes and think of what your goal would look like. Think about the kind of person you would be if you had achieved the goal. Think about how much you would enjoy the achievement of that goal or objective. This ability to visualize is one of the great powers of the human mind. Your subconscious makes your outer world consistent with your inner world. To activate this power, you only need to create a "mental equivalent" of what you want to see in your outer life. Your subconscious will do the rest.

### *Activate the Law of Attraction*

As if you were running a movie projector, you should play and replay this picture continuously on the screen of your mind. This picture will then activate your subconscious and trigger the Law of Attraction. This law says that you are a "living magnet" and that you inevitably attract into your life the ideas, people, and resources that you need to achieve your most intensely desired goals.

### Change Your Beliefs

The Law of Belief says: *Whatever you believe, with conviction, becomes your reality.* You do not believe what you see, but you see what you already believe. There is a one-to-one relationship between how intensely you believe that your goals are achievable and how rapidly they appear in your life. As William James, the renowned Harvard professor and philosopher, said, "Belief creates the actual fact."

The Law of Mind says: *Thoughts objectify themselves.* When you replay the picture of your goal repeatedly in your conscious mind, you begin to believe with ever-increasing intensity that the goal is achievable for you. As your belief grows, your goal begins to take physical form in your external world sometimes far faster than you can imagine.

## Positively Affirm Your Goal as Accomplished

Create a clear statement or affirmation of your goal as already achieved. Enthusiastically repeat this statement to yourself. Imbue your statement with emotion, conviction, and emphasis. As you repeat this positive affirmation, you imprint this command to achieve the goal deeper and deeper into your subconscious mind. Use personal language, such as "I earn $75,000 per year!" Or, "I weigh 175 pounds," or "I am an outstanding salesperson." By using affirmations, you can totally reprogram your thinking about yourself and your goals. With affirmations, your potential becomes unlimited.

## Accept Complete Responsibility for Results

Accept 100 percent responsibility for doing everything that is necessary to achieve your goal. Repeat to yourself, "If it's to be, it's up to me." Refuse to make excuses for not making progress. Refuse to rationalize or explain away your lack of success. Refuse to justify the reasons for your problems and obstacles. Instead, accept total responsibility for achieving your goal. Become totally self-reliant.

Here is an interesting discovery. When you accept complete responsibility for achieving your goal, people will emerge to help you and guide you along the path to your success. But when you make excuses, blame others, and expect them to help you, they will ignore you and avoid you. When you look to yourself *first*, you are far more likely not only to be more successful, but to attract into your life the support of the people you need. If you look to other people to help you achieve your goals, you will almost always be disappointed.

## Step Out in Faith

Once you are clear about what you want, the next step is to act as if it were impossible to fail.

As Thoreau said, "Go confidently in the direction of your dreams." Act as though achievement of the goal was absolutely inevitable. Carry yourself in your daily activities with others, in everything you do and say, exactly as if the achievement of your goal was guaranteed by some great power.

## Do Something Daily

Do something every day that moves you toward your major goal or goals. By the yard it's hard, but inch by inch, anything is a cinch. When you do something every single day that moves you closer to your goal, you eventually develop an unshakable faith and belief that your goal will ultimately be achieved.

In the final analysis, every goal-setting exercise must be reduced to specific, concrete action steps that you can take to achieve the goal. If you do just one thing each day, no matter how big the goal or how far away it may be, this single action will keep you motivated and focused. It will keep your subconscious mind stimulated and active. Daily movement toward your goal will energize you and increase your confidence.

## Achieving Income and Career Goals

Here are five key ideas for setting goals for your income and your career:

**1.** *Focus on customer satisfaction.* Everybody makes a living by serving someone else. Whatever you do for a living, you are always in the business of customer satisfaction. Your job is to determine your most important customers, inside and outside your company, and then dedicate yourself to serving them better and faster.

Who is your customer? Your customer is the person whose satisfaction determines your success in your career. It is the person who depends on you for something that you do for them. Your customer is the person you have to please in order to be paid more and promoted faster.

In business, your boss is your primary customer. If you please your boss by doing the things that this person wants or needs, you will be successful. If you please everyone else in your company but you don't please your boss, your job will be in jeopardy. What does your boss need to be happy with your performance?

If you are a manager, your staff members are also your customers. Your staff has been entrusted to you to help you achieve your goals of satisfying your customers. In order for you to do your job satisfactorily, your staff must be happy with you and with the way you treat them. The very best bosses have the happiest and most productive staff members. Who are your most important staff members?

Your coworkers and colleagues, over whom you have no direct control or influence, are also your customers. Their help, or lack of help, can have a major impact on your ability to do your job well. Who are the people around you whose support and cooperation you require to get your job done well?

The primary customer for your business is the person who purchases and uses your product or service. Your ability to satisfy this customer's wants and needs in a timely fashion, at a reasonable price, and at an appropriate level of quality, is the key not only to your success, but also to the survival of your entire enterprise.

2. *Find out what your customers want.* Keep asking yourself, Who is my customer? How does my customer define satisfaction? What value does my customer expect from me? How do I best please my customer?

Every company that is successful is continually asking its customers, "What can we do to please you better? What can we do to satisfy you even more next time?" Every individual should be asking these questions as well.

One of the biggest problems in the world of work is that people are not clear about exactly what they need to do to satisfy their bosses. One of the best things you can do on a regular basis is to go to your boss and ask, "Why am I on the payroll? What is the most important thing that I do around here, from your point of view?"

You can be doing your job extraordinarily well, but if what you are working on is not important to your boss, you will actually be sabotaging your career. However, if you do the one or two things that are most important to your boss, those actions that generate the highest levels of "customer satisfaction" in his eyes, this alone can advance your career faster than anything else you could do.

To succeed at work, you must ask yourself repeatedly, "Why am I on the payroll? What results have I been hired to achieve?"

3. *Determine your primary output responsibilities.* Continually ask yourself, your boss, and the people around you, "What

are my primary output responsibilities?" In other words, what are you expected to produce as the result of your work?

There are three ways of defining an output responsibility. First, an output responsibility is measurable, concrete, specific, and it can be defined clearly on paper. You can attach a number and a standard of performance to it. An output responsibility is a certain quality and quantity of work that can be defined and measured by an objective third party, including your boss.

For example, "getting along well with others" is not an output responsibility. It may be a necessary activity for you to perform your job, but because it is neither measurable nor concrete, it is not a key determinant of your success or failure.

Second, an output responsibility is something that is under your control. It is something that you can do from beginning to end. It does not depend on someone else.

Third, an output responsibility is a task or result that serves as an input for someone else. In other words, every output that you produce serves as an input to someone else. It becomes a part of someone else's job. For example, if you make a sale, that output becomes an input to your organization, which must now produce, deliver, and service the product.

Consequently, each product or service that your company produces becomes an input to the life or work of someone else. If your company manufacturers computers or photocopiers, those machines become the outputs of your organization and inputs to other organizations, which then use them to produce outputs of their own.

The questions for you to ask are: "Who must use what I produce? What does it take to please the people or organizations that have to use what I produce? How can I best satisfy my most important customers?" The most successful people and organizations are those who please the greatest number of their customers by giving them what they want, in the way they want it, at prices they are willing to pay.

**4.** *Determine your key result areas.* In setting business and career goals, you must be continually asking, "What are my key result areas?" This is an essential question for business and career success. What is it that you and only you can do that, if done well, will make a real difference to your organization or will yield extraordinary results?

Think of a task that only you can do. If you do not do it, it will not be done by anyone else. But if you do it, and do it well, it can make a real contribution to yourself and your organization.

There are seldom more than five to seven key result areas in any job. Your ability to perform well in each of the key result areas of your particular position is the key to your overall success. You could do many of your tasks in an excellent fashion, but if they are not among your key result areas, they could actually be harmful to your career. The time you spend on them will take you away from doing the vital few things that your success depends on.

Apply the 80/20 rule to everything you do. Just 20 percent of the things you do will account for 80 percent of the value of your work. It is essential that you work on the top 20 percent of activities that account for most of your results.

**5.** *Practice management by objectives.* One of the most effective forms of corporate goal setting is "management by objectives." This technique should only be used with competent people—that is, with people who have mastered the job and know what needs to be done. This method requires that you entrust an entire task to an individual.

There are four steps to management by objectives. First, define the desired goal or result clearly, in discussion with the person who will have the responsibility of achieving it. Take the time to agree exactly on *what* is to be accomplished.

Second, discuss and agree on the plan of implementation. What steps will be taken to accomplish the goal? How is it to be done? How will you measure success? What standards of performance will you use? How will you know that the job has been done well? And especially, what will be the consequences for doing or not doing the job in an effective and timely way?

Third, agree on a time of completion, and set a schedule to review progress and problems. When is the job expected to be finished? The setting of clear deadlines and schedules is a vital part of management by objectives.

Fourth, leave the person alone to do the job. Once you have assigned a clearly defined job with output responsibilities and standards of performance to a competent person, leave the person alone to do the job in his own way.

The key to delegation is to delegate the task completely and refuse to take it back. Do not interfere. Give whatever advice, guidance, and support is necessary for the person to do the job, but make it clear that the job is the responsibility of that person.

One of the most powerful ways to build competence, confidence, and ability in other people is to assign complete responsibility to them for the achievement of an important task. When people know that they are completely responsible, it gives them a greater sense of personal power and control. It builds initiative and resolve. It develops persistence and determination. It is one of the most powerful of all people-building tools available to parents or managers. And, it is a great time saver.

## Achieving Your Goals Faster

There are four important thinking tools that you can apply to the achievement of any goal. The application and use of these tools greatly improves your competence and ability to accomplish the goals that you have set for yourself, and for your business.

**1.** *Remove the obstacles.* Identify the obstacles that stand between you and your goal. What is holding you back from achieving your goal? Why haven't you achieved it already? Write down every single obstacle or difficulty that you think is limiting your ability to achieve the goal that you have defined.

These may include internal obstacles, or obstacles within yourself. They may be external obstacles, or obstacles that are created by circumstances or the situation in the world around you.

Once you have determined the obstacles that are holding you back, identify and determine your single largest obstacle. What is the major obstacle that is standing in the way of your completing this task? Resolve to go to work on this one obstacle and concentrate single-mindedly on it until it is removed.

Peter Drucker said, "In every complex problem, there is usually a single large problem that must be solved before any other problems can be solved." Your job is to identify the biggest single problem or difficulty that is holding you back and then focus on solving *that* before you get sidetracked by smaller problems and difficulties.

**2.** *Identify your limiting step.* In the accomplishment of almost any goal (whether it's increasing your income, doubling your sales, or losing weight) or the completion of any job, there is usually one step that determines how fast you can get from where you are to where you want to go. This is the bottleneck or choke point in the process. Your ability to identify and remove this bottleneck is one of the most important techniques for efficiency and effectiveness that can move you toward the achievement of your goal faster than any other action.

The 80/20 rule applies to this principle of constraints, or limiting factors, in a special way. In this case, the 80/20 rule says that "Eighty percent of the reasons that you are not achieving your goal are contained within yourself, or your company." Only 20 percent of the constraints on your ability to accomplish what you want are contained in external circumstances or the environment around you.

The starting point of personal effectiveness is for you to, first of all, define your goal and, second, to ask yourself, "What is it in me that is holding me back?" When you look into yourself, you will almost always find that it is the lack of a particular skill, quality, or behavior that is your main constraint on achieving a particular goal or result. This is the "what" that you need to work on before you do anything else.

**3.** *Determine the knowledge and skills you will require.* Identify the additional knowledge or skills that you require to achieve your goal. What else do you need to learn? What else do you need to know? What is the most important additional knowledge, skill, or experience that you require in order to achieve the goal that you have set for yourself?

As professional speaker Les Brown has said, "In order to achieve something that you have never achieved before, you must become someone that you have never been before." To accomplish bigger and better goals, you will have to develop new skills and acquire new knowledge. You cannot achieve more than you are achieving today without developing yourself to a higher level.

Remember, knowledge is power. But only practical knowledge that can be applied toward getting desired results is true power. Ask yourself, "What practical knowledge do I need to acquire in order to move more rapidly toward the achievement of my goals and the accomplishment of my tasks?"

Sometimes the practical knowledge you need is in marketing and sales. Sometimes it is the skill of managing people. Sometimes it is the knowledge of strategic planning or organizational development. Often it is knowledge that is hard to identify, but discovering the critical knowledge you need and then going to work to acquire it can have an inordinate impact on your results.

**4.** *Determine the people whose help you will need.* Identify the people whose help, support, and cooperation will be necessary for you to achieve your goals, both personal and business-related. Whose help do you need? Who can help you to get to the goal? Who can block you from achieving your goal? Who do you need to work in cooperation with to achieve your goal in a timely fashion?

Often when you set a goal that is going to take a lot of your time, you will need the cooperation and understanding of your family. If you want to rise to a position of prominence in your company or industry, you will need the cooperation of your boss, your coworkers, and your subordinates.

Think about the people whose cooperation you will require. What can you do to get them to want to cooperate with you? What is in it for them? How will they benefit from helping you to achieve your goals? Always start with what others need and require, then work backward to identify what it is that *you* need and require.

## Asking Yourself the Right Questions

Here are some final questions that you can ask to keep yourself clear, focused, and on track in the achievement of your goals and objectives.

First, you should ask regularly, "What am I trying to do?" Exactly what is it that you are attempting to achieve as the result of your work and your efforts? Vagueness and fuzziness in your answer to this question makes it almost impossible for you to achieve your goals on schedule.

Second, you should ask, "How am I trying to do it?" Is your current method working? What are your assumptions? Are you assuming something that might not be true? Could there be a better way to achieve your goal than the method that you are currently using?

Third, you can ask, "What are my real goals?" How do these goals affect my personal life? Why am I doing what I am doing? It is absolutely essential that you be clear about the real purpose behind your goals if you want to remain motivated and energized in your pursuit of them.

Fourth, and perhaps the most important question to ask is, "What is my aim in life?" What is my aim in my work? What is my aim with my family? What do I want to accomplish as the result of being alive? What do I really want to do with my life?

These are questions that you should ask yourself over and over again to keep yourself on track.

## Developing Absolute Clarity

The starting point of time management is for you to achieve absolute clarity with regard to your goals, in every area of your life and at every level of your business. Like a photographer, you must continually focus the lens of your time and activities on exactly the most important things that you are trying to accomplish and the reasons that you want to accomplish them.

All time management skills require a clear, unambiguous agreement about goals and objectives. Decide exactly what it is that you are trying to achieve and focus single-mindedly on your most important goals and activities. This is the first step toward excellent time management.

*"There is one quality that one must possess to win, and that is definiteness of purpose, the knowledge of what one wants, and a burning desire to achieve it."*
—NAPOLEON HILL

## Action Exercises

1. Clarity is essential! Make a list of ten goals for the coming year in every area of your business and personal life. Write in the present tense, as if you have already achieved the goal.

2. Review your list and ask, "What one goal, if I achieved it, would have the most positive impact on my life, right now?" Write this goal at the top of a new page.

3. Set a specific deadline for the achievement of this goal. Set sub-deadlines, if necessary.

4. Make a list of everything you can think of to do to achieve this goal. As you think of new activities, add them to the list. Keep updating your list until it is complete.

5. Organize your list into a plan. Decide what is most important. Decide what must be done first, before something else can be done.

6. Determine the obstacles you will have to overcome, the additional knowledge and skills you will require, and the people whose help you will need. Be specific.

7. Take action on your most important goal, and resolve to do something every day that moves you one step closer to achieving it. Never give up!

# CHAPTER THREE

# The Essence of Good Time Management: Getting Yourself Organized

*"Make it a life rule to give your best to whatever passes through your hands. Stamp it with your manhood. Let superiority be your trademark."*

—ORISON SWETT MARDEN

The difference between average people and highly effective people is that highly effective people are much better organized when they work than others. Excellent personal and professional organization is a hallmark of highly effective and well-paid people.

Fortunately, organizing is a skill, and all skills are learnable. You can learn to be an extremely well organized, efficient, and effective person. When you do, you will produce vastly more in the same period of time than the people around you.

One of Murphy's Laws states that *before you can do anything, you have to do something else first.*

The one thing that you have to do first, before you can do any productive work, is to get yourself organized completely. The core function of good time management is planning and organizing yourself, and your work, for maximum productivity. It is only possible to get the best out of yourself when you have brought together everything you need before you begin work. You must then determine a place for everything and make sure that everything is in its place.

## Plan Everything in Advance

The top 3 percent of high achievers are all persistent, continuous planners. They are forever writing and rewriting their lists of goals and activities. They think on paper and are continually analyzing and reevaluating their plans.

I used to wonder why it was that so many successful people seemed to spend so much of their time planning. Over time, I learned that the more time you spend planning, the better and more foolproof your plans become. By continually reworking your plans for achieving your goals, your goals become increasingly believable and achievable.

As you think about and plan each step, your confidence in your ability to accomplish those goals increases. When you break down even the biggest goal into its individual parts, and then organize those parts into a step-by-step series of specific actions, the task seems much more manageable and under your control. The more you plan, the more you program your goal deeper and deeper into your subconscious mind, where it takes on a motivational power of its own.

## Get a 1,000 Percent Return on Investment

The payoff from good planning is enormous. It is estimated that each minute spent in planning saves ten minutes in execution. To put it another way, your investment in planning pays you a 1,000 percent return on the time and energy you invest.

In life, all that we really have to sell is our time. The more productive our time usage, all things being equal, the more we will eventually be paid. Your job is to invest your time where you can get the highest ROL, or "return on life." Where else can you get a 1,000 percent return on your investment?

Sometimes people say that they are too busy to sit and plan. The fact is that even if you force yourself to plan out everything in detail, you will find it hard to spend more than a few minutes per day in the planning process. The only way that you will ever create the time you need is by planning your activities carefully in advance. Remember, you save ten minutes for every minute that you spend planning before you begin.

## The Reason for Most Failure

Peter Drucker said, "Action without planning is the reason for every failure." If you look back over the major mistakes you've made in your life, they will almost all have one factor in common. It was that you rushed into the decision or situation without giving it enough thought. You either did not get enough information, or you did not take the time to weigh and balance the pros and cons before acting. In every case, the failure to plan carefully can be very expensive.

At the same time, you will also find that almost every one of the most successful accomplishments of your life, from planning a business start-up or a business project, all the way through to planning a vacation, was accompanied by a good plan, worked out thoroughly in advance. The more time you took to think through what you had to do, and the likely consequences of your actions, the more efficient you were and the more satisfying was the end result.

The fact is that the better and more complete your plans are before you begin, the greater will be your likelihood of your success once you start.

There is an old saying: "Success is tons of discipline." One of the best exercises in self-discipline is for you to take the time to think through and plan out everything you do before you begin.

## Four Ideas for Personal Organization

Here are four ideas you can use to help yourself get organized:

**1.** *Neatness is a key habit.* Remember that neatness is a key habit for personal productivity. You can dramatically increase your productivity and output simply by cleaning up and organizing your workspace. You've heard it said that "Order is heaven's first law." Order is earth's first law as well. You need a sense of order to feel relaxed and in control of your environment and your life. You actually get a feeling of pleasure and satisfaction each time you put some part of your life or work in order.

When you clean up your desk or office, you feel more on top of your work. When you clean out your car, you feel more in charge of your personal life. When you organize your purse or briefcase, or even your home and your closets, you feel like a more effective human being. Your self-esteem goes up. Your self-confidence and self-respect increase. You feel more powerful as a person. You generate more energy and feel an increased determination to get on with the job.

**2.** *Stand back and evaluate yourself.* Here is a good exercise for you: Stand back from your desk or work area and ask, "What kind of person works at that desk?"

Look in your purse or briefcase and ask, "What kind of a person would have a purse or briefcase like that?" Look at and in your car. Look in your closet. Look in your house, your yard, and your garage and ask, "What kind of a person would live that way?"

Would you entrust that person with an important task? Why or why not? Honestly evaluate yourself through the eyes of a neutral third party. What do you see?

In a series of interviews with senior executives, fifty out of
fifty-two of the respondents said that they would not promote a
person with a messy desk or a cluttered work environment. Even
if that person was producing good work, these executives said
that they would not trust a position of responsibility to a person
who could not get organized. Don't let this happen to you.

**3.** *Refuse to make excuses.* Many people working in a messy
environment use their intelligence *against* themselves. They use
their cleverness to justify and excuse themselves for the messi-
ness of their workspaces. They say things like, "I know where
everything is." Or they say nonhumorous things such as, "A
clean desk is a sign of a sick mind."

However, every time-and-motion study of efficiency in the
workplace concludes that these are exercises in self-delusion. A
person who says she knows where everything is turns out to be
using a large amount of her mental capacity and creative energies remembering where she placed things, rather than doing
the job.

People who say they work well in a cluttered environment
are usually wrong. If they worked in a neat, well-organized environment for any length of time, they would be surprised at how
much more effective and productive they were. If you or a person you know has a tendency to justify and attempt to explain a
cluttered desk or work area, challenge yourself, or the other person, to work with a clean desk for an entire day. The result will
amaze you.

**4.** *Work from a clean desk.* Direct mail entrepreneur Joe
Sugarman once wrote a book explaining his five rules for success. One of his five principles was, "End every day with a clean
desk." He made this a rule throughout his organization. This
policy forced all employees to work more efficiently and complete their work by the end of each day. It made a major contribution to success.

When I learned this, I introduced this rule into my own company. I told everyone that they would be expected to clean up their desks and leave them neat and orderly at the end of each day. When they argued with me, I told them that if they didn't follow this rule, I would go from office to office after they left and throw everything on their desks into the wastebasket to be taken away by the night janitors. I only had to follow through on this threat once before everyone realized how serious I was.

One manager, probably the messiest executive in my company, gave me every excuse possible for working in a cluttered and chaotic environment. But I refused to listen or compromise. He had no choice but to clean everything up and put it away before leaving at the end of each day. Within one week, he came to me and apologized. He said, "All my life, I have thought that I worked better in a messy environment. In the last week, I have accomplished two and three times as much as I ever accomplished at work before. I am absolutely astonished at how much more I get done when everything is put in its proper place throughout the day."

## Three Steps to Organizing Your Workspace

Here are three things you can do to organize your workspace:

**1.** *Clear your desk.* Begin your process of getting organized by clearing your desk of everything but the one thing that you are working on at the moment. If necessary, place things in drawers, on the credenza behind you, in the wastebasket, in cupboards, or even on the floor. Do whatever is necessary to turn your desk into a clear, clean, uncluttered work area, with just one thing—the most important thing—before you when you begin.

**2.** *Assemble everything you need.* Arrange to have everything you need at hand before you begin any task. Just like a good cook gets out all the ingredients necessary to prepare a dish before he begins, or a master craftsman arranges all of his tools, as a professional, you should assemble all the tools of your trade before you start on a particular job.

Get all the information and files you will need. Get pens, notepaper, stick-it notes, calculator, ruler, dictating machine or recorder, file folders, and everything else you can think of before you commence work. The rule is that you should be able to reach out and touch everything you need to do the job.

**3.** *Handle each piece of paper only once.* Resolve to handle every piece of paper only once. Make a decision to do something with it when you pick it up, and don't pick it up unless you are ready to act on it. It is better to stack it up and put it aside for appropriate action later than to continually shuffle and reshuffle it on your desk.

## How to Handle Paperwork

There are four things you can do with any piece of paper:

**1.** *Throw it away.* One of the best time management tools at home or office is the wastebasket. The fastest way to save time in reading anything is to simply throw it away and not read it at all. This applies to junk mail, unwanted subscriptions to catalogs, sales circulars, and everything else that is not relevant to your goals.

Use the wastebasket to get rid of reading materials that have been hanging around for months. Ask yourself, "If I did not read this, would there be any negative consequences?" If the answer is no, then throw it away as fast as you can. You can also ask yourself, "If I ever needed this information, could I get it somewhere else?" If the answer is yes, throw it away.

My rule for keeping my workplace clean is, "When in doubt, throw it out!"

**2.** *Delegate it to someone else.* You can refer or delegate the task to someone else. When you pick up a piece of paper, ask yourself if there is someone else who should be acting on this matter. Is there someone else who can handle it better than you? One of the keys to success in personal management is for you to delegate everything that can possibly be done by anyone else. This is the only way that you can free up your time to do more of the things that are most important to you and to your job.

**3.** *Take personal action.* You can take action on the piece of paper. These are the letters, proposals, and messages that you must personally do something about. Get a file folder and put the word "action" on the tab. Even better, get a red file folder where you put all of your action items, and place it where you can see it clearly.

Keep this action folder handy. When you come across something that you need to do something about, simply put it in your action file to work on later. If it is something to be done immediately, take action quickly and put it behind you.

**4.** *File it for future reference.* You can file it away. But before you file anything, remember that 80 percent of papers filed are never needed, used, or seen again. Designating something to the files creates work. Before you decide to put something in your files, ask yourself, "What would happen if I couldn't find this piece of paper?" What would be the negative consequences of not having this information available?

If there are no negative consequences, or if you could get the information somewhere else, then throw the piece of paper away. Keep your desk clear, and keep your files clear as well.

When I first began using the wastebasket to clear off my excess papers, publications, and reading material, I found it difficult. But with experience, I found that very little that I have thrown away has ever been needed again. The habit of throwing things away rather than saving and filing them has been a big time saver for me, as it has been for many others.

The most important thing is that you take some kind of action on a piece of paper when you pick it up. Do something, do *anything* with the piece of paper. Move it along at least one step. One of the greatest time wasters of all is continually picking up the same piece of paper, reading it, putting it down, and having to come back to it, over and over again.

## Put Things Away

When you are finished with something, put it away. Complete your transactions. Finish your jobs. Discipline yourself to stay at it until the job is 100 percent complete. Remember, start with a clean workspace and end with a clean workspace.

There is something deeply satisfying and psychologically rewarding about task completion. Your brain is structured in such a way that you get an "endorphin rush" every time you complete a task of any kind, large or small. The larger or more important the task is to you, the greater will be the feeling of happiness and exhilaration you experience when you complete it. Each time you complete a task, you condition yourself to complete subsequent tasks. In no time at all, you find yourself internally driven and motivated to start and complete more and more important tasks and responsibilities.

Make a habit of finishing what you start. Teach and encourage others to finish their work and put it away as well. Especially, teach your children to complete their tasks by setting a good example, and by rewarding them when they do finish something important. One of the hardest behaviors for people to learn is the habit of completing tasks and putting things away, but this is a habit that serves them all their lives.

## Time Management Tools and Techniques

There are five time management tools and techniques that you should practice for maximum productivity and good personal organization. Each of them takes a little time to learn and master, but pays you back in greater efficiency and effectiveness for the rest of your life.

As Goethe said, "Everything is hard before it is easy." Good habits are hard to form but easy to live with. Once you have developed them, they become automatic and easy. They serve you for the rest of your career.

**1.** *Use a time planner*. The first time management tool that you need is a time planning system that contains everything you need to plan and organize your life. The best time planners, whether looseleaf binders or electronic versions, enable you to plan for the year, the month, the week, and for each day. A good time planner will contain a master list where you can capture every task, goal, and required action as it comes up. This master list then becomes the core of your time-planning system. From this master list, you allocate individual tasks to various months, weeks, and days.

The second part of the time-planning system is a calendar that enables you to organize your time and plan several months ahead. With the right system, you will be able to transfer individual items from your master list to the exact day when you intend to complete them.

The next part of your time-planning system is a daily list. This daily list is perhaps the single most important planning tool you can have. Some people call it a "to-do list." Winston Churchill headed his daily list with the words, "Actions This Day."

**2.** *Always work from a list*. Every effective executive works from a daily list. It is the most powerful tool ever discovered for maximum productivity.

Ineffective executives, those who are overwhelmed with too many things to do and too little time, either do not use a list or do not refer to a list if they have one in the first place. They often resist the idea of writing everything down. As a result, they find themselves continually distracted by ringing phones, interruptions, unexpected emergencies, and e-mail requests.

When you create your daily list, you begin by writing down every single task that you intend to complete over the course of the day. The rule is that you will increase your efficiency by 25 percent the very first day that you start using a list. This means that you will get two extra hours of productive time in an eight-hour day from the simple act of making a list of everything you have to do before you start work. You can bring order out of chaos faster with a list than with any other time management tool.

If ever you feel overwhelmed with too many tasks, you can immediately impose order on your list by writing down every single thing you have to do for the foreseeable future. The very act of making a list of ten, twenty, or thirty items allows you to exert control over your time and your life. You immediately feel more relaxed and confident. You feel back in charge of your work.

Once you have written up your daily lists and begun work, new tasks and responsibilities will come up. Telephone calls will have to be returned. Correspondence will have to be dealt with. In every case, write it down on the list before you do it.

Sometimes a task or demand on your time will seem urgent when it comes up. But something that might distract you from your other work regains its true importance when you write it down. An item that is written down on the list next to all your other tasks and responsibilities often doesn't seem so important after all.

**3.** *Organize your list by priority.* Once you have a list for your day's activities, the next step is for you to organize this list in order of priority. We will dedicate Chapter 4 to the different ways that you can determine your top priorities.

Once your list is organized, it becomes a map to guide you from morning to evening in the most effective and efficient way. This guide tells you what you have to do and what is more or less important. You will soon develop the habit of using your list as a blueprint for the day. Refuse to do anything until you have written it down on the list and organized it relative to its value in comparison to the other things you have to do.

4. *Use any time management system you like.* The variety of personal digital assistants (PDAs) and computer-based time management systems available today is absolutely wonderful. No matter what you do, in whatever field, there are digital time management systems that you can tap into or load onto your personal computer to help organize every part of your life. You can upload, download, transfer, merge, purge, and share your files and information throughout the company and around the world. In addition, there are countless time management systems that provide you with an array of forms for writing out your goals and plans by hand.

What I have discovered is that it doesn't matter what time management system or planner you decide to use. They are all good. They have all been developed by experts and contain virtually everything you need to double and triple your productivity. The most important part of any time-planning system is that you use it regularly until it becomes a habit, like breathing in and breathing out. It takes a certain amount of time to master a time-planning system, but once you have learned it, you become more productive and efficient every time you use it.

5. *Set up a 45-file system.* There is a simple method of organizing your time and your schedule for up to two years in advance. It is called the "45-file system." This is a tickler file that lets you plan and organize your activities and callbacks for the next twenty-four months. This is how it works.

First, you get a box of forty-five files with fourteen hanging files to put them in. The forty-five files are divided as follows: There are thirty-one files numbered one through thirty-one for the days of the month. There are twelve files for the months of the year, January through December. The last two files are for the next two years. This is a wonderful system that you can also use with hanging files in your desk drawer.

When you have an appointment or responsibility for six months from now, you simply drop it into that monthly file. At the beginning of each month, you take out all of your responsibilities for that month and sort them into your daily files, numbered one through thirty-one. Each day, you take out the file for that day and that becomes the starting point of your planning.

This system takes a few minutes to set up. It then assures that you never miss or forget to follow up on a distant call, task, or appointment. It helps you to take control of your time and impose order on your future.

## Seven Tools for Personal Organization

Here are seven more ideas that you can use to help get yourself organized for maximum productivity. The more of these tools you learn to use, the more that you will get done each day.

**1.** *Prepare the night before.* First, prepare your work list for the following day the evening or night before. The best exercise is for you to plan your entire next day as the last thing you do before coming home from work. When you plan your day the night before, your subconscious then goes to work on your plans and goals while you are asleep. Very often you will wake up in the morning with ideas and insights that apply to the work of the day.

Sometimes, the answer to a problem that you are working on will pop into your mind when you wake up or when you are getting ready for work. Often that's when you will gain a new perspective on a problem or job, or see a different or better way that it might be accomplished.

A major benefit of preparing your daily list the night before is that this exercise lets you sleep more soundly. A major reason for insomnia is your lying awake trying not to forget to remember everything that you have to do the following day. Once you have written down everything you have to do on your list, it clears your mind and enables you to sleep deeply.

2. *Schedule your time*. Scheduling your time reduces stress and releases energy. The very act of planning and organizing your day, week, and month gives you a greater feeling of control and well-being. You'll feel in charge of your life. It actually increases your self-esteem and improves your sense of personal power.

3. *Get an early start on the day*. Start your day early. The more time you take to sit, think, and plan, the better organized you will be in every area of your life. In the biographies and autobiographies of successful men and women, almost all of them have one thing in common. They developed the habit of going to bed at a reasonable hour and rising early.

Many successful people arise at 5:00 A.M. or 5:30 A.M. so that they can have enough time to think and plan for the coming day. As a result, they are always more effective than those who sleep in until the last possible moment.

A few minutes of quiet reflection before you begin any undertaking can save you many hours executing the task. When you get up early and plan your day in advance, you tend to be more calm, clear-headed, and creative throughout the day.

4. *Use an organized filing system*. Resolve to use an organized filing system both at home and at work. As much as 30 percent of working time today is spent looking for misplaced items. These are things that are lost because they have not been filed correctly. Does this sound familiar to you? There are few activities so frustrating as spending your valuable time looking for misplaced materials because no thought was given to a filing and retrieval system.

The best and simplest of all filing systems is an alphabetical system. In conjunction with a filing system, you should have a master list or record of all your files in a single place. This master list gives you the title of each file and tells you where the file is located.

One of the finest tools for an office filing system is a Rolodex. There are many different uses for a Rolodex at home as well. You can purchase them in any stationery store and they will allow you to keep track of a variety of files, in a variety of ways.

**5.** *Do important work during prime time.* Organize your life so that you are doing creative work during your *internal* "prime time." Your internal prime time is the time of day, according to your body clock, when you are the most alert and productive. For most people, this is in the morning. For some people, however, it is in the evening. Occasionally, a writer, an artist, or an entertainer may find that her prime time is in the early hours of the morning.

It is important that you be aware of your internal prime time so that you can schedule your most important projects accordingly. Your most important work usually requires that you be at your very best, rested, alert, and creative. What time of the day do you most feel this way?

You must also be aware of *external* prime time. This is the time when your customers or clients are most readily available. Each person should give some thought to structuring their day for both their external and internal prime times.

**6.** *Use a dictating machine or tape recorder for correspondence and notes.* Dictating equipment can be one of the very best timesaving devices in your business or private life. Once you learn how to use a dictating machine, you can cut your time in writing by as much as 80 percent. It takes 20 percent or less time to dictate than it takes to write something by hand, or type it personally. A dictating machine also saves the time of the person who is going to type it for you. It is usually much easier to transcribe from a tape than to interpret a person's handwriting.

When using a dictating machine, there are three keys to ensure maximum efficiency: First, write an outline of what you are going to dictate. Jot down the major headings and subheadings before you begin. Think through the sentence structure in your mind before you begin dictating onto the tape. Don't be afraid to go back, erase, and do it over again using a better choice of words.

Second, don't try to be a perfectionist. Sometimes, your natural conversational voice is the best and most correct grammatically. You can always go back and correct the major mistakes later. It's much easier to edit something that has been transcribed than to write it or dictate it perfectly in the first place.

Third, concentrate on getting your thoughts dictated as quickly as possible, and then go back and clean it up before you finalize it. In no time at all, you will be dictating perfectly correct letters and reports that need no correction or editing at all.

7. *Make air travel productive.* An important area where personal organization is important is travel, especially air travel. Some years ago, Hughes AirWest, a regional airline that once served the western U.S., hired a consulting firm to compare the efficiency of flying first-class with flying economy-class, and with working in a normal office. What they found was that one hour of *uninterrupted* work time in an airplane yielded the equivalent of three hours of work in a normal work environment. The keyword was "uninterrupted." If you plan ahead and organize your work before you leave for the airport, you can accomplish an enormous amount while you are in the air.

## Get the Most Out of Air Travel Time

Since so many people are traveling by air for business today, it is essential that you know how to make every hour of traveling time count for yourself and for your company.

### Get the Right Seat

The starting point of getting the most out of air travel time is to prebook a non-bulkhead window seat. The reason you want a non-bulkhead window seat is so that you have a tray that opens up in front of you that you can work on.

You also want to keep your briefcase handy during takeoff and landing, and with a bulkhead seat this is not possible. When you travel, your briefcase becomes your traveling office. A window seat will allow you to get out your materials and go to work without the interruption of someone who wants to get past you to go to the washroom. Be sure to specify to your travel agent that you do not want a seat opposite the kitchen or the bathroom on an airplane. These seats are too noisy and distracting for concentrated effort.

When you pack your work for a trip, organize it by subject. Sit down at your desk before you leave and go through what you are going to get accomplished while you are in the air. Before you depart, make sure that you have all materials, envelopes, stamps, and Federal Express envelopes on hand when you begin working. Your briefcase should be fully equipped with everything you require. You will be amazed at how much work you can produce on an airplane when you put your mind to it.

## Get There Early

An important technique to get the most out of your traveling time is for you to arrive at the airport at least two hours before your departure. Most business flyers arrive today with only sixty minutes to catch the plane, even with increased security measures. Studies have showed that if you arrive at the airport at the last possible minute, you experience enormous stress. As a result, it can take as long as two hours for you to relax and settle down to the point where you can concentrate once the plane has taken off.

It is much better for you to arrive at the airport relaxed, with plenty of time to spare. Then, as soon as you get on board, you can begin work and continue working away until the plane lands.

### Avoid Diversion or Distraction

Be sure to work steadily during the flight. Put your head down and concentrate without diversion or distraction. Resist the temptation to read newspapers or airline magazines. Some travelers carry a set of earphones they use to discourage conversation from the person in the next seat.

One frequent flyer I know has a great answer if his seatmate wants to make conversation. When the person next to him asks what he does, he turns to her, smiles sweetly, and says, "I'm a fund-raiser for a religious cult." This has never failed to terminate the conversation, and it leaves him free to work peacefully for the rest of the flight.

Here is one final point on air travel. The very best time to do serious, concentrated work is on the outbound flight, when you are fresh. The best time to read books or magazines, or relax and watch the movie, is on the return flight. On the way back, you are usually tired and not as capable of doing productive work. Be sure to make that outbound flight count. Use every minute to get through work that you have been unable to catch up with in the office.

Getting yourself organized is the starting point of peak performance. Careful planning and organization of your work before you begin will yield dramatic improvements in your productivity, your performance, and your results. You cannot be too well organized if you want to get the most done in the time you have. It is a key to time power.

*"You must be single-minded. Drive for the one thing on which you have decided."*

—GEORGE PATTON

## Action Exercises

1. Resolve today to become one of the best-organized people in your business. Repeat this affirmation, "I am orga-

nized and efficient in everything I do!'' until this command is accepted by your subconscious mind.

2. Write everything down before you begin. Always work from a list, and add new items to the list before you start on them.

3. Get a time planner of some kind, whichever format you are most comfortable using (e.g., digital or paper), and invest the time necessary to learn how to use it. The payoff in saved time and increased productivity will be enormous.

4. Clean up your desk or workspace and keep it clean. Discipline yourself to be a role model for others who want to know how a top-performing person works.

5. Gather everything you need before you start working, and have only one major task in front of you at a time.

6. Handle each piece of paper only once, and take some action on each item when you pick it up. Whenever possible, delegate it, defer it, throw it away, or handle it immediately.

7. Make every minute count, especially when you travel by air. By organizing properly, you can get a full day's work done on a single flight.

# CHAPTER FOUR

# Establishing Proper Priorities

*"Success is a process of diverting one's scattered forces into one powerful channel."*

—JAMES ALLEN

Your ability to set priorities among your goals, tasks, and activities is the key to personal effectiveness. It is not easy to do. The natural human tendency is to "major in minors" and to work very diligently on things that, in many cases, need not be done at all. You must learn to swim against this natural current, to violate the Law of Least Resistance, and to keep focused on those things that can really make a difference in your life.

There are several proven ways for you to set your own personal and business priorities. These are organized methods of thinking that enable you to select the relevant over the irrelevant, the important rather than the merely urgent, and the tasks with long-term consequences rather than those that are fun, easy, and give immediate gratification.

## Begin with Your Values

To set proper priorities, you begin with your *values*. What is really important to you? Of all the things that are important to you, what is *most* important? What do you believe in? What do you stand for? Developing clarity about your values, before you begin setting priorities in your business and personal life, is essential to high levels of effectiveness.

Peak performance and high self-esteem only occur together when your activities and your values are congruent with each other. It is only when what you believe and what you are doing fit together like a hand in a glove that you feel truly happy.

On the other hand, *incongruence,* or lack of alignment between your values and your activities, leads to stress, unhappiness, and dissatisfaction. Whenever you find yourself doing something on the outside that is inconsistent with your beliefs on the inside, you experience stress and conflict. Therefore, the starting point of peak performance is for you to choose, on the basis of your values, what goals and tasks are most important to you.

## Free to Choose

Human beings have been defined as "choosing organisms." You are always making choices of some kind. You are always choosing between what you value more and what you value less. The wrong choice, based on your true values, can lead to frustration, underachievement, and failure.

The best way to determine your values is to look at your actions. You always act in a manner consistent with what is most important to you at the moment. It is not what you say, wish, hope, or intend that counts. It is only what you *do* that tells you, and others, what you truly believe.

To know yourself, look at your behaviors. Observe the choices you make hour by hour and day by day. Especially, look at the way you spend your time. This is one of the best reflections of your true values and priorities in any area. Your choices tell you, and others, who you really are inside.

## Your Order of Values

You may have several values regarding your family, your work, your interactions with others, and yourself personally. The rule is that you will always choose a higher-order value over a lower-order value. You always choose the value that is the most important to you in that situation over values that are less important.

It is only when you are forced to choose between two alternatives that you reveal to yourself, and to others, what is most valuable to you. The order in which you choose your values determines the quality of your character and your personality. Changing your order of values actually changes the person you are.

Here is an example of how similar values, but in different orders of priority, make one person different from another. Imagine that you have two men, Bill and Tom. Each has the same three main values in life: family, health, and career success. But each of them has these values in a different order.

Bill's order of values is family, health, and career success. His family comes before his health and career, and his health comes before his career. Whenever he is forced to make a choice about how he allocates his time, his family comes first.

Tom has the same values, but in a different order. His order of values is career success, family, and health. Whenever Tom has to choose between career success and his family, career success comes first, his family comes second, and his health comes third.

Here is the question. Would there be a difference in personality and character between Bill and Tom? Would there be a small difference or a large difference? Which of the two would you like to have as a friend? Which one of the two would you trust more

and be more comfortable with? When you evaluate people from
the standpoint of their values, the answers become clear.

## You Are Your Values

Your true values are only and always expressed in your actions,
and your choices. Many people say that their family comes first
in their lives. But if you look at the way they organize their time
and their life, it is obvious from their actions that work, golf,
socializing, and other activities are more valuable to them than
their families, because that is how they allocate their time.

When people are single, their values are quite different from
when they get married and have children. As a single individual,
without responsibilities for others, your values may be work, socializing, travel, fun, sports, and other activities. But as soon as
you get married and have children, your values change dramatically. Almost overnight, your spouse and your children take pre-
cedence over everything else. And when your values change, you
become a different person.

The starting point of managing your time, and setting your
priorities, is for you to think through who you are and what is
really important to you. Once you have done that, you continually organize and reorganize your activities so that what matters
most always comes first.

## Listen to Your Intuition

You can use the "inner peace test" to determine whether or not
what you are doing is the best thing for you. You can always tell
if it is right for you because, whenever you are doing something
that is in complete alignment with your values, you feel happy
inside.

Sometimes people work at jobs that they don't enjoy. As a
result, they feel frustrated and dissatisfied. This is not because
there is anything wrong with the job. It simply means that this
particular job is wrong for that particular person.

This is an important point to understand. There are many jobs, and parts of many jobs, that you don't enjoy, which you instinctively avoid. It is easy to slip into the belief that there is something wrong with the job or the company when neither may be true. The job is a good job, but it is not the right job for you. The company may be a good company, but your position in it is not aligned and attuned with your unique set of values, convictions, and talents.

## Look Into Yourself

What parts of your life and work give you the greatest pleasure and satisfaction? What parts of your life are the most successful? Where are your activities out of synchrony with your basic values and convictions? Where are they in harmony?

In setting your priorities and organizing your life, imagine that you could change anything, in any way you wanted. Imagine that you owned the entire company and you could design your ideal job so that you were doing only the things that you most enjoyed all day long. What changes would you make?

Apply *zero-based thinking* to your work. Ask continually, "If I were not doing this job today, knowing what I now know, would I get into it again today?"

In my seminars, I often talk about the "C" word. This word stands for "courage." When you begin to examine yourself and your life on the basis of your values and what is really important to you, you have to develop the courage to follow wherever this line of reasoning leads. And it often leads to your making fundamental changes in the way you live your life and do your work.

If you say that one of your most important values is peace of mind, or personal happiness, then you have to be willing to stand back and look at your life honestly and objectively. Then go through your life systematically, and adjust or eliminate those situations and activities that take away your feelings of inner peace and personal happiness.

### Clear Values Lead to Clear Priorities

Once you are clear about your values, either at home or at work, it is much easier for you to set priorities. I conducted a value-setting exercise with a large national corporation some time ago. When we started, the company had 250 projects that it was working on, at various stages of completion. By the time we had determined the true values and strengths of the company, 80 percent of those projects had been crossed off and discontinued. By practicing *values clarification,* the company was able to get back to focusing on the things that it did the best and enjoyed the most.

## Apply the Pareto Principle

The starting point of setting priorities, once you have determined your values, is to apply the Pareto Principle, the 80/20 rule, to every part of your life.

This rule was named after the Italian economist Vilfredo Pareto, who formulated it in 1895. He concluded, after many years of research, that society could be divided into two groups of people. The first group, 20 percent of the population, he called the "vital few." This group included the people and families who controlled 80 percent of the wealth of Italy. The other 80 percent he called the "trivial many," those who controlled only 20 percent of the wealth.

Further experimentation proved that the 80/20 rule applied to virtually all economic activities. According to this principle, 20 percent of what you do will account for 80 percent of the value of all the things you do. If you have a list of ten items to work on at the beginning of the day, two of those items will usually be more valuable and important than all the others put together. Therefore, your job is to determine the top 20 percent of tasks before you begin.

### The 80/20 Rule Prevails in All Areas

In your business, you will find that 20 percent of your customers account for 80 percent of your revenues. Twenty percent of your products or services account for 80 percent of your profits. Twenty percent of your salespeople make 80 percent of your sales. You will even find that 20 percent of your customers are responsible for 80 percent of your problems. The 80/20 rule reigns supreme.

In your personal life, this rule also applies. Twenty percent of what you do with your family will give you 80 percent of the results, rewards, and satisfaction that you enjoy. Eighty percent of the time that you go out for dinner, you will go to 20 percent of the restaurants that you are familiar with. When you go to your favorite restaurants you will order the same dish 80 percent of the time.

In your work, before you start doing anything, you always ask, "Is what I am about to do among the top 20 percent of activities that account for 80 percent of the value of everything I do?" Every hour of every day you should apply this principle to your work. Take time to think before you act, and then concentrate on the 20 percent of the tasks and activities that represent the highest payoff for you and your company.

## Separate the Urgent from the Important

In setting priorities, it is important that you remember to separate the urgent from the important. Remember that the urgent is seldom important, and the important is seldom urgent.

An urgent task is something that must be dealt with immediately. It is usually determined by forces external to yourself, such as your boss or your customers. Very often it is a ringing telephone or an unexpected interruption from a coworker. These are all urgent because they are "in your face." But they are often not important in terms of their long-term value.

Perhaps the most important word in setting priorities is the word *consequences*. Something that is important is something that has serious potential consequences, whether or not you do it. Something that is unimportant is something for which there are few or no consequences. Sometimes, it doesn't matter if it is done at all.

Important tasks, on the other hand, are those that can be put off in the short term. These are the bigger, more difficult, and more important tasks that can have serious long-term consequences on your life and work. But they are seldom urgent, at least at the beginning.

### Your Top Priorities

The most pressing tasks on your list of things to do are those tasks that are both urgent *and* important. They have to be done immediately. There are significant potential consequences for doing them or not doing them.

First of all, you should organize your workday so that you stay on top of the tasks that are both urgent and important. These are things that must be done immediately, and they usually have tight timelines.

Once you are caught up with your urgent and important tasks, you should turn your attention to those tasks that are important but not urgent. The more time you can spend working on important tasks with serious long-term potential consequences, the more effective you become and the more you will accomplish.

# Identify Your Limiting Step

An important technique for setting priorities revolves around what is called the "limiting step principle." Between you and any goal you want to accomplish, there is almost invariably a limiting factor, or bottleneck, that determines how fast you accomplish your goal. One of the keys to personal effectiveness is to look at each job and ask, "What one factor determines how quickly I complete this job?"

Apply this principle of constraint analysis to your work hour by hour and day by day. Keep asking, "What is the constraint that determines how fast and how well I complete this task?" Whatever it is, go to work immediately in that area. This is your top priority, and alleviating this constraint will help you to accomplish your most important task faster than anything else you could do.

For example, if you want to get to work on time, you could say that the constraint is the amount of traffic that will be on the roads between your home and your work. But perhaps the traffic is always the same. Then your constraint would be how early you leave home for work, to allow for the traffic. Or perhaps your constraint is the hour at which you arise in the morning so that you can get fully prepared and leave the house on time.

## Apply Constraint Analysis to Each Task

When you examine each of your goals, small or large, short-term or long-term, and identify the constraint, choke point, or limiting factor that determines how fast you achieve that goal, you will see clearly the specific actions you will have to take to achieve your goal on schedule.

Once you have identified your limiting factor, you then concentrate all of your energies on alleviating that specific bottleneck. You focus your intelligence and creativity on finding ways to remove this constraint so that you can accomplish your goal far faster.

When you have done this, you will find that another constraint exists immediately behind the first. A key part of personal effectiveness is for you to engage in an ongoing process of constraint analysis. Keep asking yourself, "What sets the speed at which I accomplish this specific goal or complete this task?"

## Look Inside Yourself or Your Company

The 80/20 rule applies to constraint analysis in a special way. It seems that 80 percent of the limiting factors that determine your success at home or at work are contained within yourself. Only 20 percent are actually contained within the situation, the company, or the environment. This is an important observation. The average person always looks for the reason for her problems outside of herself. The experienced person, on the other hand, always looks for the reasons inside herself or inside the organization.

In most cases, the reasons that you are not achieving your personal goals are because of the lack of a skill, ability, quality, or talent. The problems or frustrations you are experiencing on the outside are almost always a result of some need that you have on the inside.

One of my rules is this: "To achieve a goal you've never achieved before, you are going to have to develop and master a skill that you've never had before." It may be that to achieve one of your important goals, you are going to have to become a different person. You are going to have to develop skills and qualities that you are currently lacking. You are going to have to become a different person if you want to get different results.

Always take a few minutes to stand back from your situation and analyze it objectively, as though you were a consultant who had been called in from the outside. Then ask, "What is it in me, or in my company, that is holding me back?"

## What Else Is Holding You Back?

When I do sales consulting for organizations, I help them think through this process from beginning to end. First, we set a hypothetical goal of doubling their sales. We then ask, "What is the limiting factor that determines how quickly you double your sales in this company?"

The first and most common answer is, "The number of sales we make." If this answer is true, we set a tentative goal to double the number of sales.

We then ask, "What is the constraint or limiting factor that determines the number of sales that you make?" The answers to this question can lead in several different directions and suggest different solutions. For example, the answer may be, "We are not making enough sales." If this is the correct answer, or constraint, then the solution is to find a way to increase the number of sales.

Perhaps the answer is, "Our salespeople are not selling enough to each of our prospects." If this were the answer, then the skills and abilities of the sales force need to be upgraded through training and development.

## Identify the Correct Constraint

Perhaps the reason we are not selling enough is because "our prospects are buying too much of our product from our competitors." If this is the answer, the solution to alleviating the bottleneck may be to change or upgrade the product or service, to focus on different customers and markets, to develop new products and services, or to use different distribution channels.

Perhaps the answer can be rephrased as follows: "Our customers are not buying enough of our products from us." In this case, the solution is to advertise more effectively, sell more professionally, explain the product to the prospect in a way that makes it more attractive, or to close more assertively. The solution to increasing sales may be to improve the effectiveness of the advertising, or to advertise in a different media. It may be to change the prices and terms of purchase. Perhaps it is to change the size, packaging, or ingredients of the offer. Whatever the answer, the time taken to correctly identify the limiting factor determines the specific actions that will be taken to alleviate that constraint and achieve the desired result of sales improvement.

The point is this: The more thoughtfully you engage in constraint analysis, the more likely it becomes that you will select the right area of focus to alleviate the choke point and achieve the goal. You will set the proper priorities and save yourself an enormous amount of time and money. Remember, the very worst use of time is to do something extremely well that need not be done at all.

## Think About the Future Consequences

In setting priorities, one of the most important thinking exercises you engage in is to consider the future impact of any action you take. One of the ways to measure the value or importance of a task is to look at what might happen if the task is done or not done. Something that has a high potential future impact on your life or work is a task of high priority. Something that will have little or no impact on your future is a task of low priority and value.

For example, if you were to read this book on time management and incorporate the very best ideas contained here into your ways of living and working, you could double your productivity, performance, and output. You could accomplish vastly more and be paid at a far higher rate. You could dramatically increase the value of your contribution to your company and become one of the top people in your field. On this basis, reading this book and becoming extremely skilled at time management is a top priority for you because of its long-term future impact.

At home, playing with your children and spending time with your family has potential long-term impact for their happiness and health. Therefore, investing time in the most important people in your life is a top priority because of the impact it can have on their future as well as yours.

On the other hand, watching television, reading the newspaper, surfing the Internet, or going out to lunch with your friends are activities of low priority because they have little or no potential impact in the long term.

Keep asking yourself, "What are the possible consequences of doing or not doing this particular task?" What are the consequences of engaging in this particular activity? If it can have significant consequences, it should be at the top of your list. Engaging in this activity should be a far better use of time than most of the other things you can do.

## Practice Creative Procrastination

An important part of setting priorities is the practice of creative procrastination. The fact is that everyone procrastinates. Everyone has too much to do and too little time. In one study, the researchers concluded that, on average, executives have 300 to 400 hours of projects, responsibilities, and reading materials stacked up that they have not been able to get to, but which they hope to get through in the future.

Because you cannot do everything, you have to procrastinate on many things, if not most things. Creative procrastination requires that you deliberately decide, at a conscious level, the items that you are going to put off doing so that you have more time to do those things that can really make a difference in your life.

Apply the 80/20 rule to procrastination. Resolve to procrastinate on the 80 percent of tasks that are of low value so that you can dedicate the limited amount of time you have to those 20 percent of tasks that have the highest value.

## Return on Time Invested

In terms of value and return on time invested (ROTI), if you have a list of ten tasks to complete, two of those tasks will be worth more than all the others put together. This means that each of those tasks will be worth at least five times more, or will give you a 500 percent return on time invested over doing any of the other eight tasks on your list, which are of low or no value. Focusing on these two tasks will give you the highest payoff possible for the investment of your time.

It has been said that *effectiveness* is doing the right things and *efficiency* is doing things right. The difference between leaders and managers is that leaders do the right things and managers simply do things right. In setting priorities, you must focus on doing the right thing, rather than simply doing things right.

As a knowledge worker, according to Peter Drucker, your first job is to decide "what" is to be done? The questions of "how" and "when" only come later. Remember, if it is not worth doing, it is not worth doing right.

## Priorities Versus Posteriorities

An important part of setting and working on priorities is for you to set *posteriorities* as well. A priority is something that you do more of and sooner. A posteriority is something you do less of, and later, if at all. Setting priorities means starting something and completing it as quickly as possible. Setting posteriorities means stopping something or even discontinuing an activity altogether.

Since you can only do one thing at a time, and you cannot do everything that you have to do, one of the questions you ask at the beginning of each day and each week is, "What am I going to stop doing?" What are you going to cut out? What are you going to eliminate? What activities are you going to delete? What are you doing today that, knowing what you now know, you wouldn't start up again today if you had to do it over?

### Stop Doing Things

The fact is that you can only get control of your time to the degree to which you stop doing things that you are doing today. You cannot simply find ways to do more things, to work longer and harder hours. Instead, you have to stand back and look at your life and work objectively and ask, "What am I going to stop doing so that I have enough time to do the most important things in my life and work?"

Before you start a new task, remember that your dance card is full. You are already overwhelmed with work. You have no spare time. You are subject to the Law of the Excluded Alternative, which says, "Doing one thing means *not* doing something else."

Before you commit to a new task or job, you must think through and decide upon the things that you are not going to do right now or that you are going to eliminate altogether. You must decide how and in what way you are going to defer, delay, or delegate certain tasks on your work list if you are to free up enough time to do other tasks that are more important. Getting into a new task means getting out of an old task. Picking up something that you haven't done requires putting down something that you were already working on.

The very act of thinking through what you are going to stop doing is a tremendous help in setting accurate priorities before you begin.

## Practice the ABCDE Method

One of the most helpful ways for you to organize your tasks by priority is for you to use the ABCDE Method. This requires that you review your list of daily activities before you begin. You then place one of these letters in front of each activity. Organize your tasks in terms of potential consequences.

### Your "A" List

An "A" task is something that you *must* do. It is very important. There are serious consequences for not doing it. Place an "A" next to every item on your work list that is urgent and important and has serious consequences for completion or noncompletion.

If you have several "A" tasks, organize them by importance by putting A-1, A-2, A-3, and so on next to each item. When you begin work, you always start on your A-1 task. This is your top priority.

### Your "B" List

A "B" task is something that you *should* do. There are mild consequences for doing it or failing to do it. The rule is that you

should never do a "B" task when there is an "A" task left undone. "B" tasks may be getting back to a coworker with the answer to a question or replying to correspondence.

### Your "C" List

These are things that would be *nice* to do, but they are definitely
not as important as "A" or "B" tasks. There are no consequences
for doing them or not doing them. Reading the paper or going
out for lunch fall neatly into the "C" category.

### Delegate Everything Possible

The letter "D" stands for *delegate*. Before you do anything, you
should ask if there is someone else to whom you can delegate
this task to free up more time for the most important tasks that
only you can do.

### Eliminate Everything Possible

The letter "E" stands for *eliminate*. There are many little tasks
that creep onto your daily list that you can eliminate altogether
and it would make no difference at all to you or to anyone else.
The rule is that you can only get control over your time to the
degree to which you stop doing things of low or no value. The
more things you stop doing or eliminate altogether, the more
time you will have to work on your "A" tasks, the tasks that determine your success or failure at work.

## Reengineer Your Work

The process of reengineering applied to your personal work can
be very helpful to you in setting better priorities. The central
focus of reengineering is *simplification*. You must continually
look for ways to accomplish a complex task or busy job by simpli-
fying the process of work on the task from beginning to completion.

In reengineering your work, you continually look for ways

to delegate, defer, downsize, outsource, or eliminate tasks. In delegating, you look for someone else who can do the job at least as well as you, but at a lower hourly rate than you earn. In deferring, you look for ways to put off parts of the task that do not have to be done immediately. In downsizing, you look for ways to reduce the size or complexity of the task. In outsourcing, you look for individuals or outside organizations that specialize in doing this particular task, and you turn over complete parts of the task to them. In eliminating, you look for ways to discontinue the task altogether, especially if it is no longer important in the current situation.

The decision to continually look for opportunities to outsource, delegate, and get things done by other people frees you up for the things that only you can do. It is a critical part of setting and achieving your top-priority tasks.

## Set Personal Priorities

Your main goal at work—and the key to self-esteem, self-respect, and personal pride—is for you to increasingly develop your personal and corporate effectiveness. The more effective, efficient, and productive you are, the better you feel and the more successful you will be. This is a central focus of time power.

To set better personal priorities, regularly ask yourself questions such as:

1. What are my unique strengths and abilities?

2. What are my natural talents?

3. What do I do especially well?

4. What have I done well in the past? What skills, abilities, and accomplishments account for most of my success in life and work up until now?

5. What are the things that I do quickly and well that seem to be difficult for other people?

6. Where do I have the ability to become outstanding if I were to upgrade my knowledge and skills?

7. What do I really love to do?

Most of your results in life come from your ability to perform well in a few limited areas. One of the characteristics of leaders is that they only choose positions and accept jobs and responsibilities where they know they have the ability to do the job in an excellent manner. They refuse to do things that they don't enjoy or that they do not do particularly well.

## Where Do You Perform Well?

Think through your past life, your past successes, your past jobs and occupations, and identify what it is that you do well. Determining those things that you perform (or could perform) in a superior fashion is one of the keys to channeling your life, your work, and your energies into areas where you can really make a difference for yourself and your company.

To be successful at any job or profession, you must develop a series of core competencies, or skills, that enable you to do your job well. But to rise to the top of your field, you must become outstanding in at least one area. In this sense, the "good" is the enemy of the "excellent." Many people become good at what they do. They then become complacent and stop growing. They compare themselves with people who are not as good as they are, rather than focusing on what they are truly capable of.

## Look for Ways to Add Value

The reason for every job, and the role of every person, is to "add value." The primary reason that you are on the payroll is to contribute value of some kind to your company. This value is then combined with the value that others contribute into the product or service that is sold to the customer or client. Your ability to contribute value determines your results, your rewards, and your success in your career.

Ask yourself, "Of all the things I do, where and how do I contribute the most value to my company?" If you analyze your work carefully, you will find that there are usually only *three* things you do that are responsible for 90 percent or more of the value you contribute to your company.

To determine your three strongest skill areas, begin with this question: "If I could only do one thing all day long, what one activity contributes the greatest value to my business?"

Once you have determined the answer to that question, you then ask, "If I could only do one more thing, what would it be?" You then ask the question one more time until you come to the third major activity.

The whole purpose of organizing your life and setting priorities is so that you can spend more time on these three tasks. You will contribute more and be of greater value to your company if you complete these tasks, and if you do an excellent job on each one of them, than everything else you do put together. What are they?

## The Secret of Success

Some years ago, I met one of the top insurance salesmen in the world. He sold more than $100 million of life insurance each year. He had a staff of forty-two people. These people handled every single aspect of his business, from scheduling through to proposal preparation, administrative tasks, banking, advertising and promotion, and client service. He focused on the one thing that he did better than almost anyone else in the world, which was face-to-face contact and interaction with prospective clients and customers.

He took two hours aside every day to study, practice, and prepare his face-to-face meetings and interactions. He became one of the most knowledgeable experts in personal insurance and estate planning in the world. His unique talent was his ability to assess the needs of a client and to help that client make the very best decisions in the areas of life insurance and estate planning for his unique situation. He delegated everything else.

## Where Do You Excel?
Analyze yourself and ask these questions:

1. What is it that I do better than anyone else?

2. What is my competitive advantage?

3. What is my area of excellence?

4. What is my unique selling proposition?

5. Where could I be excellent?

6. Where should I be excellent?

7. What skills do I need to develop to make a maximum contribution?

Asking and answering these questions is the key to personal effectiveness and high performance.

Commit to excellent performance. Make the decision today that you are going to join the top 10 percent of people in your field. Determine the most important skill that you can learn and develop, the one skill that will help you more than any other, to get into the top 10 percent in your profession. Write down this skill as a goal, set a deadline, make a plan, and work on it every day.

## Get Better at Your Key Tasks
One of the keys to setting priorities and good time management is to get better and better doing more and more of the few things you do that make more of a difference than anything else. The better you are at what you do, the more you will get done in a shorter period of time.

Set "mastery" as your goal in your career. You will only be

truly successful, happy, and paid what you are truly capable of earning when you develop mastery at what you do. Years of research have concluded that the achievement of mastery is possible for almost everyone, but it is not easy. It requires five to seven years of hard work in your field, including many hours of study and practice, to become one of the very best at what you do. And there are no shortcuts.

## Invest Time in Your Future

Whenever I bring up this subject in seminars and workshops, many of the participants moan and roll their eyes. They have somehow gotten the idea that it is possible to jump to the head of the line in life without paying the price that others have paid. They are looking for a quick, easy way to move to the top without putting in the hundreds, and even thousands, of hours of hard work that are necessary to get there.

Sometimes they say to me, "Five years is too long!" Then I tell them something that often changes their thinking completely: "The time is going to pass, anyway."

How old will you be five years from today? The answer is five years older. In other words, time is going to pass in any case. The only question is, "Where are you going to be in your field at the end of five years?"

The good news is that if you set mastery in your field as your long-term career goal, and you work toward that goal every day, continually reading, listening, and learning to upgrade your skills, you will inevitably reach the top of your field. If you are willing to make the sacrifices and pay the full price of success in advance, you will eventually reap the rewards. Nothing can stop you from getting to the top of your field except yourself, and you can only stop yourself by stopping.

## Think in Terms of Priorities All Day Long

Apply the 80/20 rule to every part of your business. Identify the most profitable products and services your company offers. Identify the top 20 percent of customers who contribute the greatest value. Identify the 20 percent of people in your company who contribute the most value in terms of their work. What are the 20 percent of possible opportunities that can account for 80 percent of your sales in the years ahead? Keep viewing your business through an 80/20 lens. Be sure you are working on those activities that can make the greatest difference of all.

What products, services, and competencies account for your company's greatest successes? Why is it that your company has grown from where it started to where it is today? The key to achieving great successes in the future is to identify the reasons for your success in the present. This becomes your springboard to market superiority in the future.

In setting priorities, you must analyze your business clearly and understand it completely. Determine the areas in which your company performs well. Decide upon the company's area of excellence, or area of competitive advantage. Where and how are your company, and its products and services, superior to your competition? In what areas are breakthroughs possible if you were to develop new products and services or to upgrade your existing products and services?

## Analyze Your Company Priorities

Practice "corporate triage" on your company, and your products and services, on a regular basis. The concept of triage comes from World War I. During the battles on the western front, there were so many wounded that the medical corps could not treat them all. There were not enough doctors and nurses. As a result, they began dividing the rooms into three groups. The first group was made up of the wounded soldiers who would die in any case, whether or not they got medical attention. They were put aside and made comfortable. The second group was the soldiers who would survive in any case, whether or not they got medical attention, because they had light wounds. These individuals were put aside and treated quickly. The third group of wounded would survive only if they got immediate medical attention. This is where the doctors and nurses focused all of their energies, to save those who would die in the absence of treatment.

### Divide Products/Services Into Three Groups

In your business, you can apply the idea of corporate triage to your products and services. They can be divided into three groups: winners, survivors, and losers. (Sometimes they are called "cash cows, stars, and dogs.")

Which of your products and your services are your winners? These are the ones that sell well, are profitable, and generate steady, predictable cash flow. They are the things for which your company is known. These are the products and services that you take excellent care of, but which do not require immediate or emergency attention.

What are the products and services that have great potential? If you spend time on these products and services, in sales and marketing, or if you redesign or repackage them, you can turn them into winners in the market. These are the products and services that require immediate attention and the best energies of your most talented people.

Then there are your losers, or your "dogs." No matter how much effort you put into marketing and selling these products or services, no matter how you repackage them or reformulate them, they are still not making much of an impression in the marketplace. They are a drain on funds and on the time and energies of your key people. These are the products and services that will die sooner or later because, for whatever reason, the market doesn't want them.

### Focus Where Excellent Results Are Possible

In setting priorities for your business, your winners represent the top 20 percent of your business activities. You must never take them for granted. You must do everything possible to upgrade and improve them and ensure that they continue to be good sellers and generators of cash.

Your potential "stars" are the products that have the potential of becoming big sellers if you spend enough time, attention, and money on them. They are your potential winners for the future. Investing time and money in these products and services is a high priority.

The products and services that will die anyway, no matter how much time or money you invest in them, become your "posteriorities." Especially in times of reduced markets and profitability, you must have the courage and decisiveness to accept that, although it seemed like a good idea at the time, this product or service does not justify the expenditures necessary to make it successful. It should be discontinued or abandoned so you can devote your energies to those products and services that represent the future of the business and the cash flow of tomorrow.

## Prioritize Your Personal Life

You can practice "personal triage" in your life, as well. There are some things in your life that give you tremendous pleasure and satisfaction. These are the high-priority uses of your time, such as your family and your personal activities. You should pay close attention to them and never take them for granted.

There are potential uses of your time, activities, and money that represent the possibilities of the future. These are areas where you need to invest more of yourself and your time if you want to maximize everything that is possible for you in those areas.

Finally, there are those people and activities in your life that, knowing what you now know, you wouldn't start up with again today. These are the time traps and activities that you should downsize, minimize, and eliminate so that you have more time for those few things that give you the greatest pleasure and satisfaction.

## Look Into the Future

A key part of personal time management is for you to take the time to look into the future. Project forward five years and think about where you want to be. Create a mental picture of your ideal future and then think about the steps that you would have to take, starting today, to make it a reality. Remember, it doesn't matter where you are coming from. All that really matters is where you are going.

Focus on the future rather than the past. Focus on opportunities rather than problems. Think about solutions and what specific actions you could take, rather than things that have gone wrong and who is to blame. Keep asking, "Where do we go from here?" As John Maynard Keynes said, "We must give a lot of thought to the future, because that is where we are going to spend the rest of our lives."

In many companies, 80 percent of the time of senior people is spent on the problems of yesterday rather than on the opportunities of tomorrow. Keep thinking of ways that you can change the things that you are doing today to ensure that your future is consistent with what you desire.

### *Project Forward Five Years*

Gary Hamel and C. K. Prahalad, the strategic planners who wrote the book *Competing for the Future,* encourage decision makers to project forward several years when they do strategic planning. They encourage executives to imagine that their company is the top company in the industry some years in the future. They then identify the products, services, markets, and especially skills, talents, and abilities that they will need to be industry leaders five years from now. Finally, they encourage business leaders to begin immediately to develop the core competencies they will need to be market leaders in the future. You should do the same.

## Focus On the First 20 Percent

In setting priorities, remember that the first 20 percent of any task usually accounts for 80 percent of the value of that task.

Once you begin working on the task, the first 20 percent of the time that you spend planning and organizing the resources necessary to achieve the task usually accounts for 80 percent of your success. In setting priorities, always focus on the first 20 percent of the task. Get on with it and get it done. The next 80 percent will tend to flow smoothly once the first 20 percent is complete.

If you are in sales, getting the initial appointment, where you meet face-to-face with the decision maker, is the first 20 percent of the transaction. But it accounts for 80 percent of the value in the sales process. The presentation, the closing of the sale, the follow-up, the delivery of the product or service, and so on, represent the second 80 percent that only accounts for 20 percent of the value.

## Forget About the Small Things

In setting priorities, never give in to the temptation to clear up small things first. Don't start at the bottom of your list and work up to the important tasks at the top. Don't allow yourself to get bogged down in low-priority activities. Don't major in minors. As Goethe said, "The things that matter most must never be at the mercy of the things that matter least."

The natural tendency of human nature is to follow the Law of Least Resistance. In time management and personal work, this means that we have a natural tendency to start on small tasks, thinking that as soon as we get warmed up, we will launch into our big tasks and we will be more productive.

Here is what I have found. When you start in on little tasks, they begin to multiply, like rabbits in the springtime. When you begin clearing up your small tasks, you seem to attract more and more small tasks to work on. The longer and harder you work, the more small tasks seem to arise. By the end of the day, you will be exhausted, and you won't have accomplished anything of value. Start with your most important work first.

# Five Key Questions for Setting Priorities

There are five key questions that you can ask yourself regularly to ensure that you are working on your top priorities and getting the very most done that is possible for you.

**1.** *Why am I on the payroll?* Ask yourself if what you are doing right now is the most important thing that you have been hired to do. If your boss were sitting across from you watching you, what would you be doing differently from what you are doing at this moment?

Here is an exercise. Make a list of everything you think you have been hired to do and take it to your boss. Ask your boss to organize this work list by priority. Have your boss tell you what is most important and what is least important. From that moment onward, work single-mindedly on those tasks that your boss considers to be more important than anything else.

**2.** *What are my highest value activities?* Remember, there are only three things that you do that account for most of the value of your work. Which of your activities contribute the greatest value to your company? If you are not sure, ask the people around you. Everyone knows the most important things that other people should be doing.

**3.** *What are my key result areas?* What are the specific results that you have to get in order to do your job in an excellent fashion? Of all those key result areas, which are most important?

**4.** *What can I, and only I, do that if done well will make a real difference?* What is the one thing, hour by hour, that only you can do and, if you do it well, will make a significant contribution to your business? This is something that no one else can do for you. If you don't do it, it won't be done. Doing this task, doing it well, and doing it promptly can have a major impact on your career.

**5.** *What is the most valuable use of my time, right now?* This is the key question in time management. Every time planning and management skill is oriented around helping you to determine the correct answer to this question at every moment of the day. What is the most valuable use of your time right now?

## The Law of Forced Efficiency

This law says that when you are under tremendous pressure to get results, you become more and more efficient at setting priorities and getting things done.

Here is an exercise for you. Imagine that your boss came to you with two first-class airline tickets and told you to take five days, all expenses paid, at a beautiful vacation resort. It is Monday at 9:00 A.M. Your boss won these tickets at a raffle the night before, but he cannot use them. He is willing to give them to you if you can get all your work for the week done by 5:00 P.M.

If you received such an offer, and it was only valid if you could get your week's work done by the end of the day, how would that change your method of working? What would be the first thing that you would want to be sure to complete before you left? What would be the second task or activity? How much of your time would you spend drinking coffee and chatting with your coworkers under such a constraint? How would you do your work differently if you only had one day to complete five days' worth of work?

If you need encouragement in setting priorities, try asking yourself, "If I had to leave town for a month, and I could only finish one task before I left town, what one task would be the most important for me to get done?"

Put the pressure of priorities on yourself. Ask yourself these questions on a regular basis. And, whatever your answer, set those key tasks as your highest priorities. Go to work on them immediately, and concentrate single-mindedly on those tasks until they are complete.

## Aim for Maximum Payoff

Your time is your life. When you are working on your highest-priority tasks, you are getting the most out of life. Anything you do other than your top priorities is a relative waste of time.

The biggest payoff of all is that when you are working single-mindedly on your highest-priority task, you experience an unending flow of energy, enthusiasm, and self-esteem. You feel more powerful and confident. You feel terrific about yourself and your life.

If you work on low-priority tasks, no matter how many hours you put in, you get no sense of satisfaction or pleasure. You merely feel tired and stressed out at the end of the day. You feel harried and overwhelmed. You feel frustrated and unhappy.

## Take Time to Think and Then Take Action

Take time before you begin work to think through and establish your priorities, using the various ideas and techniques explained in this chapter. Select the most valuable use of your time and get started on that one task. Discipline yourself to stay with that task until it is complete. When you repeatedly concentrate on your top priorities, you will soon develop the habit of high performance. With this habit, you will get two or three times as much done every day as anyone else who works around you. And you will feel terrific about yourself.

*"Success is the sum of small efforts, repeated day in and day out, without ceasing."*

—ROBERT COLLIER

## Action Exercises

1. Resolve today that you are going to become excellent at thinking through and working exclusively on your top-

priority tasks; never allow exceptions until this becomes a habit.

2. Make a list of activities each day before you begin work, and set careful priorities on your list. Divide the items by applying the ABCDE method to each one before starting. Always work on your "A-1" task.

3. Apply the 80/20 rule to every part of your business and personal life. Identify the top 20 percent of activities, customers, products, services, and tasks that account for 80 percent of the value, and focus on them before anything else.

4. Identify your key constraints to business and personal success. What sets the speed at which you achieve a specific goal, and what could you do to remove the limiting factor, either in yourself or in the situation?

5. Think about the potential consequences of doing or not doing a particular task; separate the urgent from the important, and spend more time doing those things that can have a major effect on your future.

6. Determine your personal areas of excellence, those jobs that you do easily and well, faster and better than others. These activities are where you can make the greatest contribution to your company.

7. Every hour of every day, ask yourself, "What is the most valuable use of my time, right now?" Whatever the answer, be sure that you are working on that task, the one that can make a greater difference than anything else.

# CHAPTER FIVE

# Developing the Work Habits to Get Things Done

*"Man is not the creature of circumstances; circumstances are the creatures of men. We are free agents, and man is more powerful than matter."*

—BENJAMIN DISRAELI

Good work habits go hand in hand with success in every area of endeavor. There is nothing that will bring you to the attention of your superiors faster than developing a reputation for being a good, dependable worker. How you work determines the quality and quantity of your rewards. How you work determines how much you earn, how effective you are, how much you are respected in your organization, and how much real satisfaction you get out of your job.

Unfortunately, most people are poor workers. They are unorganized, unfocused, and easily distracted. They work at about 50 percent of capacity. Sadly enough, they don't even seem to know how to work any differently. Even if they wanted to, it is like speaking a foreign language; they wouldn't know how to do it without first being taught.

Much of the blame for poor work habits goes back to the school system and the attitudes of teachers toward academic excellence and parents toward homework. If people go through ten or twelve or even fifteen years of schooling and never have to learn how to settle down and produce good-quality work, it's not surprising they will have a hard time producing high-quality work when they enter the job market.

## The Habits of Highly Productive People

In this chapter, you will learn how to develop the habits of highly productive people. To begin with, the foundations of good work habits can be summarized in two words: *focus* and *concentration*.

### Focus on What Is Important to Your Most Important Goal

Focus requires clarity concerning the desired results and the relative priority of each step that you need to take to achieve those results. When you think of focus, think of a photographer adjusting his lens to keep the key subject sharp in the center of the picture.

To be truly effective at work, you must be continually adjusting your lens to be sure that what you are working on is the most important thing you could be doing at the moment to achieve your most important goal. The worst waste of time is doing something very well that need not be done at all.

### Concentrate Your Energies

Concentration requires the ability to stay with a task until it is 100 percent complete. Concentration means that you work in a straight line to get from where you are to where you want to go without diversion or distraction. Concentration requires that you stay on task, without getting sidetracked into doing things of lesser importance.

There is a story of a traveler in ancient Greece who met an old man on the road and asked him how he could get to Mount Olympus. The old man, who turned out to be Socrates, replied by saying, "If you really want to get to Mount Olympus, just make sure that every step you take is headed in that direction."

If you want to accomplish your goals, you must be sure that everything you do is taking you in that direction. This decision alone will dramatically increase the quality and quantity of what you get done each day.

## Four Steps to High Productivity

There are four main steps to high productivity, and they cannot be repeated too often:

**1.** *Set clear goals and objectives in writing.* Think through what you are trying to accomplish before you begin. Ask yourself, "What am I trying to do? How am I trying to do it?" Whenever you experience frustration of any kind, go back and repeat these questions.

**2.** *Develop a detailed plan of work and action for achieving your goal.* Setting clear goals answers the "What am I trying to do?" question. Making detailed plans of action answers the question of "How am I trying to do it?"

**3.** *Set clear priorities with each of your work tasks organized in a hierarchy of value and importance to the desired result.* Apply the 80/20 rule over and over, day by day, and hour by hour, before you embark on any task or activity. Discipline yourself to work on your highest priority before you do anything else.

**4.** *Concentrate single-mindedly, without diversion or distraction, on the most important thing you can do to achieve the goal.* This is the real key to getting things done.

## The Benefits of Concentration

There are several benefits from learning how to concentrate. First, important task completion is a source of energy, enthusiasm, and self-esteem. On the other hand, failure to complete important tasks, or to complete them only partially, is not only a major source of stress, but it *depletes* your enthusiasm and self-esteem.

When you complete an important task, you experience a surge of energy and well-being. But when you work on an unimportant task, even if you complete it in a timely fashion, you get no feeling of satisfaction or personal reward at all.

Disciplining yourself to concentrate on a job until it is finished gives you a feeling of confidence, competence, and mastery. It gives you an experience of self-control, so you feel that you are in charge of your own destiny.

## The Habit of Task Completion

The habit of completing your tasks, finishing what you start, is an essential part of character building. You cannot imagine a fully mature, fully functioning person who is unable to finish what she begins. The development of this habit is the key to long-term success.

You can accelerate the process of becoming a highly productive person by regularly visualizing yourself as focused and channeled toward high achievement. See yourself as a highly productive, efficient person. Feed your subconscious mind with this picture until it is accepted as a command. Remember, the person you "see" is the person you will "be."

Your subconscious cannot tell the difference between a real experience and one that you vividly imagine. If you create an imaginary picture of yourself performing in an efficient and effective way, your subconscious mind reacts exactly as if that is what you were actually doing at the moment. Each time you replay this image of yourself performing at your best, your subconscious mind records it exactly as if it were happening again. It then adjusts your words, actions, and behavior so that your actions on the outside are consistent with the picture you have created on the inside.

Each time you remember an occasion when you were performing at your best with confidence, your mind imprints it into your self-concept. The more often you see yourself as the very best that you can possibly be, the more rapidly this becomes your automatic behavior. You program yourself for success by feeding your mind with positive pictures, either images that you create, or repeat pictures of previous peak-performance experiences.

## Combine Thoughts with Feelings

The principle of *emotionalization* is powerful when you use it in conjunction with visualization. There is a formula that says "thought times emotion equals result" (T $\times$ E = R). What this means is that if you create a clear mental picture of yourself working efficiently and well, and you combine that with the emotions of enthusiasm and enjoyment, your subconscious mind accepts this picture more rapidly as a command. Therefore, it more rapidly becomes your current behavior.

A powerful method for reprogramming your subconscious mind with the thoughts, feelings, and behaviors of highly productive people is for you to "act as if" you were already the efficient, effective person that you desire to be.

### Assume the Position

It turns out that there is a physical position for almost every mental or emotional state. There is body language for good work habits as well. For example, if you work at a desk and you sit up straight, erect, and lean forward, you actually trigger a feeling of being more productive. If you walk briskly, with your head up, your shoulders back, and your chin held high, you tend to feel like a more confident and productive person.

The Law of Reversibility says that if you feel a particular way on the inside, you will act that way on the outside. It also says that if you act as if you already felt the way you desire, your actions, which are under your direct control, will create the feelings, which are not.

If you want to be confident, act confidently. If you want to be courageous, act courageously. If you want to be efficient, behave as if you already are an efficient person. Your actions generate your feelings and beliefs, just as your feelings and beliefs determine your actions.

### Sit Up Straight

On the other hand, if you slouch in a chair or walk slowly with your head down, you will feel lethargic and unproductive. If you put your feet up, or lean back and relax, your energy levels will drop and you will lose your enthusiasm for any kind of productive work.

Throughout the workday, you should stop regularly and observe how you are sitting and doing your work. Ask yourself, "Would a highly effective person sit and look like this?" If the answer is no, then change your posture and your position so that it is more consistent with the way you think a highly productive person would sit and work.

### Perform Like a Genius

Some years ago, *Reader's Digest* reported on a study of geniuses. The story examined the life and habits of many geniuses over the ages in an attempt to determine what characteristics they had in common. The magazine finally concluded that all geniuses seemed to behave the same in three ways. Fortunately, ordinary people with average intelligence can develop these three qualities or behaviors and dramatically increase their mental productivity as a result.

The first quality was that all geniuses seemed to take a *systematic* and orderly approach to problem solving. Whenever something went wrong, they would stop and analyze it carefully, step by step, before jumping to a conclusion or taking action to resolve it. As a result, when they finally did make a decision, it was better than those of people who simply reacted to a problem rather than thinking it through.

The second quality that the geniuses in the study seemed to have in common was a sense of wonder—the ability to look at situations in a fresh, almost childlike way.

Geniuses keep an open mind and a flexible attitude toward all subjects. They allow their minds to "float freely," and they examine all the possible ways of approaching a situation or solving a problem before they come to a conclusion. They are continually asking themselves the question: "What *else* might be the solution?"

The third quality of geniuses is that they seem to have the ability to concentrate with greater depth and intensity than the average person. Thomas Carlyle once said, "Genius is simply an infinite capacity for taking pains." Almost anyone who can discipline himself to concentrate single-mindedly on a single subject until he completes that task or masters that subject will begin to perform vastly better in that area.

This ability to concentrate single-mindedly applies to sales, management, parenting, negotiating, or anything else. All great achievements are the results of long periods of single-minded concentration, focused on a single task or objective, until the job is complete.

## Steps to Better Concentration

There are several ways to develop the qualities of concentration common to exceptional men and women. These are all business skills, and they can be learned by anyone who possesses enough determination to practice them repeatedly until they become habits.

First, before you start work, clear your workspace of everything except exactly what you need to complete your highest-priority task. Simplicity and order tend to be more conducive to highly productive work, for average people as well as for geniuses.

Second, plan your days and organize your work so that you create blocks or chunks of time to work on completing major tasks. Use your ingenuity to find ways to take time from other activities, and consolidate this time into blocks of a minimum of sixty to ninety minutes each. Because of the time it takes you to settle into a task, it is usually not possible for most people to accomplish meaningful tasks in less than sixty-minute to ninety-minute periods. By meaningful tasks, I am referring to creative work such as writing reports and proposals, as well as holding meetings and discussions with and about people and projects. Almost all important tasks require unbroken periods of time where total concentration is possible.

You cannot rush important conversations, discussions, or negotiations. You need blocks of time. To be able to concentrate your attention, you must become creative in finding these blocks of time. There are many ways to accomplish this.

## Early to Bed, Early to Rise
One very effective technique is to work at home in the morning for an extended period, before you go in to work. You are usually fresher and more capable of concentrated effort first thing in the morning than at any other time during the day.

For example, you can go to bed early and get up at 5:00 A.M. Start work immediately, and work without interruptions for three or four hours before going into the office. You will be amazed at how much you get done in these unbroken, uninterrupted chunks of time, early in the day, when you are rested and at your best.

It is amazing how many great men and women practice this way of working. Thomas Jefferson once wrote, "The sun has never caught me in my bed."

When you get up and get going early, you can get the equivalent of an entire day's work done before the normal working day even begins. If you work from 5:00 A.M. to 8:00 A.M. and then go to the office, you will soon be on top of all your major tasks. Everything else you get done during the day will be a bonus.

## Work Without Interruptions

Many companies in large cities will often rent an apartment near the office and furnish it with desks, chairs, and office supplies so that executives can go there and work without interruption away from the telephone and drop-in visitors. This dramatically increases their productivity, especially when they are working on important tasks and projects that have to be done on a specific schedule and completed by a certain deadline.

The very fact that you know that you will not be interrupted enables you to concentrate better and produce more. If you are working at home, you should disconnect your telephone so that no calls can get through to you. Working without interruption for long periods is an extraordinarily powerful way to increase your output and get more and better results.

## Start Earlier, Work Harder, Stay Later

There are three other simple techniques that you can use to double your productivity and to accelerate your results.

1. *Go into the office one hour earlier, before the workday begins.* By leaving home early and getting into the office early, you will avoid most of the traffic. Since there is no one there to interrupt you, you can get started immediately. Often you can clear up an entire day's work in that one hour.

2. *Develop the habit of working straight through the typical lunch hour when almost everyone else has left the office.* Company policy permitting, there is no law that says that you have to go for lunch when everyone else goes. There is no law that says

that you have to eat lunch from twelve to one each day. You can take your lunch hour before noon or after one o'clock. In both cases, there will be no lunch-hour crowds or delays. You can eat quickly and be back at work with very little downtime. You can get in and out faster and you will get better service.

**3.** *Stay in the office and work one extra hour after everyone goes home.* This is one of the best ways for busy people to stay on top of their jobs. During that uninterrupted hour (which, as you know, is worth three hours during the day), you can clear up all your responsibilities, write your reports, dictate your correspondence, and plan the next day in detail. The key is to take those sixty- to ninety-minute chunks of time and work without interruption. Close the door, unplug the telephone, put your head down, and work without stopping.

### The Paradox of Work

The paradox of work is, "You can't get any work done at work." Fully 75 percent of the time in any work environment is spent in conversation and discussions with other people. There are never-ending distractions, interruptions, and telephone calls. As much as 50 percent of working time in any environment is taken up with idle chitchat among coworkers as they go back and forth throughout the day.

If you start one hour early, work through lunch, and stay one hour later, you will add three hours of productive time to your workday. You will, in effect, double your productivity, performance, and output. Your results will skyrocket. You will get vastly more done than the other people who work at regular hours. You will be so far ahead of your coworkers that people will be amazed at how much you get done.

Hard, sustained, concentrated effort is essential to high productivity and the successful achievement of anything worthwhile. Every great accomplishment in human history was preceded by an extended period of concentrated effort for a long, long time, sometimes for months or even years. Your job is to create these chunks of time.

## Minimize Idle Conversation

Some of the great time wasters or time savers, depending on how you handle them, are conversations and discussions with coworkers and staff. Since conversation and interaction are inevitable and unavoidable, the way you handle discussions can have a substantial impact on your overall productivity and results.

When you have a meeting with someone, arrange your office and organize your time so that you concentrate single-mindedly on that person during the meeting. Do not allow the conversation to go off on tangents. Listen intently to the other person when he speaks and resist the temptation to digress from the topic being discussed.

The very act of listening with intense concentration dramatically *reduces* the amount of time that it takes a person to communicate his full message. It is amazing how much time is wasted or lost because of continuous digression from the subject or distractions, such as a ringing phone or people walking in. The more you can control these interruptions, the less time it will take you to have a high-quality conversation that achieves the results you desire.

## Develop a Compulsion for Closure

There is something in the human brain that thrills to any completed task. One of the most important habits you can develop is that of closure, or completion. Set specific deadlines for yourself, and use them as a "forcing system" that enables you to concentrate single-mindedly on tasks. Discipline yourself to do one thing at a time, and then to complete that one task before you begin something else.

Each time you satisfy your brain's needs for closure, it releases endorphins into your bloodstream. These endorphins give you a sense of happiness and well-being. They increase your energy and creativity. They improve your personality and make you feel good about yourself. Disciplining yourself to complete important tasks improves the overall quality of your life and dramatically increases your productivity.

## Reward Yourself Regularly

One of the ways that you can condition yourself for task completion is to set up a structure of rewards for each thing that you do. Just as animals are trained by their handlers giving them a sugar cube or a biscuit when they perform a particular trick, you can condition yourself by giving yourself a little reward each time you complete part of a task. You can then give yourself a large reward for the completion of the total job.

Psychologists have found that 85 percent of your motivation to engage in a particular action is determined by the benefit that you anticipate enjoying as the result of taking that action. When you set up a reward system for yourself, you motivate yourself, both consciously and subconsciously, to continue working without distraction toward task completion.

### *Share the Rewards*

When you need the cooperation and understanding of members of your family while you are working on a big task or completing a major assignment, discuss and agree upon a reward for the entire family when the job is done. It can be something as simple as going out for dinner or to a movie. It can be a vacation or a trip to Disneyland. When everyone knows that there is a reward at the end of the road, the people around you will be more understanding and supportive, and they will even encourage you to keep working at the job until it is finished.

Many companies with sales forces use this system of family rewards with great success. They organize their sales contests and quotas in such a way that the top producers get a trip to a resort in Hawaii or the Caribbean if they hit their targets. They send the brochures describing the resorts to the spouses of the salespeople at their homes. The spouse at home, who is now also motivated by the idea of the reward, will constantly encourage the salesperson to make the sales necessary to qualify for the trip.

Rewards are wonderful incentives to high performance. You should create as many of them for yourself as you can think of. Even if it is something as simple as going for a walk after finishing a report, the anticipation of the reward will drive you onward and help you to concentrate on the task.

## Talk to Yourself Positively

You can improve your ability to concentrate on any task by using *positive affirmations*. Whatever commands you repeat to yourself are eventually accepted by your subconscious mind. Your subconscious then motivates and drives you to behave in a way consistent with that command.

When you talk to yourself in a positive way, with the emotions of enthusiasm and conviction, you find yourself *internally* driven toward higher productivity. You can develop a trigger phrase when your attention wanders. Keep repeating, ''Back to work! Back to work! Back to work!'' whenever you find yourself getting distracted or you feel like procrastinating. This will jolt you into getting back on task, and keep you working on the job until it is done.

When someone else wants to talk to you or distract you from your work, you can break away by simply saying, ''Well, I guess I have to get back to work!'' Whenever you say that you have to get back to work, the other person will usually stop talking and leave you alone.

Each time you repeat these words, you will be surprised at how easy it is for you to return to your work and start concentrating again.

## Practice Single-Handling

One of the most powerful methods for getting things done is to practice what is called ''single-handling.'' Single-handling means that once you start a task of any kind, you resolve to stay at that task until it is 100 percent complete.

If you pick up a letter, begin a report or proposal, or initiate a sales call or conversation, discipline yourself to stay at it until it is finished. This simple technique can increase your productivity by as much as 50 percent the first day you start using it. It is one of the most powerful habits of time management you will ever learn.

### Get Onto the Learning Curve

Take advantage of what time-and-motion experts call the "learning curve." When you do a group of similar tasks together, the amount of time it takes you to do each subsequent task declines. If you have to make ten or twenty telephone calls or distribute that many reports, you can decrease the amount of time necessary for the completion of each of these tasks by as much as 80 percent by using the learning curve. Every time you do one of these tasks, you get better at it, so it takes you less time to do it even better next time.

The learning curve only works when you do similar tasks one after the other, repeatedly, until they are all done. This is why it is essential to bunch your tasks and do them all at once rather than sporadically through the day.

## Personal Productivity Techniques

There are a series of techniques you can practice to increase your productivity and performance, and improve the rate at which you get things done. These are methods used by the highest-paid and most productive people in every field.

**1.** *Concentrate your powers.* Use the principle of "concentration of power." This requires that you concentrate your talents and abilities where they will yield the highest payoff to you at the moment. It is the key to personal productivity and is essential to success in personal strategic planning.

In corporate strategy sessions, managers focus on the goal of increasing "return on equity" (ROE). The purpose of business strategy is to allocate the company's resources in such a way that they yield the highest possible financial return on the equity invested.

Here is another kind of ROE for you. In setting personal strategy for yourself, your goal is to get the highest "return on energy." Your job is to allocate your talents and abilities in such a way that you achieve the highest possible return on the mental, emotional, and physical energies that you invest in your work. Your highest return on energy is almost always that task where you combine your unique talents and abilities with the specific needs of the situation. You then focus and concentrate single-mindedly on that one task, which is the key to high productivity.

Whenever you have a new job to do, ask yourself: "Does this job give me my highest return on energy invested?" Discipline yourself to apply your skills where you can achieve the greatest results and rewards for both yourself and your company.

**2.** *Concentrate where superior results are possible.* Resolve to concentrate on the few areas where superior performance will bring outstanding results. Usually less than 5 percent of what you do accounts for most of your results. Continually ask yourself, "What can I, and only I, do that, if done well, will make a real difference?"

Discipline yourself not to work at those tasks that, no matter how well you do them, cannot help you or advance you in your career. They do not give you as high a return on energy as something else.

**3.** *Do things you're better at.* When you do things at which you excel, you get more done, make fewer mistakes, and achieve greater personal productivity. Not only that, you enjoy your work more when you are doing things that you do well. What are the few things that you do better than anyone else? What is it that you do easily that seems to be difficult for others? Focus on your unique talents and concentrate on those few areas where you can achieve superior results. This is the key to peak performance.

**4.** *Focus on opportunities.* Concentrate your strengths, and the strengths of others, on your major opportunities. Focus on the opportunities of tomorrow, rather than the problems of yesterday. Concentrate your best talents and energies, and those of your best people, on those few areas where major breakthroughs are possible.

Many companies make the mistake of putting their best people to work to salvage the mistakes of yesterday, rather than deploying them to maximize the opportunities of tomorrow. Keep asking yourself, "What are my biggest opportunities for the future? Where can I make a real breakthrough if I concentrate?"

**5.** *Fish for whales.* Fish for whales, not minnows. Remember that if you catch 1,000 minnows, all you have is a bucketful of fish. But if you catch a single whale, you will pay for the whole voyage.

In business, you must look at your marketplace and try to determine who or what the whales might be. You then make a plan to go after them. Sometimes, landing one big customer, or selling one whale of an order, will be enough to make a business or an individual successful.

**6.** *Focus on key result areas.* Identify the key results you are expected to get by answering the question: "Why am I on the payroll?" Once you've identified your key result areas, work in them exclusively.

Each person has five to seven key result areas where they can make an important contribution to their job and to the organization. It is only when you concentrate your efforts on your key result areas that you will achieve the most significant results possible for you in the shortest period of time.

**7.** *Set and keep deadlines.* Set deadlines for important goals and stick to them. Deadlines force you to work harder and more effectively as the deadline approaches.

A goal or an assignment without a deadline is usually an exercise in futility. It has no motivational force behind it. It creates no compulsion for closure. It is something that you easily procrastinate on and put off until the last minute.

Set deadlines for everything you do. Promise other people that you will finish certain jobs by the deadline. When you promise others, you motivate yourself to fulfill the promise. When you place your honor and your ego on the line by making promises to others, you find yourself internally driven and motivated to get the job done exactly as you said, on schedule.

**8.** *Allow enough time.* Allow enough time to do everything well. Take the time to complete the job in an excellent fashion. Practice the "30 percent rule," which says to always allow yourself an extra 30 percent of time to complete any task. Build in a cushion for unexpected difficulties, delays, or setbacks. Highly productive workers always allow enough time to do the job right.

**9.** *Maintain a steady pace.* Don't hurry or rush around frantically to get the job done. Maintain an easy pace and work steadily. Remember the fable of "The Tortoise and the Hare"? Highly productive people work with a certain rhythm that allows them to flow through enormous amounts of work without becoming stressed or anxious. As Thomas Carlyle said, "Our great business in life is not to see what lies dimly at a distance, but to do what lies clearly at hand."

A hallmark behavior of successful salespeople, executives, and entrepreneurs is that they do one thing at a time. They do the most important thing in front of them, and they stay with it until it is complete. They set priorities and they single-handle their tasks.

**10.** *Think about results.* Result orientation, the ability to get things done, is a key quality of all peak performers. You can develop the ability to concentrate single-mindedly through practice and repetition, over and over, until it becomes an ingrained habit of success. Once you develop the skill of getting things done, the skill will serve you for the rest of your life.

*"Whatever you can do, or dream you can, begin it. Boldness has genius, power, and magic in it."*
                                            —JOHANN WOLFGANG VON GOETHE

## Action Exercises

1. Plan your work thoroughly in advance; have everything you need before you begin work, and then resolve to focus and concentrate.

2. Bunch your tasks; do repetitive or similar jobs all at once, one after the other, taking advantage of the learning curve.

3. Work on those tasks that give you the highest return on your investment of mental, emotional, and physical energy.

4. Create blocks of time when you can work for extended periods without interruptions. This is the key to the accomplishment of important tasks.

5. Set deadlines for yourself for each task, and give yourself rewards for task completion.

6. Develop a compulsion for closure. Discipline yourself to work steadily, without stopping, until the task is complete.

7. Keep repeating the words "Back to work!" throughout the day to keep yourself focused and concentrated on your key result areas.

# CHAPTER SIX

# Managing Multitask Jobs

*"America is unique because it offers you an economic ladder to climb. And here's what's exciting: It is the bottom of the ladder that's crowded, not the top."*

—JIM ROHN

Ⅱll of life is a series of projects. A project is a complex task. It is often called a *multitask job*. This type of job requires the coordination of the efforts of several people, each of whom is responsible for part of the job, with every part of the job being necessary for successful completion. Your ability to handle these multitask jobs is a critical skill for success.

All achievements of consequence are complex, and they involve the cooperation of many people. An example would be the race to put a man on the moon. Tens of thousands of men and women had to coordinate their activities for its successful accomplishment.

Even simple tasks like planning a party, or producing a brochure or newsletter, require the ability to plan multiple tasks. This type of planning and organizing is one of the core skills of time management. Your ability to put together and work with a team of people on a project is the most important skill for advancement in your work.

## The Key Management Skill

A study by Stanford University on the qualities that companies look for in promoting people into the position of chief executive officer concluded that the ability to put together a team to accomplish a task was the single most important identifiable quality of an executive who was destined for the fast track in her career.

Take the example of the spectacular success of a man like Lee Iacocca, who saved Chrysler Corporation from bankruptcy. One of the reasons he was hired into the presidency of Chrysler was because of his ability to bring senior executives together from a variety of different areas to turn the company around. In his first thirty-six months at Chrysler, he replaced thirty-five out of thirty-six senior vice presidents. His ability to assemble this team made all the difference. In his autobiography, he gives full credit to the men and women on those teams who revived the company.

Your ability to put together teams to do multitask jobs or complete complex projects will determine the course of your career as much as any other factor. It will enable you to multiply yourself times the talents and efforts of others, and accomplish vastly more than you ever could on your own.

## A Learnable Skill

Fortunately, project management is a learnable skill, like riding a bicycle. It can be divided into a series of steps, each of which you can master, one at a time.

### Start with the End in Mind

In managing any project, you begin by defining the *ideal desired result* of the project. What exactly are you trying to accomplish? What will the project look like if it is a complete success?

Start by defining the successful completion of the project, the ideal desired result. Write it down and clarify it on paper. Then, work backward to the beginning of the project. Do this exercise in conjunction with the team members involved whenever possible.

How will you be able to tell if you have completed this project successfully? This step, of thinking through and defining your ideal end result, is one of the most valuable of all mental and physical planning tools for any project.

### Start at the Beginning

Once you are clear about your desired result, you then start from the beginning. Determine what you are going to have to do to get from where you are to the completion of this project, on schedule and on budget. Determine a specific deadline or target to aim at. Make sure that it is realistic and achievable.

### Assemble the Team

Bring together all the people whose contributions will be necessary for the success of the project. Sometimes you need to assemble the team before you can even decide upon the ideal result and the schedule. Remember that people are everything. Take ample time to think carefully about the people who are going to be the team members. Fully 95 percent of success in everything that you accomplish as a leader will be determined by your ability to select the people who are going to help you to do the work. If you make the mistake of selecting poor team members, you will almost invariably find it more difficult to achieve the goals that you have set for yourself.

Jim Collins, in his best-selling book *Good to Great*, says: "The key to success is to get the right people on the bus, and get the wrong people off the bus. Then, put the right people in the right seats on the bus."

Focus on the people before the task. Remember that because all productivity comes from people, the people are the most important ingredient.

## Share the Ownership

Instill ownership of the project in the team members by sharing the job with them. There is a direct relationship between how much a person feels a sense of ownership for the job and how committed he is to making the project a success. One of the key jobs of leadership is to instill this feeling of ownership in each member of the team, so that each person feels personally responsible for the accomplishment of the overall project. You accomplish this by discussing every detail of the project with the people who are expected to carry it out.

## Develop a Shared Vision

A shared vision is an ideal future picture of success that everyone buys into. How do you develop a shared vision? You sit down with the members of your team and work with them to answer the question, "What are we trying to accomplish?" You encourage everyone to contribute, to visualize, and to imagine the ideal outcome or desired result of the project. Once this vision is clear and shared by everybody, you move on to the development of "shared plans" to achieve the vision.

## Create Shared Plans

Shared plans are essential to successful project completion. This step requires that everyone on the team work together to discuss and develop the plans. Plans include the step-by-step activities that will be necessary to complete the project. Everyone knows what has to be done, and even more important, everyone knows what each team member is supposed to do. The more time you spend planning with the members of your team in the early stages, the more committed and creative they will be in accomplishing the task once you get started.

## Set Schedules and Deadlines

Once you have a shared vision and shared plans, and everyone knows exactly what is to be done and what the ideal result will look like, the next step is for you to set a deadline for project completion based on the consensus of your team. You may require sub-deadlines as well. Achieving consensus is extremely important in building a peak-performing team. Ask people how long they think it will take to complete each part of the task and to complete the task overall. As the result of discussion and exchange, everyone should agree that the project can and will be completed by a certain time. One of the biggest mistakes in project management occurs when the project leader sets a date or deadline that is arbitrary and with which the team members do not agree. In each case where this happens, problems arise and the deadline is not met. If the deadline is met, the result is often so full of mistakes and problems that it would have been much better to have agreed on a reasonable deadline before you began. Set your deadlines based on the consensus of your team, or even a majority decision, if that works for you. Get everyone to agree on the timing and scheduling for each job or task that they will be expected to contribute to the overall project.

## List Everything That Must Be Done

List every task, function, and activity that must be completed, right down to the smallest job. The more that you can break the project down into individual jobs and tasks, the easier it is for you to plan, organize, supervise, delegate, coordinate, and get the project finished on time.

## Identify the Information You Will Require

Identify any additional information that you will need to complete the project. List the acquisition of the information as a separate task. Assign it or delegate it specifically to one of the team members. Set a deadline. Remember, a decision without a deadline is merely a meaningless discussion. Nothing gets done.

## Identify the Limiting Factor

Determine the *limiting step* in the completion of the project by answering the question, "What part of the project—that is, what task or activity—determines the speed at which the project can be completed?" In other words, what part of the task is the bottleneck that sets the speed for everything else?

For example, when my company decides to do a public seminar for 1,000 people, the limiting step that determines everything else is finding and booking a hotel or convention facility in a particular city. Finding and finalizing the space for the seminar is almost always the most difficult bottleneck in the whole project. Once we have confirmed a location, we can then begin marketing, sales, advertising, promotion, ticket sales, the shipping of products and materials, staffing, and everything else.

In every project, there is a bottleneck. There is always one task that determines the schedule for everything else. Start off by identifying your limiting step, and then make alleviating that constraint your top priority. Put your most talented and capable people, and even yourself, to work on that task. Nothing can be done until that job is done first.

## Organize the Project

Organize the different parts of the project in two ways: *sequential* tasks and *parallel* tasks. You organize by sequence when you determine which jobs must be done before other jobs can be done, with each task in order. Sequential organization is necessary where a particular task requires that another task be completed before it can be started. In almost every case, before you do anything, you have to do something else first. Organize the tasks sequentially with a logical process of activities from beginning through to the end of the project.

The second way to organize the tasks is through parallel activities. Parallel activities exist when more than one task can be done at the same time. Two or more people can be working on two or three different tasks independently of each other.

### A Typical Multitask Job

For example, let us imagine that you are going to be renting and moving to a new building. The limiting factor or constraint is the decision on the space that you are going to rent, the determination of the exact address, and the signing of the necessary rental or lease documents. Once the location has been determined and secured, several other tasks can be done both sequentially and in parallel.

Some sequential tasks are determining the exact requirement for furniture and fixtures in the new offices, packing up the old offices, arranging for a moving company to transfer the furniture, and the actual moving in.

Some parallel activities could be arranging for new telephones; ordering new stationery; informing your customers, vendors, and suppliers of the new address; and other activities that can be done independently of each other.

### Think on Paper

Create or acquire a simple project management form. Fortunately, because of the recognized importance of project management, there are numerous books, workbooks, planning forms, and computer-based project management systems. They can be used for projects as simple as throwing an office birthday party and as complex as the building of a shopping center or football stadium.

The simplest model is something that you can draw by hand and can carry in your mind as a template for any project that you become responsible for in the future. Start with a blank sheet of paper. Graph paper or lined paper is ideal. Down the left-hand side of the paper, you list every single task that has to be accomplished, up to and including the completion of the project, in the order that the tasks have to be done. Across the top of the page, you write the dates of completion for each phase of the project. The times listed across the top may be in days, weeks, months, or even years. You may have one column for each week or one column for each month. If it is a short-term project, you may have a column for each day, with specific tasks to be completed every twenty-four hours.

### *Planning a Party*

Imagine that you were going to have a Christmas party at your home. The most important first step is to book the caterer for the day that you have planned. Once you have a caterer and a date, you can then proceed through the project to select the menu, confirm the prices, send out the invitations, and make arrangements for chairs and tables. Confirming the caterer and the date puts the project into motion.

You make a list down the left-hand column of every step, from determining the date and the caterer all the way through to the final detail in setting up the Christmas party. Across the top you may put in weeks and months. Under those weeks and months you create columns. Now you have a picture of the project with the first step in the project at the upper left-hand corner and the final completion of the project in the lower right-hand corner.

This project planning form gives you a simple picture that you can review and refer to regularly to be sure that each task is completed on schedule. This simple project planning form can be used and reviewed by everyone who is involved in and responsible for any part of organizing the Christmas party. The clarity of this project management process dramatically increases the likelihood that everything will be done on time, with no unexpected delays or glitches.

Developing and using a chart such as this, or any chart that you find in any time management system, will save you more time and increase your effectiveness more than you can imagine. This chart will show you where all of the bottlenecks or problems may arise. It will enable you to anticipate problems in advance and to take steps to ensure that those problems don't occur.

### Delegate Responsibilities and Deadlines

Once you have the project planned, the team assembled, and every task delineated and laid out in the order in which it must be completed, you then delegate each task with a specific deadline. Build a "fudge factor" into your schedules and aim for the completion of each task comfortably before the deadline. The more important the final date, the more important it is that you build in a cushion of time to ensure that the project is completed on schedule. Most people aim to finish a project at least 10 percent of the time before it is due. If it is a project that takes three weeks and must be completed by, say, Friday, three weeks from today, set a goal to have the entire project complete by Wednesday or even Tuesday of that week. Expect that there will be last-minute mistakes, unexpected setbacks, and unavoidable delays. This is the mark of the superior executive.

Many of history's great endeavors, battles that determined the fate of empires and other significant turning points, have failed because a single person did not build in that little bit of extra time needed to ensure success. Don't let this happen to you.

### Practice Crisis Anticipation

One of the most important parts of project management is crisis anticipation. This is what you do when you study the overall project and assess the things that can possibly go wrong. Murphy's Laws were developed by people who worked on projects of all kinds. These laws state that "Whatever can possibly go wrong, will go wrong. And of all the things that possibly can go wrong, the one thing that will go wrong will be the worst possible thing, at the worst possible time, and cause the most amount of money." Another of Murphy's Laws is that "Everything takes longer than you expect." Still another is that "Everything costs more than you budget for." The key to crisis anticipation is to think through, *in advance,* the different delays and setbacks that can possibly knock the project off schedule. Where could you have an obstacle or setback that would threaten the successful completion of the project? Once you have determined the worst possible thing that can happen, make sure that it doesn't happen. Address problems before they occur and take steps against them in advance.

## Develop "Plan B"

Develop alternative courses of action. Chancellor Otto von Bismarck, the great European statesman who assembled the many principalities of Germany into a single state, was famous for his diplomatic skills. No matter what happened, he always seemed to have a detailed backup plan as an alternative. This became known as the "Bismarck Plan" or "Plan B." You should always have a Plan B as well. You should always imagine that something unexpected will happen, and that you will have to do something completely different from what you set out to do. The more time that you take to develop a fully functioning alternative, the greater strength and resilience you will have, no matter what happens.

### *Continually Develop Options*

In life, you are only as free as your options. You are only as free as your well-developed alternatives. If you do not have options or alternatives already developed, you may find yourself trapped into a single course of action. If something goes wrong with that plan or course of action, you can be in serious trouble.

Many of the greatest successes in history were possible because the person in charge took the time to think through what might possibly go wrong and then made provisions against it. When it did go wrong, that leader was ready with a second plan.

It is important that you never trust to luck when you plan a project. Hope is not a strategy. Remember the words of Napoleon. When asked if he believed in luck, he said, "Yes, I believe in luck. I believe in bad luck. And I believe that I will always have it, so I plan accordingly."

## Four Problems to Avoid

There are four main problems in project management. Each of them can be avoided by taking the time to think carefully before embarking on a new project.

**1.** *Not Allowing Enough Time.* The first is not allowing enough time to complete a multitask job. This is the primary reason projects fail and people's careers get sidetracked or torpedoed. They hope for the best, trust to luck, and don't allow a sufficient cushion of time to complete every step of the project. As a result, the project fails.

**2.** *Assuming the Best.* The second problem is assuming that everything will work out all right. As author Alex McKenzie said, "Errant assumptions lie at the root of every failure." Never assume that everything will work out all right. Assume that you are going to have problems. Allow yourself sufficient time and resources to solve those problems and keep the project on schedule.

**3.** *Rushing at the End.* The third problem in project management is when the project team ends up rushing at the end. When you rush to complete a project because you have run out of time or money, you almost invariably make mistakes and do poor quality work that you have to go back and correct later. It actually takes less time to finish a project correctly if you work at it slowly and steadily, doing it properly in the first place.

**4.** *Trying to Do Several Things at Once.* The fourth problem in project management is trying to do several things at once, and ending up doing nothing well. You either take on too many responsibilities yourself, or you assign too many responsibilities to other people. In either case, various parts of the project fall through the cracks, and sometimes all the effort is lost. Do things one at a time, and do each thing well before moving to the next task.

## Plan Your Projects Visually

One of the most powerful methods for designing and managing a project is called "storyboarding." The technique was originally developed by the Walt Disney Company to plan cartoons and movies, and it was eventually used in every part of the entertainment business. In storyboarding, you create a visual image of the project, mounted on the wall, so that everyone can see it and comment on it. You begin with a large corkboard. You then get boxes of pins or thumbtacks and stacks of three- by five-inch and five- by eight-inch index cards. Get several felt pens with different colors. You are then ready to begin.

Across the top of the board, write the major parts of the project in one or two words, on the five- by eight-inch index cards, with the colored felt pens. These are very much like the titles of the chapters of a book, and they are called "headers." You may have anywhere from three to ten different headers as the main parts of the project.

Under each of the headers, you place the three- by five-inch index cards. You list an individual step in the completion of the task on each of these cards. When you are finished, you will have created a visual representation of the entire project, showing what needs to be done and in what order. You can then write the name of the person who is responsible for each of the jobs on the card listing the job.

With this layout, you can move headers and job descriptions

around. You can change their order and schedule. You can change the person who is responsible and the deadline.

You can also use storyboarding with a sheet of paper. You can write a series of larger boxes across the top, then write a series of steps for each of those tasks in boxes underneath. The more visual you can make the project, the easier it is for you to see relationships between the various tasks and to make whatever changes are necessary to ensure that you complete the project on time.

### Storyboarding Individual Job Descriptions

One way that you can use storyboarding is to pin a series of five-by eight-inch cards across the top of the corkboard and put the names of a team member on that card. Below each person's name, on three- by five-inch index cards, write the specific tasks that that person will be expected to complete, along with the deadline. This gives everyone a visual representation of their relationship to everyone else on the team, and it makes it clear what is to be done, by whom, and by what time.

Next, you list each person's tasks in order of priority, from the first thing she will be expected to do, to the last thing.

Each time you have a staff meeting, you compare each person's various tasks and functions as they are represented on the corkboard. With this visual picture, you can revise responsibilities and move the various cards around. This form of visual representation of a project stimulates creativity, and it dramatically increases the clarity of the project to everyone involved in completing it. Planning your project visually increases the likelihood that the project will be completed successfully, on time, and in a quality fashion.

## Example of a Multitask Job: Mailing a Newsletter

Here is an example of a multitask job that my company completed using the project management system described in this chapter. In this case, it was a newsletter. We brought together the team that was going to be responsible for the various jobs that had to be done to send out a newsletter successfully. We then listed all the tasks in sequential order, and the time frame, or schedule, within which they would have to be completed.

These were the tasks that we concluded had to be done: First, we defined the desired results, the goal that we had for producing and sending the newsletter in the first place. We asked ourselves, "What would be the ideal result?" We then used this result as our target or our goal, and everything that we did in the design of the newsletter was aimed at achieving that result.

Second, we determined the market that we were aiming at and arranged to acquire mailing lists for those people and businesses. We immediately realized that arranging for mailing lists was a separate multitask project, so we set this task aside with a separate project management team responsible for it.

Third, we designed the format and the layout of the newsletter. We determined the advertising copy, the photos we would use, and how it was going to be laid out. We determined the emphasis to be placed on both articles and product sales. We then determined who would be responsible for producing each part.

Fourth, we wrote and assembled the copy and the photographs, and we laid them out in a draft for review and revision.

Fifth, we had the newsletter typeset and laid out professionally, so it had the look and the appeal necessary to achieve the desired sales.

Sixth, we determined the printer for the newsletter. We got three different bids, compared them, and selected the best printer.

## Determine Separate Multitask Jobs

Having decided that arranging for the mailing list was a separate multitask project, we broke it down into four steps. The first step was to define the market population. Who were we going to send the newsletter to? One thing we needed to do was to contact a list broker. We went through our own mailing lists and the mailing lists of others that we work with until we were clear about the size of the market population. The people on these selected lists were the targets of the newsletter.

The second thing we had to do was assemble and acquire all of the names so that we knew the total that we would be mailing to. The third step was to select a mailing house that would handle the envelope stuffing, labeling, and the actual mailing. The fourth and final step was to print the list, print the brochures, deliver them all to the mailing house, then have the mailing house send the newsletter out to our selected lists.

This may sound like a simple project. Yet from start to end—deciding on a newsletter, determining the layout and design, selecting the mailing lists and mailing house, getting it printed, and mailing it out—the project took almost four solid months, and it involved the activities of five different people who invested between 200 and 300 hours. The reason that we were able to do it successfully was because we organized it like a project, step by step, with each responsibility, each task, and each function tying into every other task and function.

## Regular Review and Evaluation

The final requirement necessary to excel in project management is to schedule regular review sessions to measure progress, solve problems, and reassign responsibilities. This was a key element in getting the newsletter out on time and on budget. In every project, you must inspect what you expect. Once you have decided upon the project team and the project, and you have delegated the different tasks and responsibilities, you must set up a regular schedule to meet, review, and discuss how you are doing.

No matter how well you plan at the beginning, you will receive a continuous flow of feedback that will necessitate regular revision of your plan to make the project come out successfully.

# Successful Project Management

There are several factors that make project management successful. The first and most important of these is good communications among the various team members who are responsible for various parts of the project.

## Clarity Is Essential

The first necessity for good communication is *clarity*. This means that you say exactly what you mean. You explain what you want done clearly and unambiguously. You never assume understanding. You never assume that people understand clearly what is said or what is expected of them. You always ask for feedback and double-check with your team members. Ask team members to explain what you have just said, in their own words. Encourage questions and open discussion. Encourage people to challenge and disagree. The more involved and active people are in discussing the project as it evolves, the more committed they will be to making it successful when it is underway. The more the job is discussed, the clearer it becomes to everyone.

## Consistency Is Important

The next part of good communication is *consistency*. The team leader must be patient, optimistic, determined, and persevering. Being a good project leader requires that you have, or develop, the best qualities of leadership and managerial excellence. You must keep cool when things go wrong. You must continually remind yourself that if you don't stay on top of project tasks, they probably won't get done. If the project is important enough, you must accept complete responsibility for inspecting what you expect. Don't assume that everything is going according to plan, unless you have taken the time to check on it yourself.

## Deal with Conflict and Poor Performance

Another part of good communication as a team leader is that you must deal with *conflict* and *poor performance* in a direct, straightforward manner. If a person does not do the job he has committed to do, you cannot ignore it. You cannot pretend that it is not happening. You cannot hope it will go away. The best bosses are very demanding when it comes to both deadlines and quality work. You must be the same. Encourage everyone to openly discuss the project and the progress that you are making. If necessary, be prepared to reassign jobs and tasks. Give different jobs to different people. If one person is overloaded and another person seems underworked, be prepared to reassign the tasks so that everybody feels they can achieve their jobs in an excellent fashion.

### Develop the Courage of Your Convictions
The fourth quality of good communicators, and the great quality of leadership, is *courage*. As Winston Churchill said, "Courage is rightly considered the foremost of the virtues, for upon it, all others depend." The most important type of courage is for you to take full responsibility for the results and to resolve to persist until the task is satisfactorily completed.

## You Can Learn Any Skill

It is not easy to begin to use a systematic project management system if you have not done it in the past. But the development of project management skills will save you more time and do as much (or more) to advance your career than almost any other skill you can develop. You can use this project management skill at home. You can use it in planning vacations. You can use it in starting and building companies and organizations. You can use it to start your own business, become a successful salesperson, move onto the fast track in your life, and in many other ways.

Your ability to plan, organize, manage, and complete projects is central to your success and vital to your realizing your full potential in life, work, and leadership. Fortunately, project management is a learnable skill that you can master with practice and determination. There are no limits.

*"If you only care enough for a result, you will almost certainly attain it. Only you must then really wish these things, and wish them exclusively, and not wish at the same time a hundred other incompatible things."*

—WILLIAM JAMES

## Action Exercises

1. You only learn by doing. Select a project, business or personal, that can have a positive effect on your life if completed successfully, and apply the methods taught in this chapter to complete it.

2. Begin each project by defining the ideal or perfect result you desire from accomplishing it successfully.

3. Make a list of every ingredient and step that you will have to include or take to complete the project in an excellent fashion.

4. Draw up a project planning form. Organize every task and activity that will have to be done, in order of sequence, from first to final job.

5. Assemble the people whose help and cooperation you will need to complete this project. Discuss the project in detail with them, and get each of them to commit to complete their individual tasks by a certain time.

6. Practice crisis anticipation and determine the setbacks or difficulties that could occur to delay successful completion of the project; look for ways to solve these problems before they occur.

7. Accept complete responsibility for the completion of projects that are vital to your future success, and that of your organization. Resolve to become absolutely excellent at project management for the rest of your career.

# CHAPTER SEVEN

# Time-Saving Techniques—and How to Deal with the Six Biggest Time Wasters

*"Concentrate all your thoughts on the great desire in your life. This concentration must be continuous, unceasing—every minute; every hour; every day; every week."*

—CHARLES E. POPPLESTONE

T ime is the one indispensable ingredient of accomplishment. Everything you want to achieve requires time. The only way you can get enough time to do the things that can really make a difference in your life is by conserving time that you would normally spend somewhere else. You are surrounded by people and circumstances that waste your time and undermine your effectiveness all day long. Only by practicing rigorous self-discipline can you free yourself from these thieves of time.

# The Seven Major Time Wasters

There are seven major time wasters in the world of work, based on hundreds of studies and opinion surveys. Your ability to deal with them effectively will largely determine how successful you are in your career.

**1.** *Telephone Interruptions.* Telephone interruptions lead the list. The telephone rings and breaks your train of thought, interrupts you, and distracts you from what you are doing. When you hang up the phone, you are often distracted and find it hard to get back to the work in front of you.

**2.** *Unexpected Visitors.* Unexpected or drop-in visitors can be extremely time-consuming. These are people from within your company or from the outside. They drop by your office, disrupting your work, breaking your train of thought, and impairing your effectiveness. Sometimes they talk endlessly about unimportant matters and keep you from your work.

**3.** *Meetings.* Meetings, both planned and unplanned, consume 40 percent or more of your time. They can be formal or ad hoc, with groups or one-on-one, in an office or in the hallways. Many meetings are unnecessary or largely a waste of time.

**4.** *Fire Fighting and Emergencies.* A major time consumer (and time waster) is fire fighting and handling emergencies and the inevitable crisis. Just when you get settled in to work on something important, something totally unexpected happens that takes you away from your main task, sometimes for hours—or longer.

**5.** *Procrastination.* Procrastination is the thief of time. The tendency to procrastinate is universal for a variety of reasons that we will deal with in detail in Chapter 8.

**6.** *Socializing and Idle Conversation.* Socializing takes up an enormous amount of time. It has been estimated that as much as 75 percent of time at work is spent interacting with other people. Unfortunately, half of this time is spent in idle chatter that has nothing to do with the work. Socializing takes time away from getting the job done.

**7.** *Indecision and Delay.* Indecision costs more time than most people realize. It can generate unnecessary paperwork, correspondence, and tasks. Indecision wastes your time and that of others.

In this chapter, you will learn several proven techniques to deal with each of these time wasters, except for procrastination. This subject is so important that we will cover it in depth in Chapter 8.

# A Quick Review

Let us take a moment to review the keys to effective time management that we've covered so far in this book.

### Changing the Way You Think

First, we talked about the psychology of time management. This requires that you make a firm decision to become excellent at the way you use your time. Think of yourself continually as well organized. Visualize yourself as efficient, effective, and highly productive.

### Setting Clear Goals and Objectives

To perform at your best, you must set clear goals and objectives that are consistent with your highest aspirations and your innermost values and convictions. The more goals you set for yourself, the more likely it is that you will manage your time well, especially when your goals are in harmony with your values.

The Law of Forced Efficiency says that the more work you take on, the more efficient you will become in completing the most important parts of that work. You will be *forced* to be efficient just to keep on top of your responsibilities.

This law also says that "There is never enough time for everything, but there is always enough time for the most important things." The fact that you have a large number of tasks almost guarantees that you'll become more and more efficient.

## Planning Out Your Work in Detail

You need detailed plans of action, organized by sequence and priority, for productive work. You will save ten minutes in execution for every minute that you invest in planning and organizing before you begin.

## Setting Clear Priorities on Your Tasks

You must establish clear priorities and always work on your highest-value tasks. Apply the 80/20 rule to everything. Separate the urgent from the important. Always concentrate on the most valuable use of your time.

## Working All the Time You Work

It is essential that you develop good work habits and learn to concentrate single-mindedly on one thing, the most important thing at any given time. Good work habits enable you to produce vastly more than the average person, and they are the key to great success in life.

## Managing Multitask Jobs

You must think through and carefully plan large jobs or complex tasks that involve several people, using everything that you have learned so far. Think on paper, and develop the habit of planning and organizing every detail before you begin.

# The Way You Spend Time Today

How do you use your time? According to time management specialist Michael Fortino, over an average lifetime, you will spend seven years in the bathroom. You will spend six years eating. You will spend five years waiting in lines. You will spend four years cleaning your house. You will spend three years in meetings. You will spend one year searching for things. You will spend eight months opening junk mail. You will spend six months sitting at red lights. You will spend 120 days brushing your teeth. And here's the big surprise: You will spend four minutes per day conversing with your spouse and thirty seconds per day conversing with your children.

## Get Focused and Stay Focused

In order to change some of these ratios in a positive way, you will have to learn how to cut out the time wasters and save time in every area of your life. To save time at work, for instance, you must continually ask yourself questions such as the following:

Why am I on the payroll?

What have I been hired to accomplish?

What is my major goal or objective right now?

What am I supposed to do, or be doing, at this moment?

What results have I been hired to achieve?

Is what I am doing right now contributing to the accomplishment of my most important goals and objectives?

The most important of these questions to continually ask yourself, from the time you start work to the time you finish, is: "Why am I on the payroll? Is what I'm doing right now what I have been hired to do?" The greatest time saver of all is the word "No!" Make it a habit to say no to any demands on your time that do not move you toward your most important goals.

## Seven Ways to Deal with Telephone Interruptions

Here are seven ideas to help you deal with the tyranny of telephone interruptions:

**1.** *Use the telephone as a business tool.* Get on and off the phone fast. Don't socialize on the phone when you are working. Make your calls as efficient as possible. When you were a teenager, the telephone became a social tool for you. It was your connection to your friends and members of the opposite sex. You became accustomed to spending a lot of time on the phone in idle conversation. As an adult, you still associate the phone with socializing, with idle chatter. It has become a habit. However, when you enter into the world of work, you have to break that habit and begin to view the telephone as a means of business communication. You must discipline yourself to use the telephone as a business tool during the hours from nine to five.

**2.** *Have your calls screened.* Find out who is on the phone and what he wants before you answer. Overcome the natural curiosity that wells up in you when people you don't know call you. Find out why they are calling before you take the phone call.

**3.** *Have your calls held.* Whenever possible, set aside periods of the day when you take no interruptions. Don't become a slave to a ringing phone. One of the best tactics you can use is to actually disconnect your phone when you are working on something important. If it is important enough, whoever is calling you will call back again later.

**4.** *Set clear callback times.* When you call people and they are not there, leave a message and the time that you will be available to take the return phone call. When someone calls you and you can't take the call, make sure that your secretary or receptionist gets a callback time. This is the time when you can get a hold of the caller so that you don't play telephone tag back and forth.

**5.** *Batch your calls.* Use the learning curve. Make all of your telephone calls at once. Don't spread them throughout the day. Sometimes you can accumulate your phone calls up to 11:00

A.M., then return them all between the hour of eleven and noon. Or you can accumulate them up to 3:30 P.M. and then return them all by 4:30 P.M.

**6.** *Plan your calls in advance.* Think about a business call as a meeting, and write out an outline or agenda for your telephone meeting or discussion. Don't waste time by picking up the phone and calling, and then forgetting the reason you are calling and the things you wanted to discuss.

**7.** *Take good notes.* Take complete notes of telephone conversations. The power is on the side of the person with the best notes. Never answer a telephone without a pad of paper and a pen in your hand. Keep careful notes of the things that you agree to. Write down what the other person agrees to, including the numbers, times, dates, amounts, and so on that are discussed on the phone. These notes can be extremely important to you in the future.

## Dealing with Drop-In Visitors

Here are five ways to deal with the next of the major time wasters, drop-in visitors.

**1.** *Create a quiet time for work.* First, specify a quiet time during the day when you will concentrate on your work. During this time, allow no interruptions. Get yourself a DO NOT DISTURB sign from a store or a hotel and put it on your door. Make it clear that when that sign is out, you do not want to be disturbed for any reason by anyone, except in an emergency.

**2.** *Stand up quickly.* Deal with unwelcome visitors by standing up when they come into your office. Some years ago, I worked in a company with a manager who would go from office to office making conversation. He was one of the most boring talkers in the world. He was a nice fellow, but when he came in, you knew that if he sat down, he was going to be there for a half hour. I finally learned how to handle his unwelcome visits. The instant he came in the door, I would immediately stand up and come around my desk as though I was just on my way out. I would say, "It's nice to see you, but I am just leaving. I'll walk out with you." I would then walk him to the door and lead him back out into the hallway. Then, I would keep on going myself. I would go to the washroom or to some other office until he was gone, and only then would I go back to my desk. This saved me an enormous amount of time that the other executives in the company were unable to avoid losing.

**3.** *Bring the discussion to a close.* When the meeting has gone on long enough, say, "There's one more thing before you go." You then stand up and lead your visitor to the door. Finish off the conversation with anything you can think of, shake hands, and then go back to work. One variation of this technique is to say, "One more thing before you go; I want to show you something." You then take the visitor out of the office and show him a plant, a book, a new piece of furniture, or anything that you can think of. Then, turn around and go back to work, leaving him there to carry on.

**4.** *Arrange specific meeting times.* To deal effectively with drop-in visitors, you can arrange specific times to meet that are convenient for both of you. Make appointments to get together with the people in your office. Make appointments with your staff, and let them know that, at certain times of the day, your door is open and you will be available.

**5.** *Avoid wasting the time of others.* Make every effort to avoid being a drop-in visitor on others. If you do drop in on someone else, always be polite enough to ask, "Is this a good time, or can we get together later?" Encourage others to extend the same courtesy to you by asking when you have time available. It is amazing how many people unconsciously waste the time of others and are unaware of it.

# Saving Time in Meetings

Meetings are the third major time waster in the world of work. As much as 50 percent of working time is spent in meetings, either group meetings or one-on-one meetings. In the estimate of almost everyone, at least 50 percent of this time is wasted. This means that as much as 25 percent of all working time is lost in meetings of one kind or another.

However, meetings are not an evil. Meetings are a necessary business tool for exchanging information, solving problems, and reviewing progress. But they must be managed and they must be used effectively.

### Determine the Cost of the Meeting

Each meeting costs the *hourly rate* of the people attending, multiplied by the number of hours spent in the meeting. Meetings should therefore be treated as an actual dollar expenditure with an expected value or rate of return on investment.

Imagine that you have ten people in a meeting, and the average person is earning $20 per hour. Ten times twenty equals $200 per hour. This is the cost of that meeting. If you are going to spend $200 on something in your business, which is exactly what you are doing in this meeting, you should have a very good reason for it.

Think through in advance the justification of spending this amount of money. Why are you bringing these people, at these hourly rates, together for this period of time?

Continually think of meetings as an investment with an expected rate of return. Treat them exactly as if you were spending the company's money because, directly or indirectly, that is exactly what you are doing.

### Seven Ways to Make Meetings More Efficient

Here are seven ways to increase the efficiency and improve the results of meeting time.

**1.** *Is the meeting necessary?* Many meetings turn out, in retrospect, to be unnecessary. There are other ways to achieve the same goal. Sometimes you can achieve it by circulating a memo. You can have a conference call. You can speak to people individually. You can even postpone it to another meeting or another time altogether. If a meeting is not necessary, avoid holding it whenever possible. If the meeting is necessary, then ask, "Is it necessary for me to attend this meeting?" If it is not necessary for you to attend, don't go in the first place. If it is not necessary for someone else to attend a particular meeting, make sure that he knows he does not have to be there.

**2.** *Write an agenda.* If you have determined that the meeting is necessary, establish a clear purpose for the meeting, and write up an agenda. An excellent time management tool is for you to write a one-paragraph statement of purpose for the meeting. Start with this sentence: "We are having this meeting to achieve this specific goal." Then, write out the objective of the meeting.

This is a tremendous discipline. Make out an agenda or a list of everything that has to be covered in the meeting. Next to each item, put the name of the person who is expected to address that particular issue. Distribute the agenda, if possible, at least twenty-four hours in advance so that each person knows what she will be expected to contribute. You want everyone to know what the objective of the meeting is and what will be discussed. This applies to one-on-one meetings with your boss, with your subordinates, with your customers, with your suppliers, and whoever else.

One of the most helpful techniques you can use in business is to draw up an agenda for each meeting with your boss. I learned this many years ago as a junior executive. Before I started using this technique, my boss and I would spend an hour talking around in circles with no clear beginning or end. Once we had an agenda to work from, we could cover more information with

greater clarity in fifteen minutes than we used to cover in sixty
minutes.

Sometimes I would type up the agenda before the meeting.
On other occasions, I would just write it up by hand, photocopy
it, give my boss a copy, keep a copy for myself, and then say,
"These are the things I want to discuss with you." We would
then go down the list, item by item, and get resolution of each
point. I would then be out of his office and back to work. My
boss really appreciated this approach. As a result, he was always
willing to see me because I took up so little of his time.

**3.** *Start and stop on time.* Set a schedule for the beginning
of the meeting, and set a time for the end of the meeting. If the
meeting is going to run from eight until nine, start it at eight
o'clock sharp and end it at nine o'clock sharp. The worst type of
meetings are the ones that start at a specific time but have no
clearly determined ending time. Here is another rule: Don't wait
for the latecomer. Assume the latecomer is not coming at all and
start at the designated time. It is unfair to punish the people who
are on time by making them wait for the person who gets there
late, if at all. Many companies establish the policy of locking the
meeting room from the inside at the exact time the meeting is
scheduled to start. The people who show up late are not allowed
in. You can be sure that they don't show up late the next time.

**4.** *Cover important items first.* When you draw up the
agenda, apply the 80/20 rule. Organize the agenda so that the
top 20 percent of items are the first items to be discussed. This
way, if you run out of time, you will have covered the items that
represent 80 percent of the value of the meeting before the time
runs out.

**5.** *Summarize each conclusion.* When you discuss each item
on your meeting agenda, summarize the discussion and get closure. Get agreement and completion on each item before you go
on to the next one. Restate what has been decided upon and
agreed to with each item before you proceed.

**6.** *Assign specific responsibility.* If you have made a decision, assign responsibility for the specific actions agreed upon
and set deadlines. Remember, discussion and agreement without an assignment of responsibility and a deadline for completion is merely a conversation. Be clear about who is going to do
what and by when.

**7.** *Keep notes and circulate minutes.* A key to getting maximum effectiveness from meetings is to keep accurate notes and
to circulate the minutes of the meeting within twenty-four hours,
whenever possible. The person who keeps accurate minutes
from a meeting that can be pulled out a week or a month later
can resolve a lot of potential misunderstandings. Agendas prepared in advance, followed by meeting minutes prepared shortly
afterward, ensure that everyone is clear about his agreed-upon
responsibilities and deadlines.

## Putting Out Fires

Another major time waster in work is called *fire fighting,* or dealing with the unexpected crisis. It is a major time consumer in
personal life as well. One way to deal with these unexpected
crises is to engage in what is called "crisis anticipation." We
talked about this previously in Chapter 6. Crisis anticipation requires that you look down the road into the future and ask,
"What could possibly go wrong, and what would we do if it did?"

More specifically, you should be asking, "What is the worst
possible thing that could happen in the next three, six, nine, or
twelve months? What are the possible crises that could occur?"

### Plan for the Worst

One of the characteristics of great leaders throughout history is
that they developed the ability to think ahead and determine all
the things that could possibly go wrong. They would then plan
for contingencies in advance. When something did go wrong,

they were ready to move quickly. They had already thought it through.

Poor leaders, on the other hand, don't take the time to think of all the things that could go wrong. They trust to luck. They then become overwhelmed by circumstances. Sometimes, the inability to think through a possible crisis in advance can be fatal to a job or career.

Crises are normal, natural, and unavoidable in the history of any company or organization. But the recurrent crisis, the crisis that happens over and over again, is a sign of poor management and inefficient organization. If you have the same crisis happen more than once, it is important that you stand back and take a close look at your systems. Why does a crisis keep occurring? You then take the steps necessary to ensure that it does not happen again.

## Crisis Management Strategies

When an emergency or a crisis occurs, here are five steps to follow:

**1.** *Think before acting.* Remember, action without thinking is the cause of every failure. Take a deep breath, calm down, and remain objective. Refuse to react or overact. Instead, just stop and think. Take the time to find out what happened. Be clear about the problem before you act.

**2.** *Delegate responsibility.* There is a rule that says, "If it is not necessary for you to decide, it is necessary for you not to decide." If you can possibly delegate the responsibility for handling the crisis to someone else, by all means do so. Someone else might be much better qualified to deal with the situation than you, or it may be someone else's responsibility in the first place.

**3.** *Write it down.* Whatever the crisis, write it down on your list before you take action. When you write down a problem, it helps to keep your mind cool, calm, clear, and objective. Write down exactly what has happened before you do anything.

**4.** *Get the facts.* Don't assume anything. The facts are perhaps the most important elements of all in a crisis. Ask questions such as:

What has occurred?

When did it happen?

Where did it happen?

How did it happen?

Why did it happen?

Who was involved?

Again, get the facts. Remember, the facts don't lie. The more facts you gather, the more capable you will be of dealing with the problem when you take action.

**5.** *Develop a policy.* When you are dealing with a recurring crisis, develop a policy that is simple enough so that it can be implemented by ordinary people. When a crisis occurs for the first or second time, it may require tremendous intelligence, experience, and energy to deal with it effectively. But, if a crisis has a tendency to occur more than once, and you cannot find a way to eliminate the crisis in advance, you should by all means develop systems so that an average person can handle it in your absence.

## Socializing Can Hurt Your Career

Another major time waster in the world of work is socializing. Too much socializing can sabotage your career if you become well known for it. Most people are time wasters and time consumers. They are working well below their capacity. So, they have lots of time to socialize and engage in idle chatter. Here are some ideas you can use to avoid getting trapped into excessive socializing.

## Socialize at Appropriate Times

Arrange to do your socializing at coffee breaks, lunch, and after work. Whenever you find yourself being drawn into a nonwork-related conversation with coworkers, say to yourself, "Back to work." Break off the conversation by saying, "Well, I've got to get back to work," and then do it. It is amazing how often the use of these words will cause other people to get back to work as well.

Always be asking yourself, "Is this what I'm being paid to do?" If my boss were standing here right now, would I be doing this? If my boss were sitting right in that chair, would I be carrying on this conversation in this way? If you wouldn't do it if your boss were there, it is probably not what you have been hired to do.

## You Are a Knowledge Worker

There is one exception with regard to socializing. It is that relationships with knowledge workers are unavoidably time-consuming. Some of the most valuable time you spend at work is talking through and working out problems and solutions to the challenges facing your business. But these conversations must be focused on *results,* not on the latest football game or sharing stories about fishing or summer holidays. Relationships, communications, and discussions with knowledge workers must be continually focused on the results that you and your work colleagues are trying to accomplish.

Socrates is reputed to have said, "We only learn something by [engaging in dialogue] about it." In certain work environments, the time that you take to dialogue about and discuss the work is an essential part of developing clarity about exactly what is to be done before you begin the work itself.

## Indecision and Poor Decision Making

A major time waster in work is indecision or poor decision making. Indecision and poor decision making can have enormous costs in terms of money and lost time. A basic rule with regard to decision making is that 80 percent of decisions should be made the first time they come up. Only 15 percent of decisions should be made later, and 5 percent of decisions shouldn't be made at all.

### Four Types of Decisions

There are four types of decisions that you will have to deal with on a regular basis in the course of your career.

**1.** *Decisions Only You Can Make.* This is the decision that no one else can make, and it is the decision that's your responsibility to make. It is therefore unavoidable.

**2.** *Decisions You Can Delegate.* Some decisions can be made by someone else. One of the very best ways to develop other people—to build knowledge, foresight, wisdom, and judgment in your subordinates, and in your children, for that matter—is to allow them to make important decisions. Whenever you can delegate a decision to someone else, or whenever the potential negative consequences of poor decisions are small, by all means, let someone else make that decision.

**3.** *Unaffordable Decisions.* The third type of decision is the one you cannot afford to make. The negative consequences of this decision are too great if it turns out poorly. Some decisions, if they turn out wrong, can lead to the bankruptcy of a company. Some commitments of resources can be so serious that they become irretrievable. The worst possible outcome is too serious an outcome to accept. That is a decision that you cannot afford to make.

**4.** *Unavoidable Decisions.* The fourth type of decision is the one you cannot afford *not* to make. This is a decision to act on an opportunity where delay can be very expensive. The positive upside for you or the organization can be enormous. But remember, when it is not necessary to decide, it is necessary not to decide.

## Making Better Decisions
Here are some key ideas that will help you become a better decision maker.

### Delegate Decision Making
Delegate decision making whenever possible. Remember, once you have made a decision in some particular area, you almost invariably have to make a series of related decisions in that same area. Avoid making decisions if you possibly can. Delegate them to other people.

### Set a Deadline for Decision Making
If you can't make a decision immediately, set a deadline for the decision. For example, if someone comes to you needing an answer, and you can't give an answer right away because you don't have enough information, say, "I can't give you an answer right now; but I will give you an answer by Thursday at noon." Then, whatever happens, at noon on Thursday you make the decision, one way or the other.

### Get the Facts Before Deciding
As I said earlier, get the facts. Get the real facts, not the assumed facts, or the apparent facts, or the hopeful facts. But get the real facts. If you collect enough accurate facts and information in any area, decision making becomes far easier and more effective.

Most poor decisions are made because the person has acted without getting enough information. The very act of gathering information will greatly improve your decision when you finally make it.

### Dare to Go Forward

Decision making requires courage. This is because every decision involves a certain amount of uncertainty. With every decision, there is the possibility of failure. But it is not possible for a person to advance in life unless he is willing to make decisions, with no guarantee of success. All successful leaders and managers are firm decision makers. In fact, you cannot even imagine a successful person who is indecisive and wishy-washy.

### Overcome the Fear of Failure

A study done not long ago, and reported in the American Management Association magazine, compared managers who had been promoted regularly and managers who had not. The one quality the authors found among the managers who got promoted over the others was that they were decisive in their work and in dealing with problems. The managers who did not get promoted were unwilling to make decisions for fear of making a mistake.

They then took these two groups of managers and put them through a series of written tests where they were asked what they would do to solve a particular business problem. Both of the groups turned out to be equally accurate in their answers on written tests. They both demonstrated the same decision-making ability in a classroom setting.

The difference between those who were promoted, and those who were not, was that those who got promoted were willing to make decisions and act on their judgment. They were willing to make a mistake, if necessary, rather than to hesitate or delay. The others were so afraid of making a mistake that they did nothing. Even though they were equal in ability, those who were afraid of making decisions in the first place were not entrusted with positions of higher responsibility.

One of the most important ways to improve your decision-making ability is to avoid perfectionism. Avoid the need to know every detail and to be absolutely correct before you make a decision and move ahead. An imperfect decision made immediately is usually superior to a perfect decision delayed indefinitely.

## Five More Ways to Save Time

Here are five additional timesaving ideas that you can use in your personal life.

**1.** *Shop all at once.* When you go shopping, do it all at once. Don't shop at one store one day, and another store on a different day. Go out and do all of your shopping on a single day in a single trip. By the way, the very best time to shop for groceries is Tuesday afternoon and evenings. Why? Store shelves are restocked on Monday after the weekend. By shopping on Tuesday, you can get in, get the greatest selection, and get out fast.

**2.** *Bunch your errands.* When you have several errands to do, bunch them and do them all at once, rather than doing one today, one tomorrow, and so on through the week.

**3.** *Don't waste the time of others.* Ask yourself, "What do I do that wastes the time of others?" Wasting the time of other people is usually not deliberate. It comes from not thinking about how valuable their time is. We often waste the time of others through lack of consideration.

If you are a boss or manager with people reporting to you, avoid the tendency to waste the time of your staff by keeping them waiting or being late for meetings. The more respect you show for the time of your staff, the more valuable and important they will feel. The same applies in your personal life. Show the same respect in the same way with your family and friends.

Ask yourself, "How do I waste the time of my boss? My co-workers? My subordinates? My spouse? My children? And others?" And then make efforts to avoid doing it. If you are curious, go and ask people. Say, "What do I do that wastes your time? How could I change the way I use my time so that it would be more efficient for you?" Don't be surprised by what they tell you.

**4.** *Be punctual.* Only 2 percent of people are punctual all the time, and these people are recognized and respected by everyone. Punctuality is professional and courteous. Make a habit of being on time. Remember if you're not early, you're late. There is no such thing as being fashionably late. It is really just being inconsiderate and disorganized.

**5.** *Move quickly.* Develop a fast tempo. Pick up the pace. Remember, fast tempo is essential to success. Move quickly in cleaning up your house, putting things away, getting ready to go out—in all possible household tasks and responsibilities. The more things you do, and the faster you work to get them done, the more energy you have and the more you actually get done. The faster you work and the more you get done, the better you feel. Most successful people work at a higher tempo of activity than unsuccessful people. They don't necessarily do different things, but they get more things done in a given time than the average person. They produce more in less time, and as a result, they get paid more and promoted faster. Fast tempo is essential to success.

The best advice is to always focus on saving time. Continually look for ways to save time by cutting down or eliminating the major time wasters from your life at work or home. Only then will you have enough time to work on the goals that are central to your success and happiness. Only then can you become an excellent time manager.

*"Nothing can add more power to your life than concentrating all your energies on a limited set of targets."*

—NIDO QUBEIN

## Action Exercises

1. Resolve today to minimize and eliminate the time wasters in your life and work that take you away from doing the things that can be responsible for your greatest successes.

2. Plan every meeting before you hold it or attend it. When creating a meeting agenda, concentrate on the most important items, and always finish with clear responsibilities and deadlines.

3. Don't be a slave to a ringing telephone; have your calls screened. Prepare an agenda for every business call.

4. When you work, work all the time you work. Don't get bogged down with idle socializing that contributes nothing to your results.

5. Make decisions quickly, whenever possible. Be prepared to accept feedback and self-correct. Any decision is usually better than no decision.

6. Deal with problems and crises as they occur; get the facts, analyze the information, and take action.

7. Pick up the pace. Move fast. Develop a sense of urgency. Keep your mind focused on results and on doing the most important things for which you have been hired.

# CHAPTER EIGHT

# Overcoming Procrastination

*"Above all be of single aim; have a legitimate and useful purpose and devote yourself unreservedly to it."*

—JAMES ALLEN

**P**rocrastination is the thief of time. We have all heard that many times before. The tendency to procrastinate is the primary reason that many people lead lives of quiet desperation and retire poor. It is not that people do not know what to do to be more successful. Most people are quite clear about the steps they could take to improve their lives or their work. The problem is that they continually find reasons not to do it today until it is too late. They procrastinate until there are no more tomorrows left.

One of the most valuable habits you can develop in life is a *sense of urgency,* an inner drive to get on with it, to get the job done now. A sense of urgency is the opposite of procrastination and its most powerful overriding factor. A sense of urgency can help you as much as any other habit you can develop.

## Move On to the Fast Track

In a survey, 104 chief executive officers were asked what specific qualities would most mark a young person in their companies for rapid promotion. They were given a list of fifty qualities and behaviors to choose from.

Surprisingly enough, 84 percent of them agreed that two of the fifty qualities were more important than any of the others.

The first of the two qualities was defined as "the ability to separate the relevant from the irrelevant." It was the ability to set priorities on the use of time. Every manager has had the frustrating experience of coming upon one of his staff working away at something that is of low priority when something of higher priority is being left undone. Many organizations are overstaffed yet underefficient, simply because so many people in the organization spend so much time on items of low priority.

The second quality identified by the CEOs was "the ability to get the job done fast." It was the ability to take the ball and run with it, without hesitation or delay. Everyone intends to do good work, but the road to failure is paved with good intentions. It is only actions that count, and only those actions aimed at accomplishing the most important tasks.

## When You Get 'Round to It

I was a speaker at the annual convention of a successful national sales organization recently. As each person came into the room, he was handed a small wooden disk with the words *To It* printed on either side. The salespeople called these disks "round to-it's." They are handed out generously to people who are going to do something as soon as they get "'round to it." Once you have been given one of these round disks, you no longer have any excuses for procrastination or delay.

The ability to select your most important task and then to get it done quickly will do more to move you on to the fast track in your career than any other habit you can develop.

## Developing a Reputation for Speed and Dependability

Whether you work for an organization or run your own business, or if you work in sales, when you develop a reputation for speed and dependability, you will never have to worry about being successful, promoted, or rich. With a reputation for speed and dependability, you will be able to write your own ticket. When you can separate the relevant from the irrelevant and get the job done fast, you move to the front of the line in terms of success and opportunity.

### Ways to Alleviate Time Poverty

The single biggest shortage among employed people today is time. People suffer time poverty. They may have the money they need, but they don't have the time to enjoy it. As a result, free time is becoming more important than higher pay for many people.

Today, organizations will pay more for people or services that save them time. When you call another company to supply your business with a product or service, you value and respect suppliers far more when they move fast. We consider speed of response to our needs indicative of higher-quality products and services. People who move quickly are thought to be more intelligent than those who move slowly. We will buy from them faster and pay a higher price, with less resistance.

On the other hand, when we deal with an organization that moves or responds slowly to our requests, we automatically assume that organization to be poorly run. We assume that a slow company is managed by inefficient and ineffective people. We assume that its products are worth less than the products and services of companies that do things more quickly.

## Time Is of the Essence

One of the final clauses in almost every contract written in business today is a clause that says, "Time shall be of the essence of this agreement." Today, time is of the essence of virtually everything we do.

Learning to overcome procrastination is a vital step upward on the ladder of success. Without this ability, you simply cannot succeed at anything worthwhile. Fortunately, procrastination is a habit that can be overcome. Developing a sense of urgency is a habit as well, which can be learned.

# Developing a Sense of Urgency

There are seven steps you can take to program your mind with a sense of urgency. They will motivate you to overcome procrastination, get started on your most important job, and stay at it single-mindedly until it is complete.

## Set Worthwhile Goals

Set worthwhile goals for yourself, goals that you intensely desire to achieve. All motivation requires "motive." A major reason for procrastination is that there is no specific goal that the person wants badly enough to get started and then to persist until the job is complete.

Many people procrastinate and delay because they don't really *want* to do what they are doing. As a result, they find every excuse to delay and put off getting started. To counter this tendency, you can use goals as a motivator. The more goals you have, the less likely you will be to procrastinate on the tasks necessary to achieve them. When you set a large number of goals for yourself, you trigger the Law of Forced Efficiency. You find yourself moving faster and working more efficiently simply because you have so many things that you have to get done in a limited period.

## Visualize Your Tasks as Completed

Program your mind to overcome procrastination by continually *visualizing* your tasks as completed. Visualize your goals as already achieved. Imagine how you will feel with the job behind you. Imagine the satisfaction you will have when the task is accomplished. The more pleasurable the feeling of completion that you can create in your mind, the more focused you will be. The greater clarity you have of your finished task, the more energized you will be. Clear mental pictures of a desired future reality sharpen your mind and allow you to concentrate better.

For example, if you set an income goal that you want to achieve in a certain time period and you vividly imagine how you are going to enjoy the extra money, what you will buy, where you will go, and what you will do, you will find yourself internally motivated to do the things necessary to achieve this goal. Every time you visualize your goal as complete, you increase the intensity of your desire and strengthen your resolve. You will then develop the willpower to do whatever is necessary to transform your mental image into reality.

## Practice Positive Affirmations

Use the power of positive affirmations to program a sense of urgency into your subconscious mind. At the beginning of each major task, repeat and affirm the words, "Do it now! Do it now! Do it now!"

Starting as a fatherless boy selling newspapers on the streets of Chicago, W. Clement Stone built an insurance fortune worth more than $800 million. In his book *Success Through a Positive Mental Attitude,* he wrote that the repetition of the affirmation "Do it now!" was a key factor in his rise from poverty to great wealth. By constantly disciplining himself to "Do it now," he became one of the richest men in the world.

Throughout his company, Combined Insurance Company of America, which had branches in the United States and around the world, the entire staff would come together each morning and shout "Do it now! Do it now! Do it now!" fifty times before starting the day. This repeated affirmation had a tremendous impact on the salespeople and staff. Even after people went on to other jobs and companies, they still repeated it to themselves. Many successful men and women all over the world today trace their success back to their association with W. Clement Stone and his motto: "Do it now!"

You can develop any mental habit you desire by using repeated suggestions, in the form of conscious affirmations and mental pictures. At a certain point, your subconscious will accept these words and pictures as new commands. These commands will then become your new operating principles. Soon, you will find that acting with a sense of urgency is just as much of a habit for you as breathing.

## Set Clear Deadlines for Yourself
Set deadlines for yourself on all important tasks. Put yourself on record. Tell other people that you will have the job done by a specific time. You will find that promising others motivates you. We all work very hard to fulfill our promises and to avoid disappointing other people. Often, promising others that you will have something done by a certain time and date is more powerful than promising yourself.

Setting a clear, specific deadline also programs the task or goal into your subconscious. You will then find yourself internally driven toward getting the job done. When you set a deadline for yourself, your subconscious mind installs an automatic override on your tendency to procrastinate.

## Refuse to Make Excuses

All procrastination seems to be accompanied by rationalization. And rationalization is best defined as "attempting to put a socially favorable interpretation on an otherwise socially unacceptable act."

Rationalizing is explaining away and making excuses for unproductive behavior. People who procrastinate always have what they think is a good reason to let themselves off the hook. Don't allow yourself the luxury of making excuses. Commit yourself to completing a particular task by a certain time, and then burn your mental bridges. Refuse to consider the possibility of not working on your task. Never look for reasons to justify noncompletion of a task.

## Reward Yourself for Completion of a Task

Create a reward system for yourself. Give yourself a reward for successful completion of each part of the job, as well as for successful completion of the whole job. You can actually program yourself to feel eager to start a job, and to continue with it until it is finished. Just give yourself a reward at each step.

In behavioral psychology, this is called *operant conditioning.* It is a technique used to train both humans and animals. Behavior is shaped by designing a specific result or consequence that follows every act of the individual. Rewards tend to reinforce and encourage specific behaviors. Punishments tend to discourage those behaviors. Over time, the habits of the individual can be shaped and her responses made automatic with repeated rewards.

### *Using Rewards to Develop Positive Habits*

Fully 95 percent of everything you do, or fail to do, is determined by your habits, either good or bad. One key to success is to develop good habits and make them your masters. You develop the habit of overcoming procrastination by rewarding yourself every time you do something positive until you rewire and reprogram your subconscious mind permanently.

Creating a reward system for yourself only requires a little imagination on your part. For example, if you have a big task to do and there are five parts to the task, give yourself a reward when you complete each step. The reward can be something simple, such as a coffee break, a break where you get up and walk around, or even lunch. If it is a major task, or a major part of another task, you can reward yourself by going shopping, buying something you like, taking yourself out for dinner, or even taking a vacation with your spouse or family.

When you put a reward system in place and you discipline yourself not to take the reward until you have completed the task or part of it, you eventually find yourself internally motivated to start and to finish your tasks and responsibilities. In a way, your attention moves away from the difficulty of the task itself and onto the enjoyment you'll get from the reward.

### Overcoming Call Reluctance with Rewards
A simple reward structure can be used to help salespeople overcome the fear and reluctance associated with cold-calling on the telephone. The salesperson sets a specific time and place for phone calls. He sets a specific goal for a number of calls, appointments, or sales. He then gets a fresh cup of coffee and puts it in front of him. Every time he makes a call, he is allowed to take a sip of coffee. Soon, he becomes motivated to make as many calls as possible so that he can drink the coffee before it gets cold.

Here's another technique: Take a cookie and break it up into small bites, or place a bowl of jellybeans in front of the salesperson. Each time the salesperson makes a call and gets through to a prospect, he is allowed to eat a piece of cookie or jellybean. In no time at all, in a Pavlovian response, the salesperson becomes eager to make calls and enjoy the reward. It sounds simple and even childish, but it is extraordinarily effective in developing the habit of overcoming procrastination.

You can practice operant conditioning with your children to train them in the good habits that they will need as adults. Offer to take them to McDonald's or to let them watch television if they clean up their room or complete their homework. Refuse to allow them the reward until the job is done satisfactorily. You will be amazed at how quickly they get started and keep going until the job is finished.

### Accept Full Responsibility for Completion of a Job

Program yourself to overcome procrastination by accepting 100 percent responsibility for the completion of the task on schedule. Look only to yourself. Rely only on your own ability. No matter what the obstacle in your way, resolve to find a way over, around, or past it. Refuse to make excuses.

Accepting complete responsibility for results, and never allowing yourself the luxury of a mental escape hatch, is the equivalent of putting your own feet to the fire. It is amazing how much more you will get done when you eliminate your excuses and reasons for putting off something.

## Five Ways to Get Yourself Started

Overcoming procrastination permanently requires that you use every method and technique possible to get yourself organized and motivated to start and complete the job. Here are five things that you can do in advance to reduce your tendency to procrastinate.

**1.** *Create a detailed plan of action.* Begin by creating a clear, written plan with each part of the plan and each step organized in order of priority. Put an "A," "B," or "C" next to each step. Determine the most important thing that you can do to get started and put a circle around that item.

A written plan leads you into action. It gives you a track to run on, a blueprint to follow. The more you break down your goal into individual steps and then list those steps, the easier it is for you to take the first one. Often, that's all you need to get going.

**2.** *Clean up your workspace.* Begin with only one thing, the most important thing, in front of you. A clean workspace is a real motivator to action. A good time planner can be very helpful in this regard because it keeps you focused on the next task.

**3.** *Separate the urgent from the important.* Remind yourself that important tasks are usually not urgent. An urgent task is usually not important. Start off working on the tasks that are both urgent and important, the tasks that have short time fuses and must be done immediately. Then move on to the tasks that are merely important, but not urgent. It is these important (but not urgent tasks) that contain the greatest potential consequences for your career and your future.

**4.** *Start with your most important tasks.* You always tend to procrastinate on large, important tasks with considerable future value. Successful completion of these major tasks can make a major difference in your life. There seems to be a universal tendency to delay working on, or completing, the most important tasks until the last moment.

Some people say that they work better under pressure. This may be true in some cases, because then you have no time for excuses. The heat is on. The consequences of not completing the job are too serious to delay. It is always better to have the job done well in advance of the deadline.

**5.** *Practice creative procrastination.* This requires that you consciously procrastinate on those tasks that contribute little or nothing to the accomplishment of your major, high-value goals. Since you can never do everything that you have to do, you are going to have to procrastinate on something. The difference between effective and ineffective people is that effective people procrastinate on the things that don't really matter.

On the other hand, ineffective people always procrastinate on the tasks that could make a real difference. Use your willpower and self-discipline to put off and delay doing minor, irrelevant tasks in favor of major, important tasks.

Many small jobs, left to themselves, have a tendency to become unnecessary. If you don't do them for a while, you eventually reach a point where they don't need to be done at all. These are the tasks that are the best candidates for creative procrastination. Before you start on a job, ask yourself, "What would happen if this task were not done at all?" If the answer to this question is "not much," then put it off as long as you can. Often you won't have to do it at all.

## Sixteen Ways to Overcome Procrastination

Because procrastination is such a major concern of so many people and has been a bugaboo for people throughout the ages, methods for overcoming procrastination have been developed over the years. Here are sixteen of the most powerful techniques ever devised to help you overcome procrastination in your work and personal life. Think about which one of these ideas could be most helpful to you right now, in your current situation.

**1.** *Think on paper.* Prepare thoroughly. List every step of the job in advance. Break the job down into its constituent parts before you begin. Simply writing out every detail and thoroughly preparing in advance will help you to overcome procrastination and get started.

**2.** *Gather all the materials and work tools that you will need before you begin.* When you sit down to work or to begin a task, make sure that you have everything at hand so that you won't have to get up or move until the task is done. Being fully prepared is a powerful motivator for staying with the task until it is finished.

**3.** *Do one small thing to get started.* There is an 80/20 rule that says that the first 20 percent of the task often accounts for 80 percent of the value of that task. This is probably what Confucius meant when he said that, "A journey of 1,000 leagues begins with a single step." Once you have taken even one small step to start the job, you will often find yourself continuing on with the task to completion.

**4.** *"Salami slice" the task.* Just as you would never try to eat a whole loaf of salami at once, don't try to take on all of a job from the start. Sometimes the best way to complete a major job is to take a small slice and complete just that piece, just as you would take a single slice of salami and eat it.

When you select a small piece of the task and then discipline yourself to do it and get it behind you, it will often give you the momentum you need to counter inertia and overcome procrastination.

**5.** *Practice the Swiss cheese technique.* Just as a block of Swiss cheese is full of holes, you treat your task like a block of cheese and you punch holes in it. Select a five-minute part of the job and do only that. Don't worry about the whole job. For example, if you want to write an article or a book, break the task down into small pieces that take an identifiable amount of time to complete and do just one small piece at a time whenever you get a chance. Many authors begin by writing one page a day. If you are doing research, you can read one article per sitting. Many people write complete books on airplanes, or complete their college degrees with snatches of time between other activities. If you wrote one page a day for a year, you would have a 365-page book by the end of the year.

**6.** *Start from the outside and complete the smaller tasks first.* Often there are preparatory steps you must take before you can tackle the main part of the job. In that case, starting from the outside by doing all the little tasks first will help you to overcome procrastination, and it will get you started on the big tasks.

**7.** *Start from the inside and do the larger tasks first.* This is the opposite of suggestion number six. Look over your list of everything that you have to do to complete the job and ask yourself, "What is the biggest single task on this list?" What is the one item that will take the most time or require the most effort? Discipline yourself to start with that item, and stay with it until it is complete. All the other, smaller tasks on the list will then seem easier by comparison.

**8.** *Do the task that causes you the most fear or anxiety.* Often, it has to do with overcoming the fear of failure or rejection by someone else. In sales, it may be associated with prospecting. In management, it may be associated with disciplining or firing an employee. In relationships, this may have to do with confronting an unhappy personal situation. In every case, you will be more effective if you deal first with whatever is causing you the greatest emotional distress or fear. Often this will break the logjam in your work and free you up mentally and emotionally to complete all your other tasks.

**9.** *Start your day with the most unpleasant task first.* Get it over with and behind you. Everything else for the rest of the day will seem easier in comparison.

A recent study compared two groups of people. One group started an exercise program in the morning. The second group started an exercise program in the evenings after work. The researchers found that the morning exercisers were much more likely to still be in the program six months later. Starting the day with exercise was much more likely to lead to the habit of regular exercise than putting it off until the end of the day when it was easier to make excuses and procrastinate.

Mark Twain once wrote that, "The first thing you should do when you get up each morning is to eat a live frog; then you will have the satisfaction of knowing that that is probably the *worst* thing that can happen to you all day long."

Your "live frog" is your biggest, most difficult, most unpleasant task. When you start and finish this task before doing anything else, you will have the satisfaction of knowing that the rest of your day is going to proceed much more smoothly.

**10.** *Think about the negative consequences of not doing the job or completing the task.* What will happen to you if this job is not done on schedule? Both fear and desire are great motivators of human behavior. Sometimes you can motivate yourself by the desire for the benefits and rewards of task completion. Sometimes you can motivate yourself into action by thinking about the negative consequences and what will happen to you if the job isn't completed as promised.

**11.** *Think about how you will benefit from doing the job and completing the task.*

Write down all the reasons why it would be helpful for you to get this job done on time. The more reasons you have for completing the task, the more intense will be your desire to begin, and the greater will be your internal drive to complete what you've started.

If you have one or two reasons for getting a job done, you will have a mild level of motivation. But if you have ten or twenty reasons for completing the job, your level of motivation will be considerably higher, and so will be your persistence and self-discipline.

**12.** *Set aside fifteen minutes during the day when you will work on your project.* Set aside a specific time—say, from 10:00 to 10:15 A.M., or 2:00 to 2:15 P.M.—and resolve just to work for that brief fifteen-minute period without worrying about anything else. This technique will launch you into the task so that completion will be much more likely.

To get the most out of this technique, you must make an appointment with yourself and write it down. Then, at the designated time, have your tools and materials at hand and begin the fifteen-minute work session. At the end of the fifteen minutes, you may want to continue to work. If not, put the work aside and schedule another fifteen-minute appointment at another time. And then keep your appointment with yourself.

**13.** *Resist the tendency toward perfectionism.* Since perfectionism is a major reason for procrastination, decide not to worry about doing the job perfectly. Just get started and work steadily. You can always go back and make corrections and revisions later. Nothing worthwhile has ever been done perfectly the first time anyway.

Not long ago, a friend of mind started a consulting business. I asked him how it was going. He said he had not done anything yet because it was going to take a full month before he got his brochures, business cards, and letterhead back from the printer. I told him that his brochures, letterhead, and business cards would never get him a nickel's worth of business. What he should do is write his new telephone number on the back of his existing business cards, or get some cards made up at a quick copy center, and then just get out and talk to prospective clients. I told him that this would do him more good than all the brochures he would ever design.

He phoned me a week later and told me that this advice had transformed his thinking about himself and his business. He had started calling on prospective customers that very day and was already doing business and making money.

**14.** *Pick one area where procrastination is hurting you.* Select a single identifiable area where you know your tendency to procrastinate is holding you back. Pick the most important area, and resolve to conquer that specific example of procrastination. Set your priorities, and then concentrate single-mindedly on the one area where overcoming procrastination can make the greatest contribution to your success. Always attack the most difficult tasks first. Challenge yourself to confront the hardest parts of your work, and then get them done before anything else.

**15.** *Develop a compulsion for closure.* Once you have launched and begun to work on your task, refuse to stop until it is completed. When you develop the discipline to start a major task and then stay with it until it is finished, you will be laying down the foundation for a life of persistent, purposeful work. Force yourself to finish the last 5 percent of the job. That is the part that is worth all the rest in terms of personal satisfaction.

It is amazing, and somewhat sad, the number of people who overcome procrastination sufficiently enough to get started on a task, but they never carry it through to completion. As they get closer and closer to the end of the task, they find more and more reasons and excuses to put off the last 5 percent or 10 percent of the job. This is the reason most university theses and dissertations to complete masters or doctoral degrees never get completed and submitted. A person may spend years of study in college and leave without the degree because he was unable to push through and complete the last 5 percent or 10 percent.

You only experience the joy, satisfaction, and exhilaration of finishing the task when you bring it to completion. As you wrap up the last detail, you feel a tremendous sense of relief and accomplishment. Your brain releases endorphins, and you get a surge of happiness. But this is only possible when you complete the task 100 percent.

**16.** *Maintain a fast tempo.* Fast tempo is essential to success. Resolve to work at a brisk pace. Walk quickly. Move quickly. Write fast. Act quickly. Get on with the job. Consciously decide to speed up all of your habitual actions.

It is amazing how much more you will get done when you push yourself to move faster rather than moving at your normal pace. In fact, if you continually force yourself to work harder and faster, you will start to feel the magic of the *flow experience*. When you get into this "flow," you will experience an enhanced feeling of confidence and competence. When you are in flow, you will start to plow through enormous quantities of work in a much shorter period of time than you've done in the past.

Deliberately organizing your life, work, and tempo so that you regularly trigger this experience of "flow" is a key to great success. All truly effective people enjoy this mysterious flow of energy on a regular basis. It is activated by consciously speeding up the tempo of your work and keeping up the pace until you lift off, like an airplane clearing the ground.

## Your Greatest Challenge in Time Management

It takes courage and self-discipline to break the habit of procrastination. It takes hard work and determination. But the rewards are great. You will experience greater self-esteem, self-confidence, and personal pride. You will achieve lifelong success. By overcoming procrastination and becoming a focused, effective person, you will accomplish more than anyone else around you and more than you can possibly imagine today. There is no other decision that will be more life-enhancing and satisfying than your decision to "Do it now! Do it now! Do it now!"

*"Concentrate . . . for the greatest achievements are reserved for the man of single aim, in whom no rival powers divide the empire of the soul."*

—ORISON SWETT MARDEN

## Action Exercises

1. Select one major task where procrastination is holding you back. Resolve to learn all these methods and techniques by starting and finishing that one project.

2. Make out a detailed list of every single thing you will have to do to complete that task; think on paper.

3. Select the single most important item on your list, and gather everything you will need to start and complete that item.

4. Set a specific time when you are going to start and work single-mindedly on that task until it is finished.

5. Break your largest tasks and goals down into bite-size chunks, and concentrate on starting and completing one part of the job at a time.

6. Accept 100 percent responsibility for starting and finishing your major task; refuse to make excuses or rationalize putting it off.

7. Visualize yourself working with a sense of urgency; program your mind by repeating the words "Do it now!" over and over.

# CHAPTER NINE

# Keeping Up and Getting Ahead by Making the Most of Your Time

*"Mastery is not something that strikes in an instant, like a thunderbolt, but a gathering power that moves steadily through time, like the weather."*

—JOHN C. GARDNER, JR.

We live in a knowledge-based, information-driven society. Successful people today are simply those who *know more* than their competitors. One of your most important responsibilities is to keep up with your field and stay ahead of the pack by continually taking in new information and ideas.

The amount of knowledge in every field today is doubling every five to seven years, sometimes every two to three years. This means that you must double your knowledge on a regular basis just to keep even. The basic rule today is, "To earn more, you must learn more." You are earning all that you possibly can today, with what you now know. If you want to earn more in the future, you will have to learn and apply new knowledge and skills.

You must be continually absorbing new information if you want to achieve and maintain excellent performance in your field. If you want to be the best, you must pay the price in terms of reading, listening, learning, and growing. Your outer life will always be a reflection of your inner life. If you want to improve your life on the outside, you must begin with yourself, by improving yourself on the inside.

## One New Idea Can Make the Difference

One new idea or piece of information can change the direction of your life. For example, think of the Nobel Prize for Physics that was awarded for research on superconductivity in 1987.

Once upon a time, a group of IBM scientists working in the IBM laboratories in Switzerland reached an impasse in their research on superconductivity. They could not find or develop the formulas they needed. They finally gave up, putting the work aside so they could concentrate on other activities with more immediate commercial applications.

One of the scientists on this project decided to take a break and go down to the company library. While he was browsing through the reading materials, he came across a French journal on applied ceramics. In that journal, there was an article discussing several experiments that had been done in conductivity with ceramics. The scientist suddenly realized that this was the key that they had been looking for. The article and the information contained in it approached the subject of superconductivity from a completely different direction than the one they had been working on.

He immediately took the article and the information back to the laboratory and began applying it to their experiments. Within twelve months, the IBM scientists had discovered the secret to superconductivity. Not long after, they were awarded the Nobel Prize for Physics. They are now recognized and esteemed as two of the most important scientists of the twentieth century, George Bednorz and Karl Alex Mueller.

By keeping their minds open, and by continually reading and gathering information from difference sources, the scientists found the one piece of information they needed to make all of their other knowledge and information work together to achieve a single, large goal.

# When Your Mind Collides with a New Idea

It turns out that every change in your life comes about when your mind collides with a new idea, like a billiard ball colliding with another ball on a pool table. This is why people who regularly expose themselves to new ideas tend to move ahead more rapidly than those who do not.

Most of life can be explained by the Law of Probabilities. This law says that there is a probability that virtually anything can happen. In many cases, this probability can be calculated with considerable accuracy. Most of the calculations in the worlds of finance, investments, and insurance are based on some kind of estimates of probability.

### Increase Your Probabilities of Success

Your aim should be to increase the probabilities that the things you want will happen to you, and that you will achieve the goals that you have set for yourself. One of the ways that you increase the probabilities of success in any endeavor is by using your time in an excellent fashion. When you set clear goals, make detailed plans of action, establish clear priorities, and then focus single-mindedly on your most valuable tasks, you dramatically increase the likelihood or probability that you will be successful.

In the information age, the more ideas and information that you take in and expose yourself to, the more likely it is that you will come across exactly the idea or insight that you need, at exactly the right time for you. As a result, you will greatly increase the probability of success in whatever you are doing.

# Keeping Up and Getting Ahead

One of the fastest ways of getting ahead is learning how to make the most of your time. Here are a series of ideas that you can use to keep up with, and get on top of, your job, career, and field of expertise.

## Readers Are Leaders

Read at least one hour per day in your chosen field. One hour a day will translate into approximately one book a week. One book a week will translate into approximately fifty books over the next twelve months. If you read an hour a day, one book per week, you will be an expert in your field within three years. You will be a national authority in five years, and you will be an international authority in seven years. All leaders are readers.

Over the years, I have shared this simple concept with many thousands of my seminar participants. I receive a continuous stream of letters, faxes, and e-mails from people all over the world who tell me that their lives have changed profoundly as the result of developing the habit of reading for one hour or more in their fields each day.

### *Give It a One-Month Trial*

Try this out for yourself. Give yourself one month to test whether it works. In all likelihood, one month from now, if you read one hour each day in your field, your whole life will begin to change. Reading is to the mind as exercise is to the body. When you read in your field every day, you will become brighter and more alert. You will become more positive and focused. You will become smarter and more creative. You will see possibilities and opportunities in the world around you that you would have missed completely in the absence of your reading.

The average adult reads less than one book a year. According to the American Booksellers Association, 80 percent of households have not bought or read a book in the last twelve months.

If you read one book per week, fifty books per year, that adds up to 500 books in the next ten years. This habit of regular reading will give you an edge in your field, and move you faster toward the front of the line than perhaps anything else you can do.

Just think, if you were reading at this rate to become more effective and productive, would it affect your income? Do you think it would affect your career? Do you think this amount of reading would change your whole life? Do you think it would give you an edge over your competitors? The answer is obvious.

## Read Magazines and Trade Journals

Read the business and trade publications that contain articles and stories relevant to your field. Subscribe to them all. They only cost a few dollars a year, but one article with one key idea can save you years of hard work. Sometimes, a single insight in a single article written by a specialist in your field can change the direction of your career. Remember the Law of Probabilities. The more ideas that you expose yourself to, the more likely it is that you will expose yourself to the right idea at the right time.

Read publications such as *Forbes, Fortune, Business Week, The Wall Street Journal, Investor's Business Daily,* your local newspaper and business section, and all the specialty magazines in your field. One good idea is all you need.

### *Falling Further Behind*

A friend of mine is a management consultant. He was hired to advise a company on how it could turn around its business. Sales and profitability were falling. Competitors were surging ahead. Company management needed help desperately.

My friend asked them a few questions about their business and then said, "Can you give me the names of the major magazines, books, and newsletters that are written on and about this industry?" The president of the struggling company looked at him with surprise. He said, "I have no idea what books or magazines to recommend to you. I don't have any time to read that stuff. I can't even attend the annual conventions for this industry. I am too busy."

My friend stood up and said, "Well, I can save you a lot of money. I will tell you what your problem is right now, without further investigation. You have no idea what is going on in your industry. If you are not reading and keeping current with the changes in this business, you have no future."

It is the same with anyone in a fast-changing, hard-driving, competitive business. If you are not aggressively keeping up and ahead of your field, you have no future in it.

## Invest in Your Most Precious Asset

Decide today to invest 3 percent of your income back into yourself, into upgrading your knowledge and skills. Spend 3 percent of what you earn on your own personal and professional development. Subscribe to every magazine in your field; buy every book written that can help you in your business; listen to educational audio programs in your car; watch educational videocassettes, alone and with your staff; and take all the additional training and seminars that you can find.

Here's my promise to you: If you invest 3 percent of your income back into yourself, within a few years, you will not have enough time in the year to spend the amount of money that 3 percent represents. Three percent does not seem like a lot, but the impact that investing this small amount will have on your life and career will be so extraordinary it will amaze you.

A cross-section of New York professionals in business and academia was asked this question: "If you had managed to accumulate $100,000 from your job, what would be the very best way to invest that amount of money?" The business people, academics, teachers, doctors, journalists, and other specialists gave a variety of answers, but the most popular answer was different from what most people would expect. The very best investment that you could make would be back into yourself, and into becoming even *better* at what you had done to earn the money in the first place.

## The Guaranteed Formula for Getting Rich

Sometimes, during my speaking engagements, I will ask my audience this question: "If I could give you a guaranteed formula to become rich, would you be interested in hearing it?" Of course, everyone says yes and raises their hand. I then tell them the "guaranteed formula" for success and lifelong riches. It is this: Invest as much in your mind each year as you do in your car. That's it. Simple. Guaranteed. Obvious. And it works every single time.

The average driver spends $600 per month on his car between purchase payments, insurance, fuel, maintenance, and so on. If you are a high earner, you probably spend much more. But whatever the amount, resolve from this day forward to invest that same amount back into your mind, into becoming even better at what you are doing today. In the first year of practicing this formula, your income will increase 25 percent to 50 percent, or more, and your entire career will take off.

## Appreciating Assets Versus Depreciating Assets

An automobile is what is called a *depreciating asset*. It is subject to what accountants call "straight line depreciation." This means that, from the time you acquire the car, the value of that car depreciates a certain amount each year until it reaches a value of zero. At a certain point in the life of a car, it becomes a piece of scrap metal, suitable only to be melted down and turned into a new car.

Your brain, on the other hand, is an *appreciating asset*. The more money you invest in it, by reading and acquiring additional knowledge and skills, the more valuable you become. No matter how much you invest in your car, it will soon be worth nothing. But when you invest in your brain, you increase your "earning ability" with every new idea or concept that you can apply to producing value or results for someone else.

This is why people with more knowledge and experience earn more than people with less knowledge or experience. Their earning ability is greater. They have turned their brains into appreciating assets that are worth more and more each year in terms of the quality and quantity of results they can achieve by applying their minds to their work. You should do the same.

## Practice the "Rip and Read" Technique

It is essential that you be alert and aware to what is going on in the world of business, and in your business in particular. However, we are overwhelmed with a deluge of information that pours into our lives from all sides every day. You cannot get through it all. It is estimated that the average executive has 300 to 400 hours of reading stacked up around his home or office. You have to find a way to sort the relevant from the irrelevant and read the most important material.

One method you can use is called the *rip and read method*. Instead of reading a magazine the way it is written and laid out, you instead go to the table of contents, identify the articles of interest to you, and then turn straight to those articles. You then rip them out and place them in a file folder for reading at a later time.

### Carry Articles with You

Many people keep a "rip and read" folder in their briefcases that they carry with them to read during "transition time," such as in taxis or waiting rooms, airports and airplanes. You can keep this file handy and read the articles, one at a time, whenever you have a few spare minutes. You will be amazed at how efficient you become in plowing through huge quantities of key information using this method.

Remember, magazines and newspapers are written and designed to sell advertising. For this reason, you must resist the temptation to read a magazine from front to back, from cover to cover. Instead, approach each newspaper or magazine with the assumption that most of the material it contains is of no use or value to you. The best way to save time in reading an article is to determine if it will be of any use to you, and if it won't, to not to read it at all.

### The Way Adults Learn

Here is an important point about learning. The adult brain is designed so that you only learn and remember something if it is immediately *relevant* and *applicable* to your current situation. No matter how interesting it might be, if you cannot connect the information to your current life or work situation, and visualize how you might apply the idea immediately, it will slip through your mind, like water through a grate, and you will not remember it at all.  .

For this reason, you should not waste time reading subjects that may be of interest to you "someday." Remember the Law of the Excluded Alternative, which says, "Doing one thing means not doing something else." If you are reading something that has no immediate relevance or applicability to your work, you are simultaneously *failing* to read something that may help you immediately. Especially when reading well-laid-out magazines and newspapers, you must discipline yourself to keep focused on only those subjects that are relevant to your current work.

## Use Gifts of Time Wisely

Take advantage of every gift of time that you receive. These are short periods, sometimes just a few minutes, which you receive during the day. Always carry reading material to go through when you get these unexpected moments of waiting or inactivity.

Many people harbor the secret desire to read the classics of literature. They even purchase the "great books" and keep them on their bookshelves, hoping someday to sit down and read them. This seldom happens.

Here is a great idea for you: Purchase a paperback version of a classic book that you have been wanting to read. Tear out twenty pages and put it in your briefcase or purse. The next time you have a gift of time you can read a few pages. When you have finished reading the torn-out pages, replace them with a new set of pages from the paperback and put a rubber band around the old pages.

If you read a book a month in this way, you will read twelve books a year, 120 books in the next ten years. You will become one of the best-read people in the world by using this method. Or, if you read the classics for fifteen minutes a day, over the course of a few years, you would have read all the great books of literature.

## Learn from the Experts

Read the books written by experts in your field. Read books that contain practical information that you can use immediately to improve the quality of your work and your life.

How do you know what books you should read? Here is a simple technique. With few exceptions, you should only read books written by people who are active practitioners of their craft. Books written by university professors are usually theoretically true, but practically useless in the course of operating a real, live business or living a successful life.

When you see a book that interests you, immediately read the biography of the author. Find out what the author has done and accomplished, where she has worked, what kind of experiences she has accumulated in the course of her career. You are looking for books by people who have established a successful track record in your field.

Once you have determined that the author is a credible source of information, look at the table of contents to be sure that what the author is writing about is relevant and applicable to your field today. Avoid theory whenever possible. Look for practical ideas with practical solutions to common problems.

That is, if the book doesn't offer something practical, then the best way to save yourself is to not read it at all.

Another way to determine whether you should buy a book is by looking at the number of books that have sold, especially if the book has come out in a paperback version. Any book that goes to paperback has usually sold well in hardcover. This is a helpful guideline, although not a guarantee of quality. Some of the best-selling business books are written by academics. They are full of ideas that are completely impractical. No one is ever able to achieve improved business results applying an academic's ideas in a real corporation. The material looks wonderful on paper, but it has no relevance to the real world.

## Build Your Own Library

We are all creatures of habit. When we are young, we often develop the habit of going to the library, checking out books, reading them, and then returning them to the library. There are many adults who still do this, even when it makes no sense at all.

Your time is your most precious resource. If you earn $50,000 per year, divided by approximately 2,000 working hours, this means that your time is worth $25 per hour. You must think continually in terms of your "hourly rate" in the way you use your time. Why spend two or three hours going to a library, browsing, checking out a book, taking it home, and then returning it to the library? It is much cheaper and more efficient for you to buy the book, take it home, and have it at your fingertips for the rest of your life.

When you read, get over the idea you were taught in school that you must not leave any marks in your textbook. Instead, use a red or blue pen to underline and mark the key ideas and concepts that you come across. Turn down the corners. Write exclamation points and stars in the margins. Personalize everything you read so that you can quickly go back and access the most important ideas.

Many people will read a book, making notes throughout of

the important points. They will then go back through the book with a dictation machine and dictate all the key ideas. They will have a secretary type up this synopsis of the book, which they will then three-hole punch and put in a binder. If you use this method, you can go to that binder and quickly review all the key points that you discovered in your reading. Then, each time you review these points, you will have new ideas and insights on how to apply them to your work or business.

### Join Book Clubs

Join the book clubs in your field. Get on their lists. You will often receive solicitations in the mail offering you three or four free books when you join a new book club. Take advantage of the offer. Each month after that, you will receive recommendations on what are considered to be the top books published in that area in the last few months.

Book clubs tend to be very selective in the books they choose and recommend, because they depend entirely for their income on selecting books that you will buy and keep. An enormous number of books have to be screened before they select the ones that they recommend to you.

### Read and Listen to Book Summaries

Subscribe to SoundView Executive Book Summaries. This company selects and condenses three or four top business books each month and sends them to you in a six- to eight-page condensation that enables you to quickly get the best ideas in the book in just a few minutes. With book condensations, you can pick out the most practical and usable ideas that the book contains, and then determine whether you would like to read the entire book. You can also get book summaries on audiocassette or CD each month,so you can listen to them in your car as you drive to and from work. Each time you do, you will pick up some of the most current ideas on effective business operations.

## Open Internet Accounts and Use Them

Open accounts with Barnes&Noble.com and Amazon.com. Put in your address and credit card number. Whenever you hear about a book that may be of interest to you, pull it up on the Internet and read a brief synopsis. If you like what you read, you can order the book online and it will be delivered to you in three to four days. This is a great time-saver instead of visiting the library or driving around to the bookstores. You can accomplish the same results that might take you an hour or more in one or two minutes.

## Take a Speed-Reading Course

One of the most valuable things you can do in your adult life is to take a speed-reading course to learn how to accelerate the amount that you read and retain. Most speed-reading courses are based on similar principles. You can actually triple your reading speed in the first lesson or class. These courses are given in every city, and they are usually advertised on the Internet or in the yellow pages.

With a good speed-reading course, you will quickly learn how to read 1,000 words per minute with about 80 percent retention. You will learn how to plow through large quantities of magazines, newspapers, and books. You will learn how to get through more reading material in two hours a day than many people get through in a week.

## Learn How to Read Efficiently

Learn how to read a nonfiction book efficiently. Perhaps the best method I have found is called the *OPIR method*. OPIR stands for Overview-Preview-Inview-Review. Here's how it works.

### Start with an Overview

When you pick up a book for the first time, instead of opening it up and reading it from front to back the way you normally would, you instead begin with an "overview." Read the front and back covers. Look at the flaps inside each cover, which contain important information about the book and the author. Read the table of contents from beginning to end, looking for a subject or heading that is of special interest to you at the moment. In the OPIR method, you then flip through the pages quickly, one at a time, to get a feel for the way the book is structured.

You look at each chapter heading and the way the pages are laid out. Read the subtitles and look at the charts, graphs, or visual elements. Get a sense for how the material flows in the book. This entire overview will not take you more than about ten minutes. As a result, you can now read "on purpose." You can establish a clear purpose for reading the book by deciding in advance what it is that you want to get out of it.

### Preview the Book Before You Read It

In the second part, the "preview," you flip through the pages one at a time to get an even better feeling for the layout and content of the book. During the preview phase, stop and read an occasional sentence or paragraph, usually the first sentence or paragraph of each section. If there are questions or summaries at the end of the each chapter, read them through carefully to get a better sense for what you will learn when you start to read the book seriously.

### Read the Book in Depth

In the "inview" stage, you sit down and read quickly from page to page. The overview and the preview will have aroused your interest and triggered your curiosity. In the inview phase, you will be looking to fill in the gaps in your knowledge. You will actually be engaging in what is called *anticipatory learning*. You are searching for information and ideas that are contained in the text.

During the inview, use your hand to move down the page just below the sentence you are reading. Read with a colored pen in your hand, and make notes whenever you come across an idea that you find interesting or important. Turn down the corners of pages if the material is important and you want to come back to it later.

### Review What You Have Read
In the final phase, the "review," you go back through the book again, from cover to cover, page by page, and reread the parts that you noted are most important to you. Remember that repetition is the mother of learning. It usually takes between three and six exposures to a new piece of information before you internalize it and transfer it to your long-term memory.

This four-step method, Overview-Preview-Inview-Review, will reduce the amount of time it takes you to read a 300-page book from six to eight hours to two to three hours. The more often you practice this method, the faster and more efficient you will become and the more you will actually remember and retain from each book. Using the OPIR method repeatedly will enable you to read two to three books per week. If you follow through, and then dictate the key notes from each book you read, you will develop a personalized library of notes that you can reread months or years later, in just a few minutes.

## Increase Your Intelligence and Learning Ability
The more you learn, the more you can learn. Your mental capacity grows and expands, as if adding more microprocessors to your mental computer. And the faster you read a book, the more information you get. The faster you read, the more you retain. The faster you read, the more you are forced to focus and concentrate your mind, which actually makes you smarter. The intense concentration required by speed-reading drives more blood to your brain, and it activates more of the neurons and ganglia in your neocortex, your thinking brain.

There is a direct relationship between the number of words that you know the meanings for and how well you think. There is a direct relationship between the size of your vocabulary and the amount you earn. There is a direct relationship between your understanding of the differences in meaning between similar words and how smart you are.

You can increase both the quality of your thinking and the quantity of your income by disciplining yourself to read intensely on a regular basis. Just as you become fitter physically when you engage in physical exercise, you become fitter mentally when you use your brain to read material that increases your knowledge and skills.

## Cancel Useless Subscriptions

Over the years, I have received solicitations to subscribe to every type of magazine, newspaper, newsletter, and journal. If it seems to be of interest to my life and work, I always take out a trial subscription and read the publication when it arrives. Over the years, I have accumulated as many as fifty to sixty weekly, bi-weekly, and monthly subscriptions of all kinds.

At a certain point, you have to stand back and ask, "Does this publication help me to achieve my goals?" Does it help me to achieve my goals better than other publications that I receive in the same area?

Remember, you simply do not have time to read everything that comes to you in the course of a day, week, or month. If a publication is not helping you achieve your goals, or is not serving some other important part of your life, cancel the subscription.

## Eliminate Your Stacks

One of the problems that you face today is called "stackaphobia." This occurs when you receive an unending stream of reading material that you don't want to part with. You begin to create stacks in your office and at home. Sometimes, you consider it a sign of progress when you begin a new stack because the existing stack is too high. You often spend a good deal of time rearranging your office or home so that you can accommodate ever-higher stacks of material.

Once a year, I apply an important rule to my stacks. I ask the question, "Is this more than six months old?" In other words, has it been here for more than six months without me reading it? The rule is this: "If you haven't read it within six months, it's junk!"

To keep your mind clear and operating at maximum efficiency, you must develop the habit of going through your stacks and throwing things away. When in doubt, throw it out! If you haven't read it in six months, you will probably never read it. Whatever it contains is probably obsolete. Think of business or financial magazines commenting on business conditions or industries. Sometimes, all the information in those publications is obsolete within a month. Throw them away.

### *Don't Worry About Missing Something*

Here is another point. If the article is on a subject of importance, someone else will rewrite the article in a different way at a later time in a different publication. Don't worry about missing an important idea. The more important the idea is, the more likely it is that it will come back to you from a different source. Throw the article out.

Always ask, "If I did not have this information, and I needed it, could I get it somewhere else?" The fact is that almost any information you need is available with a few clicks on the Internet. You can go into the archives of the major business magazines and retrieve articles that were written several years ago, print them out, and have them at your fingertips in a few seconds.

## Listen to Audio Programs in Your Car

Develop the habit of listening to audio programs in your car when you drive from place to place. Audio listening is perhaps the greatest breakthrough in education since the printing press.

With audio listening you can become one of the best-educated people in America by simply turning driving time into "learning time."

The average car owner in America drives between 12,000 and 25,000 miles each year, according to the American Automobile Association. This translates into 500 to 1,000 hours per year that you spend behind the wheel of your car. This is the equivalent of twelve and a half to twenty-five workweeks (based on forty hours), or three to six months of forty-hour weeks. This is equal to between one and two full-time university semesters.

### Attend Automobile University Full-Time

Imagine if your boss came to you and said, "I am going to give you three to six months off each year to engage in personal and professional development activities," and if you knew you'd be paid more money in the end as a result. According to a study at the University of Southern California, you can acquire the same educational benefits of full-time university attendance just by listening to audio programs in your car as you drive from place to place.

The rule is this: Never allow your automobile to be moving without educational audio programs playing. You cannot afford *not* to be listening to educational audio programs. Turn your car into a university on wheels. Turn your car into a mobile classroom.

### Knowledge and Ideas Condensed and Compressed

The information contained in audio learning programs can be enormous. The average program contains the best ideas of thirty to fifty books. The author of the audio program has probably invested hundreds, if not thousands, of hours studying, reading, researching, and teaching the material contained in the cassettes or CDs. You can "hire" this expert for pennies a day. You can have him drive around with you, stopping and starting instruction at your leisure, sharing the best ideas he has learned over the years.

To learn the equivalent of the information contained in a good audio program, you would have to purchase thirty to fifty books and read them. This would cost you $500 to $1,000 and take 300 to 500 hours of study. Even then, you would not have the ideas and information organized as helpfully as you can find in an audio program.

### *Increase Your Income from the First Day*

Over the years, I have produced dozens of audio learning programs. Many of them have been translated into as many as twenty languages and have now been used successfully by millions of people. Having spoken in twenty-four countries and met countless people whose lives have been changed by audio listening, I can say I have not met a single person, in more than twenty years, who has not seen his income increase dramatically from the day he began listening to audio programs in the car. No exceptions.

In my experience, audio listening becomes addictive. When you begin listening to an audio program in your car, you are struck by the number of great ideas that you can learn so easily and enjoyably. Because of the Law of Attraction, according to which a person is like a living magnet, you will almost invariably find an opportunity to use or benefit from these ideas shortly after you learn them, and almost immediately you will see results and improvements in your life. This motivates you to listen more consistently. As a result, you get even better results. Your performance improves and your income increases. Audio listening affects certain parts of your brain in a remarkable way. You actually become more intelligent. Try it and see.

## Attend Seminars and Courses Regularly

Attend seminars and courses given by people with practical experience and successful track records. In a seminar or workshop given by an expert, you can learn a tremendous amount of practical information in a short period of time. This is because of the way seminars and workshops are developed.

When I conduct a full-day seminar on sales, leadership, management, or strategic planning that lasts six or seven hours, I will usually invest several hundred hours of reading, study, research, consulting, and practice to get the information that goes into it. I will read anywhere from twenty to 100 books, underlining and taking notes. When I design the seminar, I will take the very best ideas that I have learned on that subject from every source. I will organize the seminar around the key concepts that can be immediately applied to get better results.

Most people in the field of professional speaking and training follow the same procedures in designing seminars. What you learn in three to six hours when you attend one of these seminars may have taken the facilitator ten or twenty years of hard work to learn and condense. And the pressure is always on the speaker to include more value in a seminar by seeking out even more helpful ideas.

So, by all means, attend every seminar you can find. Be willing to travel across the country if necessary to spend several hours with an expert in his field. Your attendance at one seminar, if it is the right one for you, at the right time, on the right subject, can save you years of hard work in your field.

### Join the Professional Associations in Your Field
Join professional associations where you can meet other people in your field. Join the organization or association that represents your business, or that the top people in your field belong to. Join the chamber of commerce in your community and attend their regular meetings. Join business groups that welcome people who are in the same field as you or work in similar fields. Attend every meeting you possibly can. As Woody Allen once said, "Eighty percent of success is just showing up."

Business associations are designed to be "self-help" groups.

Everyone who belongs to these associations is there because they are looking for ways and opportunities to improve their businesses and their results. They join professional associations because they know that the very best way to help themselves is to look for ways to help other people.

At each meeting of your professional association, you will meet people who can help you, and whom you can help, to achieve business goals. In my experience over the years, having addressed hundreds of business and association meetings, I have found that the very best people in every industry belong to these groups, and they attend regularly.

### Get Involved and Offer to Help

When you join your local association, resist the temptation to simply show up for meetings. Instead, decide to get involved in some way. Offer to help. Offer to serve on a committee. Offer to do something that needs to be done on a voluntary basis. Again, the most important and respected people in every business association are those who actively contribute to the activities and success of that organization. Make sure that you are one of them.

Almost everything that you accomplish in life will be determined by the people you know and the people who know you. When you offer to serve on the committee of your professional association, you get a chance to meet and work with some of the best people in your industry. They get a chance to meet and work with you as well. Over the years, your willingness to volunteer your time and effort will allow you to build a wider and wider network of contacts that you will be able to draw upon to help you to achieve your business and personal goals. There is a saying, "The more you give of yourself without expectation of return, the more that will come back to you from the most unexpected sources."

## Network with the Top People in Your Business

Make it a habit to network regularly with people in your business and in your community. Introduce yourself to people who can help you, and whom you can help in return. The most successful people in any business or organization are those who network effectively on a day-to-day, week-to-week, or month-to-month basis. Your success in life will always be determined by the quality and quantity of the people who know you and who think of you in a positive and favorable way.

The more people you know, and who know you, the more successful you will be. People like to deal with people they know.

### Trigger the Law of Reciprocity

The key to networking, and to building a wide range of contacts is called the Law of Reciprocity. This law says that people are always looking for opportunities to return favors to people who have done favors for them. Therefore, you should always be looking for ways to help or to do favors for people who can be helpful to you sometime in the future.

One study found that the most successful managers, those who were promoted regularly, spent as much as 50 percent of their time interacting and networking with other people, both within their business and industry and outside of it. More people knew them, and more doors opened up to them as a result.

### The Success Formula That Never Fails

Here is a simple formula that you can use to save an enormous amount of time in achieving your career goals. It is simply this: T × R = P. In this formula, T stands for *talent*. These are the talents, abilities, skills, knowledge, and experience that you bring to your work. R stands for *relationships*. These are the number of people you know, and the number of people you can affect or influence in some way. P stands for *productivity*. Your productivity is the quality and quantity of your results, what you produce, and what you get paid for. Talent times relationships equals productivity.

In other words, constantly work to become better at what

you do. Continuously network to expand your number of contacts and relationships, and your productivity or value will continue to increase.

## Take a Course in Public Speaking

One of the most helpful career decisions you will ever make is to take a course in public speaking. Take the Dale Carnegie course, or join a local chapter of Toastmasters International. Attend each week, and follow the directions they give you to learn how to speak on your feet.

The way to overcome your fear of public speaking is by learning how to prepare and deliver a talk. Once you learn how to deliver a speech, you will attract into your life opportunities to speak in front of small groups of people, and then larger groups. When you do your homework and become more knowledgeable on your subject, and then express yourself clearly and effectively to others in public forums, you will attract to yourself the attention of people who can help you.

One of the most admired skills in the world of work is the ability to speak well on your feet. As you develop this skill, new doors will open for you. You will feel more courageous and confident. You will have higher self-esteem. People will respect you and admire you. You will be given opportunities to use your developing skills at higher and higher levels.

## Invest the Golden Hour in Yourself

One of the very best ways to get ahead in your field is to arise early, by 5:30 or 6:00 A.M., and invest the first hour of your day in yourself. This is often called the *golden hour*. It sets the tone for your entire day. If you get up and read something uplifting or educational for one hour each morning, you will start off your day mentally prepared to perform at your best in the hours ahead. One hour each morning spent reading a book in your chosen field, or otherwise educating, motivating, and inspiring yourself, will improve your performance in everything you do.

## Three Keys to the Future

Here are three final points for keeping up and getting ahead. They are repeated throughout this book because they are the pivotal points of high productivity and personal success.

First, plan every day in advance. Start off every day with a written plan, clearly organized with tasks, activities, and priorities. Always begin work with your most important task.

Second, listen to audio programs in your car. Always have your audio player on when you are driving. Take every opportunity to learn new ideas that can help you in your life and work.

Third, commit yourself to lifelong personal and professional development. Reading, learning, listening, and growing can save you many years of hard work achieving your career goals and your desired income. Sometimes, one new piece of information, at the right time, can change the whole direction of your career.

## Become a No-Limit Person

There are no limits on what you can become, except for the limits that you place on yourself. There is nothing that you cannot do, if you are willing to prepare yourself long enough and hard enough in advance.

Your decision to keep up, and keep ahead of what is going on in your field, will ensure that you reach your full potential. It's one of the most important decisions you can make. By becoming the best at what you do, you will become everything that you are capable of becoming. Never stop learning and growing.

*"I kept six honest serving men. They taught me all I knew. Their names are What and Why and When, and How and Where and Who."*

—RUDYARD KIPLING

## Action Exercises

1. Resolve today to dedicate yourself to lifelong learning; decide to pay any price, invest any amount of time required, to be the best at what you do.

2. Build your own personal library of books that can help you to be even more effective at what you do; take time each day to learn something new.

3. Listen to audio programs in your car from now on. This habit alone can make you one of the best-educated and highest-paid people in your field.

4. Take a course in public speaking and learn how to be both effective and persuasive on your feet. This skill can open countless doors for you.

5. Learn to speed-read and also to read more efficiently. These are both basic skills that you can acquire and use for the rest of your life.

6. Join the business groups and associations that welcome members of your profession or business; get involved and offer to help.

7. Get up at least one hour earlier than you need to and invest the "golden hour" in yourself. Read something uplifting or educational that prepares you for the day.

# CHAPTER TEN

# Saving Time When Dealing with Others

*"Nothing is so powerful as an insight into human nature. What compulsions drive a man, what instincts dominate his action? If you know these things about a person, you can touch him at the core of his being."*

—WILLIAM BERNBACH

Your interactions with others consume as much time, if not more, than any other part of your day. Even technical workers spend up to 75 percent of their time communicating with coworkers. You can greatly increase the efficiency of your interactions by improving the quality of your communications.

Some of the biggest time wasters in life are people. These people problems can be broken down into a few critical categories.

## Common Misunderstandings

A major waste of time is caused by misunderstandings between people about roles, goals, and responsibilities. People do not know what they are expected to do, how to do it, and by what time. Misunderstandings lead to inefficiencies, anger, frustration, and unhappiness. It often requires an enormous amount of time to clear up a misunderstanding and get matters back to normal.

Most of your problems in life talk back. They come with hair on top. Perhaps 85 percent of your happiness, or unhappiness, in life involves other people in some way. Miscommunications with other people are a major source of time wastage.

## Unclear Priorities

Misunderstandings about priorities often lead to your working at the wrong job, at the wrong time, for the wrong reason, and perhaps aiming at the wrong level of quality. Or the problem may be that you are working for the wrong person. Some of the most stressful times of your life are caused by misunderstandings at work, especially miscommunications with your boss.

The single most important cause of positive feelings and high levels of motivation in work is defined as "knowing exactly what is expected." On the other hand, the number-one complaint, or demotivator, of employees is "not knowing what's expected."

In order to perform at your best, you need absolute clarity about your job and what you are expected to do. You need clarity with regard to results required and standards of performance. You need clarity with regard to schedules and deadlines. You need clarity with regard to the rewards for doing a good job and the consequences of failing to do good work. Clarity is everything.

## Poor Delegation

Poor delegation to others, or from others, leads to mistakes and frustration on the part of both the boss and the employee. It is a major time waster.

One of the rules for success in life and work is to "assume the best intentions of everyone." You can generally assume that each person does the very best he can at the job he thinks he is supposed to do. But poor delegation causes even the most sincere and talented people to do poor work or the wrong jobs. Therefore, they end up feeling frustrated and unhappy.

## Unclear Lines of Authority

Unclear lines of authority and responsibility lead to time wastage. People do not know who is supposed to do what job, when is it to be done, and to what standard of quality. People are left to wonder, Who is supposed to report to whom? Who's in charge? Who's the boss?

### A Management Game

In my management seminars, I often invite the managers to play a game with me. The game is called "Keep Your Job." The rules are quite simple.

First, the managers must write down the names of the people who report to them. Next to those names they must write the most important job that each of those people is expected to accomplish, in what order of priority, and why they are on the payroll. The next step, I tell the managers, involves interviewing each of their staff members. Each staff member will be asked to answer the question, "What exactly have you been hired to do, and in what order of priority?" If the answers given by each staff member are identical to the answers given by the managers, then the managers will be allowed to "keep their jobs."

I then ask, "Does anyone here want to play Keep Your Job?" No one ever wants to play. In years of conducting this exercise, I have never found a manager who is willing to stake his job on the sure knowledge that all of his employees are clear about what they are on the payroll to accomplish.

### The Manager Is Responsible

The fact is that each manager is responsible for making absolutely sure that each employee knows exactly what he is supposed to be doing. One of the fastest ways to increase efficiency, clear up misunderstandings, and improve communications is to take the time to sit with each person on your staff and discuss exactly what they are supposed to do, and in what order, and to what standard of excellence.

## Incomplete Information

Another major time waster in business is poor or incomplete information, which leads to erroneous assumptions and conclusions. It is amazing how often people jump to conclusions or make false assumptions on the basis of wrong information.

The very best managers take the time to ask questions, and they listen carefully to the answers before they make a decision. If there is a key piece of information that suggests a problem or difficulty, they double-check on this piece of information to make sure that it is accurate.

Always ask, "What proof do you have for this statement or fact?" Never assume that something important is true without taking the time to corroborate it.

## Aimless or Too Frequent Meetings

Too many meetings, or aimless meetings that proceed without an agenda, direction, or closure, are an enormous waste of time at work. These are meetings that start and stop without any particular resolution. No problems are solved, no decisions are made, and no responsibilities are assigned. No deadlines are agreed upon for action.

Since 25 percent to 50 percent of working time is spent on meetings of all kinds, you can dramatically increase your effectiveness and productivity by taking the time to improve the quality of your meetings, by preparing agendas in advance, and by bringing each question to closure.

# Lack of Clarity Concerning One's Job

Lack of information or unclear communications on important matters affecting a person's work causes a lot of wasted time. In one survey on employee motivation, the best companies were defined as places where each person felt that he was an insider and "in the know" about what was going on in the company. The worst places to work were described as those where no one was sure about what was really going on. In this type of situation, people were unclear about their responsibilities, unsure about their jobs, and cautious about taking any risks. When people don't know what is going on, it leads to demotivation, poor performance, and "playing it safe."

People need to know everything that is happening in the company that affects their particular jobs. The very best companies are open and honest with all employees concerning those matters affecting the health of the company. Employees know what is going on and how their jobs fit into the big picture. When employees are unclear or unsure, an enormous amount of time is lost as the result of conversations, discussions, and gossip, which leads to ineffective work behaviors and poor productivity.

### Take Time to Communicate Clearly

In one study, 84 percent of successful executives said that their ability to communicate effectively with others was the key reason for their success. Almost all successful men and women today in the world of work, business, politics, and other fields are in their positions because of their ability to communicate well with other people. Effective communication is a vital time management skill.

Here is a rule: Never assume that the other person understands what you have discussed until she has fed it back to you in her own words. Never assume that you understand something until you have repeated it back, or you have explained it in your own words, and had the other person agree.

It is a truism that we only understand something to the degree to which we can explain it to another person. The very act of articulating an assignment or decision in words clarifies it for both the speaker and the person listening.

In interacting with others, seek first to understand, then to be understood. Most people get this rule backward. They are so busy trying to get other people to understand them that they don't take the time to understand the other person first. Listen closely to the other person to be sure that you fully understand what he is both saying and meaning. Only then should you try to get the other person to understand you.

The key to effective communication in working with others is developing absolute clarity about what needs to be done, and why, and when, and to what standard. Clarity requires time, attention, and patience.

## The Law of Comparative Advantage

In 1805, the British economist David Ricardo announced what has become one of the most important principles of economics, the Law of Comparative Advantage. This law initially referred to trade between countries. It demonstrated mathematically that countries should specialize in producing those products that they made better than any other country. Ricardo showed that even if country "A" produced two products at a higher level of quality than country "B," it was still better for country "A" to concentrate exclusively on producing the one product that it made best and to let country "B" exclusively produce the other. The total value created by both countries for their citizens would be greater in proportion to the resources consumed in production than if each country tried to produce both products.

## Applying Comparative Advantage to Your Work

In business and commerce, this is an extremely important principle. It is the basis of modern wage differentials. In your work life, the Law of Comparative Advantage says that you should assign, delegate, outsource, or have someone else do any job that can be done at a wage less than you earn, or less than the wage you desire to earn.

In its simplest terms, if your goal is to earn $50,000 per year and you work 2,000 hours per year, your hourly rate is approximately $25 an hour. This means that you should hire someone else to do any task that can be done at an hourly rate less than $25, even if you can do the task better than he can. This allows you to spend more time doing more work that pays $25 an hour or more.

If you want to earn $100,000 per annum, your hourly rate is $50 per hour for every hour you work. But you cannot earn $50 per hour during the workday if you are getting your car washed, picking up your groceries, or dropping off your dry cleaning. You cannot earn $25 or $50 per hour if you are chitchatting with your coworkers, making coffee, reading the paper, or surfing the Internet. This kind of work or activity does not pay you those kind of hourly rates. The basic rule is this: If you want to earn $100,000 a year, you have to do $50-per-hour work for eight hours every single working day.

## The Key Personal Productivity Principle

This is a key personal productivity principle. If you do not focus single-mindedly on working at or above your desired hourly rate, you will not earn this amount of money in the long run.

This rule applies to hiring—whether it is someone to do bookkeeping, typing, shopping, housecleaning, or any other task. The key is effective delegation, where you outsource or delegate those things that pay a lower hourly rate than you earn. This is the only way that you will have enough time to concentrate on doing the kind of work that will pay you the kind of money that you truly desire.

Every year, hundreds of thousands of people are laid off from different jobs in different industries. In almost every case, it is because their hourly contribution to their companies has dropped below the amount of money they are receiving in wages or salary. This situation may have been caused by external circumstances, by changes in the market that render the products and services they produce less desirable.

### You Can Only Be Paid What You Contribute

In too many cases, the value of workers has dropped because they have not continually upgraded their skills. On the other hand, they are wasting too much time. They are engaging in activities or performing tasks of low or no value—tasks that no one can pay them $25 or $50 an hour to do. As a result, workers are laid off or fired, and they must make the rounds for several months before finding new jobs that pay even lower amounts than they earned before.

The focus on your hourly rate, and continually increasing the value of your work on an hourly basis, is the key to your future. Basketball coach Pat Riley said, "If you're not getting better, you're getting worse." If you are not continually learning and upgrading your skills, you are actually sliding backward, and your time is becoming less and less valuable to your employer. Don't let this happen to you.

## Delegation Is the Key to Leverage

To achieve everything you are capable of achieving, and to be able to concentrate on those few tasks that can make the greatest contribution to your life and work, you must become excellent at delegation. Whether you are a boss or an employee, you must be continually seeking ways to outsource, delegate, and get other people to do the things that pay a lower hourly rate than you desire to earn.

There are several ways to become more effective at delegating, outsourcing, or hiring other people to do parts of your work so that you can concentrate on the parts of your job that pay the most.

## Who Else Could Do This Job?
Ask the question, "Who can do this job *instead* of you?" Remember, you have to delegate everything possible in order to have enough time to do those few things that are most important.

## Who Can Do the Job Better Than You?
One of the characteristics of effective managers and successful leaders is that they have the ability to find people who are superior to them in specific tasks. You should continually look for people who can do certain parts of your work *better* than you.

## Can the Job Be Done at a Lower Cost?
Evaluate the job and ask, "Who can do this job at a *lower* cost than me?" Many companies and individuals are finding that they can outsource major parts of their operations to companies that specialize in that area. Companies that specialize in a particular function can usually do the job cheaper and faster than a company that does that work as part of its other activities.

## Can the Job Be Eliminated?
Ask yourself and others, "Can this activity be *eliminated* altogether?" What would happen if the job were not done at all? Many routine tasks and activities in a company or business could be quite easily eliminated with no loss of productivity and great increases in effectiveness.

Once upon a time, in a Fortune 500 company, a new vice president of finance took over the accounting and bookkeeping for the national organization. One of his departments consisted of twelve highly paid accountants and analysts who spent their time assembling the monthly reports from all the operating divisions into a single binder, which was then distributed to all the division heads. This department and its activities were costing the company almost $1 million a year.

The new vice president was curious. He went down the hall to one of the division heads and asked him if he had been receiving the monthly reports from his accounting department. The division head assured him that he had been getting the reports each month. The vice president asked, "What do you do with them?"

The division head said, "Come here and I'll show you." He took the vice president down the hall and into a storage room where the monthly reports, each of them about three inches thick, were neatly stacked on a set of bookshelves. "We never have time to read them, but we keep them here just in case."

The VP of finance went back to his office, called in the specialists who produced the report, and told them to discontinue their activities. They would be reassigned to other jobs where the company needed their expertise more than this department. They argued vigorously against this decision. They insisted that the company depended on their monthly reports. But the new vice president was adamant. He discontinued the reports and didn't tell anyone.

Nothing happened. Nine months later, the vice president was at an executive meeting and one of the division heads asked him in passing, "Whatever happened to those big reports we used to get from your department each month?" The vice president of finance said, "We stopped sending them out."

The division head said, "Well, we never read them anyway." That was the only comment he ever received from anyone in the company on the discontinued reports.

It is amazing how many activities go on in business, and in private life, that could be quite easily discontinued completely, with no loss or inconvenience to anyone. Rooting out these opportunities for increased efficiency can dramatically improve the productivity and profitability of an organization or department.

## Six Steps to Effective Delegation

To delegate effectively in your work with others, there are six steps that you can take. If you neglect any one of these steps, you run the risk of miscommunication, misunderstandings, demoralization, and poor performance.

1. *Match the person to the job.* One of the great time wasters in the world of work is delegating the task to the wrong person. Often the task is delegated to a person who is not capable of doing it properly or getting it done on schedule.

The best predictor of future performance is past performance. The rule is that you never delegate an important task to a person who has not performed that task satisfactorily in the past. It is unfair to expect a person who has not done a job before to perform at a sufficient level of quality when he is given the job for the first time.

2. *Agree on what is to be done.* Once you have selected the right person for the job, take the time to discuss the job with that person and agree upon what must be done. The more time you take to discuss and agree upon the end result or objective—the more effort you make to achieve absolute clarity—the faster the job will be done once the person starts on it.

3. *Explain how the job should be done.* Explain to the person your preferred approach or method of working. Explain how you would like to see the job done, and how you or someone else has done it successfully in the past.

4. *Have your employee feed back to you what you have said.* Ask the person to feed your instructions back to you in her own words. Have her explain to you what you have just ex-

plained and agreed upon. This is the only way that you can be sure that the other person actually understands the job or assignment she has been delegated to accomplish.

**5.** *Set a deadline.* Set a deadline and a schedule for completion of the task. At the same time, arrange for regular reporting and periodic inspection. Invite feedback and questions if there are any delays or problems.

**6.** *Manage by exception.* Managing by exception is a powerful time management tool that you can use to work more efficiently with other people. If the job is on track and on schedule, managing by exception means that the person does not have to report back to you. If you don't hear from him, you can assume that everything is going well. The individual only has to report back to you when an exception occurs and there is a problem with getting the job done on time, to the agreed upon level of quality.

## Seven Ways to Get More Done Each Day

There are seven methods you can use to get more done each day. Each suggestion is simple, direct, and costs no money.

**1.** *Work harder.* Work harder than you are working today. You can concentrate with greater intensity on your work. You can focus single-mindedly and discipline yourself to work without interruption, diversion, or distraction. You can work harder than anyone else, which is a secret to great success.

**2.** *Work faster.* You can work faster than you do today. You can pick up the pace. You can develop a faster tempo. You can move more quickly from place to place and from job to job. When you combine working harder and working faster, you can get more done in a single day than most people get done in a week.

**3.** *Batch your tasks.* You can batch your tasks. You can do a series of similar jobs together, taking advantage of the learning curve.

**4.** *Do more important things.* You can do more important things. You can work on higher-value tasks. You can work on tasks that have a higher potential payoff rather than those activities that have a lower payoff.

**5.** *Do things you're better at.* Do things at which you excel. The better you are in a key skill area, the more that you can get done, and at a higher level of quality. Because you are better at these tasks, they will be easier for you, so you will get them done with less effort, and you will have more energy as a result.

**6.** *Make fewer mistakes.* To get more done, you can make fewer mistakes. You can take the time to do it right the first time. You've heard it said, "There is never enough time to do it right, but there is always enough time to do it over." One of the best time management techniques is to do it right the first time, even if it takes a little more effort and concentration.

**7.** *Simplify the work.* You can simplify the work by reducing the number of steps necessary to complete the task. This makes the job simpler and easier to get done.

## Paying Attention

Life is the study of attention. You always pay attention to that which you most value. If you value another person, you listen to him intensely when he is speaking. If you value the result of a job, you pay close attention to the details that determine whether or not that job is completed successfully. Effective managers value the results of their departments and employees and pay close attention to everything that is going on around them.

# Ensuring Success at Work

The very best times you will ever have at any job or company are when you are getting along wonderfully well with your boss. On the other hand, the very worst times you will ever have at any job are when you are not getting along well with your boss. And the major reason why employees have problems with their bosses is because of a lack of clarity about what exactly is to be done, and to what standard, and in what order of priority.

Here is an excellent exercise for you. Make a list of all of the answers to the question, "Why am I on the payroll?" Write down everything that you believe you have been hired to accomplish in your work. Focus on results, rather than activities. Imagine that your work consists of a series of deliverables. Define your job in terms of the deliverables for which your company pays you a wage or salary.

Now, take this list to your boss and ask your boss to organize this list by priority, based on what is most important to her. This may take a few minutes. Be patient. As you discuss this list with your boss, ask questions so that you are perfectly clear about what she wants or needs.

## Focus on Your Boss's Top Priorities

From that day forward, focus and concentrate on doing those jobs that your boss considers to be the most important before you do anything else. Whenever your boss asks you to do something else, take out your list and ask her what order of priority the new task has, relative to the tasks currently on your job list.

If you are working at your full capacity, you will have to stop doing something old to do something new. Many bosses do not realize that your plate is full already. When your boss asks you to do something new, you should ask him what he would like you to stop doing so that you can work on the new task that he has just given you. This is a wonderful way to minimize misunderstandings and improve communications.

It is only when you are working on those tasks that are most important to your boss that you can possibly have any chance of satisfying or pleasing him, or being paid more, or being promoted more often. If you make the mistake of doing things on your list in an excellent fashion, but you work on tasks that are not important to your boss, you will actually sabotage your career. The more time you spend doing an excellent job on unimportant tasks, the further behind you will fall.

## Three Types of Decisions

There are three types of decisions in any organization or family. When decisions involve other people, it is important that everyone is clear about what kind of a decision is under consideration.

**1.** *Command Decisions.* These decisions have to be made by the boss or the person in charge. These decisions are so important that one person is solely responsible for making up his mind about what is to be done.

Hiring a key staff member, firing a poor performer, making an important investment decision, finalizing a sale or transaction, or even negotiating a new loan with the bank are all command decisions. They must be made by the person in charge.

**2.** *Consultative Decisions.* This is a decision where you, or the boss, ask for advice and take input from other people. You combine the opinions, ideas, and inputs of others, together with your own, and make a decision. Even though it invites the advice and participation of others, a consultative decision is not made based on that advice.

You may be thinking of hiring a new person, assigning someone to a particular task, spending a certain amount of money on a business activity, or embarking on a new sales or marketing campaign. If you are the boss, you can ask for advice from everyone before you finally close the door and make your final decision.

When General Dwight D. Eisenhower was the supreme commander of Allied forces in Britain, he took the advice and input of hundreds of military experts, planners, and specialists in his preparation for the D-Day invasion. This process took several months. But in the end, with a single day of calm weather predicted for the English Channel, General Eisenhower alone made the fateful decision that launched the invasion of June 6, 1944 and brought World War II to an end ten months later.

**3.** *Consensus Decisions.* The third type of decision is one that is made on the basis of consensus. This is a democratic decision where everyone gets involved, discusses the pros and cons, and then agrees on what is to be done. Sometimes, everyone is in agreement, and sometimes the decision is made by a democratic vote, where the majority rules. Once the decision has been made, everyone commits to making the decision successful, however they may have voted during the discussion phase.

## Clarify the Type of Decision

One of the problems in communications and working with others is confusion over which kind of a decision is being made at that moment. Sometimes the boss asks for input and ideas. The staff members automatically conclude that this is a consensus decision, while the boss may be viewing it as a consultative decision. When the boss makes a decision that is contrary to the expressed wishes or opinions of the others, it can lead to hard feelings and misunderstandings. Time will be wasted going back and explaining to people that their input was invited and welcome, but not necessarily followed in the final decision.

When a boss makes it clear that this is a democratic or consensus decision, he is saying that the staff can decide what is to be done in this case, and that whatever the group decides, everyone will all go along with. When everyone is clear about the kind of decision under consideration, everything proceeds more smoothly, with less friction and time wastage.

## Focus on the Solution

Often in my seminars I will say, "I know the job description of every single person in this audience." This immediately gets everyone's attention. People then smile and wait to hear what I am about to say.

"You can take your business card and cross out whatever title is below your name," I say, "and replace it with the words *problem solver*. Everyone here is a problem solver. This is what you do all day long."

One of the characteristics of top people is that they are intensely *solution-oriented*. They do not continually think and talk about the problem, and who is to blame, and how much has been lost, and why it happened. Instead, they focus on the solution and what can be done to address the problem.

Your job, in whatever position, is to solve problems. Your income, your rate of promotion, the respect and esteem of your peers, and all of your success in life will be determined by how effectively you solve the problems and difficulties that you have to face every hour of every day in the achievement of your goals.

Leadership is the ability to solve problems. Success is the ability to solve problems. Personal effectiveness is the ability to solve the inevitable and unavoidable problems of daily life. The only question is, "How good are you at solving problems?"

Here is a wonderful discovery. The more you think and talk about possible solutions, the smarter you get. The more you think and talk about what can be done to solve the problem, the more ideas you will have. You will become more creative. Your mind will function faster. The more solutions that you come up with, the more solutions there are that will occur to you. Eventually you will become like the Pac-Man of the video game, gobbling up problems as fast as you encounter them.

One of the biggest time savers in life and work is your ability to solve the right problem in the right way. It is your ability to deal effectively and efficiently with problems, to overcome them, and to keep moving forward toward the result or goal that you desire.

On the other hand, one of the biggest time wasters in life and work is the inability to solve problems. The inability to solve a single key problem can lead to underachievement, frustration, failure, and even the bankruptcy of an organization. Thinking and talking in terms of problem solving and solutions is one of the most important mind-sets that you can develop.

## Seven Steps to Effective Problem Solving

There are seven steps to effective problem solving. If you follow them for the rest of your career you'll be able to cut through any difficulty or obstacle.

### Define the Problem Clearly

Start by asking, "What exactly is the problem?" Define the problem clearly, and whenever possible, in writing. Remember, accurate diagnosis is half the cure. Sometimes, writing a problem down on a flipchart or whiteboard and having everybody agree to the definition of the problem will lead rapidly to a solution.

Very often, forcing yourself to define the problem clearly in writing on a piece of paper will trigger a logical solution. Fully 50 percent of problems can be solved in the definition phase.

### *What Else Is the Problem?*

Once you have a clear definition of the problem, you should ask, "What else is the problem?" Never be satisfied with a problem that has only one definition. Keep probing. See if you cannot develop multiple definitions to a single problem.

Sometimes a large problem is actually a "cluster problem," where the larger problem is actually made up of several smaller problems. By defining the problem clearly, you break it down into its constituent parts so that you can solve each of the smaller parts at once.

The rule is that, in every complex problem, there is usually a single problem that must be solved before any other problems can be solved. This single, large problem that must be solved is often not clear or obvious. It requires a little digging on your part to find it.

It is human nature to jump to conclusions. We see a problem and we leap to a solution. We leap quickly from the problem to the solution, without considering that we might be jumping from the pan into the fire. In defining the problem, or problems, it is important that you go slowly at the beginning to make sure that you are not working on the wrong problem. Solving the wrong problem in the right way will often create a worse situation than the one you started with.

### Identify All the Possible Causes

Before seeking a solution, ask, "How did this problem occur?" What are all the possible causes of the problem? What are the reasons for the problem? It is not enough to simply come up with a solution. It is important that you deal with the underlying causes that created the problem in the first place.

When I started my company some years ago, no matter how busy we were in the market, we always seemed to have cash flow problems. Every couple of months, the bank account would be empty and we would have to scramble around to find the funds to make payroll and cover other bills.

We finally realized that we were lacking a cash management system. I learned later that this is one of the most important tools for business (or personal) survival and success. It is a long-term monthly projection of your cash needs, based on your very best estimates of your income and expenses.

Once we had taken the time to project forward a year, based on the seasonal fluctuations in our revenues, we were able to predict with some accuracy how much was coming in, how much was going out, and what times of the year we would have cash shortfalls. Once that cash plan was in place, we organized lines of credit and financial reserves to make sure that the cash crisis did not occur again.

Very often, identifying the cause of a problem immediately suggests an obvious solution that enables you to solve the problem and stop it from occurring again.

## Identify All the Possible Solutions

Before leaping to a conclusion, ask, "What are all the possible solutions?" What are all the different things that you can do to solve the particular problem? This is a very important step in the process.

Rather than assuming that there is only one answer, write down as many different solutions to the problem that you can think of. The more solutions, the better. Beware of a problem for which there is only one solution.

In many cases, the obvious solution is not the best solution. In some cases, the correct solution is to do the opposite of your initial inclination. Sometimes, it is to do something radically different. Occasionally, the solution is to do nothing at all.

In developing different solutions to a problem, you should clearly define your *boundary conditions*. These are the constraints within which you have to work and the results that this solution must achieve. Often, you can develop better solutions by defining the minimum and maximum conditions for the solution before you begin.

What does this solution have to accomplish? If the solution were perfect, what result would it achieve? How would we know that this was a good solution? Start with the end in mind. Be clear about what you want to accomplish with the decision before you decide on the solution.

## Make a Decision

Once you have all the information, make a decision. Select the solution that looks and feels to be the very best of the solutions available. But before you go on, ask, "Why is this the best solution? Why is this solution superior to the others?" The more time you take to think about and study both the problem and the solution, the better and more accurate your answer will be.

A few minutes spent in careful analysis in problems and solutions can save you an enormous amount of time when it comes to implementation.

### Establish a Fallback Solution

Be sure to ask, "What is our alternative solution?" In other words, once you have decided on the best solution, be open to the possibility that it will not work out at all. If that were the case, what would be your Plan B? What would be your fallback position? What would be your alternative solution if your first solution failed?

The process of thinking through an alternative solution is a powerful mental exercise. It forces you to expand your view of the problem and all the possibilities. Very often, by thinking through and developing a fallback position, you actually improve the original solution. Sometimes, you change it altogether.

Remember, you are only as free as your well-developed options. The more alternatives you have developed before you take action, the more effective you will be when you finally move forward. Keep asking, "What will I do if this doesn't work? What would be my alternative if I turned out to be wrong? How would I respond if this course of action failed altogether?"

### Determine the Worst Possible Outcome

Before you implement the solution, ask, "What is the worst possible outcome of this course of action?" What is the worst possible thing that can happen if you go ahead with this solution? Very often, the second alternative you developed turns out to be better than the first choice, because the worst possible consequences of the second solution are not as severe as the worst possible consequences of the first solution.

In every decision-making process, there is a certain element of risk. There is always uncertainty as to the outcome. There are risks that you can afford to take and there are risks that you cannot afford to take.

For example, a large-scale advertising campaign can be quite expensive. Many companies have made the mistake of betting the bank and throwing all their money into advertising at the Super Bowl. Their thinking is that even if only a small percentage of total viewers tuning into the Super Bowl were to buy their product, they will make back all the money spent in advertising.

However, they fail to consider the worst possible outcome: that no one would respond to the advertising at all. And this has happened several times. As a result, a number of companies have gone bankrupt. There are some risks that you cannot afford to take.

### Assign Specific Responsibility

Once the decision has been made, either assign or accept responsibility for carrying out the decision. Set a schedule and a deadline. Make it clear to everyone exactly what is to be done, by whom, and to what schedule.

Many companies make the mistake of solving the problem, coming up with an excellent solution, assigning responsibility, and then leaving the table. Two weeks or four weeks later they reconvene and nothing has happened. Why? No deadline was set. The individual who was assigned responsibility has gotten sidetracked and busy with other projects. No action has been taken. Sometimes, this inaction can be disastrous. Once you have made a decision, assign responsibility, set a deadline, and then follow through. This is the essential part of problem solving.

## Focus on Contribution

One of the key time management techniques in working with others is called a *focus on contribution*. The focus on contribution in an organization is essential to good communications and excellent teamwork. Good human relations occur in companies when they are task-focused and aimed at achieving specific goals or solving specific problems.

If relationships in the world of work are not *task-focused*, they have a tendency to become *people-focused.* Instead of being objective and measurable, they become subjective and personal. As a result, people talk to and about others most of the time. This leads to enormous losses of time and reductions in efficiency.

## Practice Participative Management

Participative management is a great time saver in working with people. It is one of the best tools that a manager can develop. Participative management requires that you bring your team together at least once each week for a general staff meeting. At this meeting, staff members talk about what they are doing, the progress they are making, and any problems they are having. People ask questions of each other, and decisions are made and solutions are agreed to.

The interesting discovery of participative management is that when someone makes a commitment to do something by a certain deadline in front of his peers, he will be internally motivated to complete that task. Not only that, when you bring people together on a regular basis, you can solve problems, make decisions, and clear up misunderstandings faster than almost any other way. Participative management is an incredible tool that you can use as a manager or supervisor for your entire career.

## Avoid Reverse Delegation

One of the most important time savers in the world of work has to do with what is called *reverse delegation*. This is where your staff member, to whom you have delegated the task, delegates the task back to you. Work is now moving up the chain of command, rather than down the chain of command. Work is coming up from the subordinate to the boss, rather than from the boss to the subordinate.

You must consciously resist reverse delegation and be aware that employees are always trying to delegate the job back to you. They use a series of techniques to which you can become a victim if you are not careful.

One of the ways that an employee delegates a task back to you is by bringing you a problem and asking you to solve it. The employee asks, "Can you take care of this task for me, or get me this information?" Since you are the boss and more competent and knowledgeable than he is, you agree to take care of it and get it back to him as quickly as possible. But then something else comes up, and it goes onto your stack and gets buried among your other responsibilities.

### The Monkey Is Now on Your Back

Here is the rule: The person who has the responsibility for the next step in the job is the one who is responsible. When your staff members ask you to do something, the outcome of which determines how they do their job, they have delegated the task back to you. The monkey is now on your back. Soon, your staff members will be coming by to supervise you and to ask you how things are going. You will now be working for the people who were working for you. You will be promising and assuring them that you will get *their* job done and back to them as quickly as possible.

The way to resist reverse delegation is to refuse to take the task back, once you have assigned it. When your staff members ask you to do something, you instead ask, "What do you think we should do?" Whatever they suggest, you can comment upon or agree to, but whatever it is, you pass it back to them so they can get on with their job.

## Resist Your Natural Tendencies

There's a natural tendency to want to go from managing back to operating. Since you got to where you are today by doing a good job on your way up the corporate ladder, whenever you find yourself under pressure, your natural tendency is to go back to doing what you did so successfully in the past. You must fight this tendency, or you will soon find yourself at the bottom of the food chain, being delegated to by the different members of your staff.

The definition of a good manager is a person who "gets things done through others." Your job is to make sure that other people do the job correctly, rather than going back and doing it yourself. Push on to others everything that can possibly be done by them. Once you have delegated and assigned a task, don't take it back.

## Teach and Train Others

Take the time to train and to teach your subordinates (and others) how to do their jobs. The more you train them, the more you build their confidence so that you can delegate even more tasks to them. Teaching other people how to do a job gives you a high return on energy. Once you have taught someone how to do a part of your work, you can always delegate and free yourself up for other work that pays you a higher hourly rate.

## Focus on Clarity

The major problem and time waster in communication, and in working with others, is fuzzy understanding. The antidote to fuzzy understanding is clarity. Clarity is one of the greatest time management tools of all. It is only achieved through repetition, discussion, feedback, and agreement. Take the time to learn how to be a good communicator. This will pay off in tremendous timesaving, and it will increase your effectiveness in every area of your life and work.

*"Before you can inspire with emotion, you must be swamped with it yourself. Before you can move their tears, your own must flow. To convince them, you must yourself believe."*

—WINSTON CHURCHILL

## Action Exercises

1. Practice delegating everything to anyone who can do the job at a lower hourly rate than you desire to earn.

2. Be crystal-clear in explaining to others exactly what is to be done, and to what standard of performance, and by what date.

3. Sit down with your staff members and explain to them exactly why they are on the payroll and what their highest-value tasks are.

4. Keep everyone "in the know." Be sure that your staff is aware of everything that is going on that affects their jobs in any way.

5. Whenever you assign a task, ask the person to feed back to you what you have said; this clears up a lot of misunderstandings.

6. Practice participative management with your staff; hold weekly staff meetings and invite everyone to participate and ask questions.

7. Remember that your people are your most valuable asset; continually seek ways to communicate with them more clearly.

# CHAPTER ELEVEN

# Time Management Techniques for Salespeople

*"The successful person makes a habit of doing what the unsuccessful person doesn't like to do. The successful person doesn't like to do it either, but he does it because he recognizes that this is the price of success."*

—HERBERT GRAY

In 1928, the magazine *Sales and Marketing Management* surveyed American businesses to determine how efficiently salespeople were using their time. They discovered that the average salesperson in America was only working 20 percent of the time, approximately one and one-half hours per day.

This finding caused alarm bells to go off throughout the sales industry. The idea that salespeople were only working ninety minutes per day became the emphasis for improved training, better time management skills, better supervision, and better control of the activities of salespeople. It led to a greater focus on the accountability of salespeople to the company for the way they were spending their time.

In 1988, *Sales and Marketing Management* magazine reported on the results of this training over the past sixty years, which was aimed at upgrading the time efficiency of sales personnel. They reported that, in 1988, the average salesperson in America was still working 20 percent of the time, ninety minutes per day. Nothing had changed.

A Columbia University study came to the same conclusions. After interviewing thousands of salespeople, the researchers found that the first sales call of the day was made, on average, at approximately 11:00 A.M. The last sales call of the day was made, on average, at about 3:30 P.M. Salespeople spent the rest of their time preparing, shuffling papers, traveling, eating lunch, drinking coffee, and complaining about how tough the business was.

McGraw-Hill did a follow-up study in the 1990s and reached the conclusion that sales personnel spent 37 percent of their time selling. This report turned out to be based on what was called *self-reports*. This is when the individual salesperson reports a particular number, according to his personal recollection, without the benefit of notes or records. Alas, we can safely conclude that the average salesperson only works ninety minutes a day.

## Double Your Sales

In my sales programs, I teach what I call my *minutes theory*. It is based on a simple equation. If you are in sales today, 100 percent of your sales and your income are generated by the number of minutes that you spend face-to-face with prospects and customers. If you want to increase the number of sales or the amount of money you make, you must increase the number of minutes that you spend in actual selling activity, face-to-face with people who can, and will, buy from you.

My theory says that if you double the number of minutes that you spend with customers, you will double your income, even if you do not improve in any other area of sales. If you manage your time as the top salespeople do, so that you are spending more time with customers, your sales will increase immediately.

If you are in sales and reading this chapter, you are going to learn how to double your time effectiveness, and double your sales, in the next few pages. Thousands of salespeople are already using the ideas in this chapter to double, triple, and even quadruple their income in as little as six months.

Many of my graduates have doubled and tripled their sales in less than a month, as the direct result of applying these methods and techniques.

## The Job of the Salesperson

Let us begin with the job description of the salesperson. The job description of the salesperson is to *create and keep customers.* The measure of effectiveness of a salesperson is how many new customers she creates, or resales she generates, in any given time period. Everything else that a salesperson does is secondary to creating and keeping customers. Therefore, the only time a salesperson is working is when he is face-to-face, head-to-head, and knee-to-knee with a prospect or customer.

Salespeople are the only working people in America who wake up each morning unemployed. And they remain unemployed until they get in front of a person who is capable of making a buying decision. The first rule for sales success can be summarized in six words: "Spend more time with better prospects."

Sales success is in direct proportion to your ability to initiate new contacts. Because selling is a numbers game, based on the law of averages, the more new contacts you initiate, the more successful you are going to be, holding constant for all other factors. The more people you see, the more likely it is that you will make more sales.

## The Three-Step Sales Formula

There is a simple formula for outstanding sales performance. It consists of three activities: Prospect, present, and follow up. Successful salespeople are those who prospect, present, and follow up more often than unsuccessful salespeople.

A person of average talents and abilities who prospects, presents, and follows up all day long will run circles around a genius who does not. If a salesperson is not making the sales he would like to make, or is not earning the income he would like to earn, it can always be traced back to a failure in one of the three key result areas: prospecting, presenting, or following up.

Apply the 80/20 rule to all of your selling activities. In selling, this means that you spend 80 percent of your time prospecting until you have so much business that you don't have time to prospect anymore. You spend the other 20 percent of your time on everything else, including planning, organizing, doing paperwork, studying your sales material, socializing, and engaging in any other activity that is not prospecting.

Prospecting is defined as the work of taking specific actions to seek out and contact people who need, who can use, and who can afford to purchase your product or service. The only thing that you have to sell as a salesperson is your time, and your time is only worth anything when you are face-to-face with someone who can buy what you are selling.

## Begin with Clear Income and Sales Goals

Achieving peak performance and excellent time management in sales begins with your setting clear income and sales goals for yourself. The act of sitting down and deciding, in writing, how much you want to earn, and how you are going to go about earning it, makes it far more likely that you will achieve those goals than if you didn't set them at all. The goal-setting exercise I am about to share with you has led to the doubling and tripling of the incomes of many salespeople. It is powerful because it is simple and easy. You can learn it and apply it immediately.

For example, one saleswoman was just starting in real estate when she came to my seminar. She had not sold her first house or taken her first listing. Nonetheless, as a result of this exercise, she set a goal for herself to earn $50,000 in income in her first year. At the time, she had no idea how few people selling residential real estate earned $50,000 per year. But the goal setting worked for her. She passed the $50,000 mark in her tenth month of selling.

## Start with Your Best Year
You begin by taking your very best year's income to date and grossing it up by 50 percent. In other words, if your very best income year to date was $40,000, you set your income goal for the next twelve months at $60,000, or 50 percent more. If your very best income year to date was $100,000, you set your income goal at $150,000. For the sake of this example, I will use $60,000 as the income target for the year.

Once you have determined how much you want to earn over the next twelve months ($60,000), the next step is to determine how much of your product or service you are going to have to sell in order to earn that amount.

For example, if you are receiving a commission of 6 percent on your sales, you will have to sell $1 million of your product or service over the next twelve months in order to earn $60,000. That number of $1 million now becomes your annual sales goal.

Next, you determine your monthly income goal. In our example, $60,000 divided by twelve months equals $5,000 per month. You then determine how much you will have to *sell* each month to achieve that income goal. One million dollars in sales divided by twelve months equals $83,333. This becomes your monthly sales target.

Once you have determined how much you want to earn, and how much you will have to sell each month to achieve it, you then determine your weekly income and sales goals. Let us assume that you will take two weeks off on vacation. You then divide the remaining number of weeks (fifty) into your income goal for the year. In this example, fifty into $60,000 equals $1,200 per week.

You then calculate the amount that you will have to sell each week by dividing your annual sales goal by fifty. In this case, $1 million in sales divided by fifty weeks means that you would have to sell $20,000 of your product or services each week in order to earn $60,000 by the end of the twelve-month period.

You now divide the number of days per week that you work into your weekly income goal. If you work five days per week, you can use that figure. In our example, $1,200 per week, divided by five, would equal $240 per day.

To calculate your daily sales goal, you divide the amount that you intend to sell per week by the number of days that you work. In this case, using $20,000 per week as the sales goal and dividing it by five, you would arrive at $4,000 worth of your product or service that you will have to sell each day.

Finally, divide your daily rate, in this case $240, by the number of hours you intend to work each day. For example, if you work eight hours per day and you divide that into our example of $240, you would come up with an hourly rate of $30.

## Focus on Your Hourly Rate

Once you have determined your desired hourly rate, you are ready to start work. From the time you start working in the morning until the time you finish in the evening, you refuse to do anything that does not pay you $30 per hour. And the only type of work that pays you $30 per hour, or more, is prospecting, presenting, and following up.

This is an important point that many salespeople don't seem to understand. You cannot drop off your laundry, pick up your groceries, get your car washed, or chat with your coworkers during the weekday and expect to earn $60,000 per year. Those time-consuming, time-wasting activities do not pay $30 per hour.

This is a universal law. You only get out what you put in. Because of this Law of Sowing and Reaping, if you do $30-per-hour work, eight hours per day, 250 days per year, there is nothing that will stop you from earning $60,000 over the next twelve months.

If you do $60-per-hour work, you will earn $120,000 over the next twelve months. You determine your own income by the way you use every hour of each day. And the very best use of time is to invest it in prospecting, presenting, and following up.

## Determine What You Will Have to Do

Once you have broken your income and sales goals down into monthly, weekly, daily, and hourly amounts, you then define these goals in terms of the *activities* necessary to achieve them. The critical element in this calculation is the factor of *control*.

You cannot control your income or your sales on a day-to-day basis. They depend on too many other factors. But you can control your activities. You can determine and control what you do from morning to night, and as a result, you can *indirectly* control your income. If you engage in the activities necessary to make the sales you want to make, you will inevitably achieve your sales goals.

It is important to emphasize that success in sales is a numbers game. It is a matter of probabilities. The more clearly you plan out your sales strategies and tactics on paper, the more likely it becomes that you will do the things necessary to achieve the amount of money that you want. The sales will take care of themselves.

### Plan Out Your Sales Work in Detail

Start by determining the average size of a sale and the average commission that you earn per sale. Divide these amounts into your desired sales and income goals. For example, if you earn $500 per sale and your annual income goal is $60,000, you will have to make 120 sales per year, or an average of ten sales per month.

You then determine how many sales presentations you will have to make, based on your current experience and skill level, to achieve that number of sales. From there, you work backward to determine how many calls you will have to make to find that number of qualified prospects. You then determine how many prospecting calls you will have to make each day in order to get a certain number of presentations and follow-ups, which will lead to the number of sales you desire and the achievement of your income goal.

If you determine that you have to make twenty phone calls in order to get five appointments, and you need five appointments in order to get one sale, you now have a specific target to aim at. You have a specific activity goal that you can work on each day. Every morning, you begin work and focus on making a specific number of calls. You discipline yourself to do the things you need to do, to achieve the goals that you have set for yourself.

## Get Better at What You Do

Once you have determined your sales goals and worked out an activity schedule for each day, you immediately go to work on yourself to upgrade your skills in your key result areas.

One of the best uses of your time is to get better at the most important things you do. Your goal is to upgrade your skills so that you achieve more and better results in a shorter period of time.

For example, if the number of appointments you make is determined by how effective you are on the telephone, you should decide, right now, to become an expert at telephone prospecting. If your success is determined by how effectively you present your product, then practice and become an expert at presentation skills. If your success is determined by how well you handle objections, or close the sale, then you should make yourself an expert in each of these areas.

### Improve Your Ratios

When you begin, you may make only one sale for every twenty people you speak with. As you improve your sales skills, your ratio will get better and better. Soon, you will be making one sale for every fifteen people that you speak with, and then one sale for every ten people, and so on.

Some professional salespeople, by continually practicing and upgrading their skills, have reduced their call-to-sale ratio to as low as five to one, and even three to one. Just think what a difference it would make in your income if you could sell to every third person you talked to!

## Analyze Your Current Skill Level

There are seven key result areas in selling. On a scale from one to ten, you must be at a seven or better in each of these areas if you want to realize your full potential as a sales professional.

1. Prospecting: getting appointments with people who can and will buy in a reasonable period of time

2. Establishing trust and rapport: asking questions, listening, and establishing a bond of trust and friendliness that is essential to making any sale

3. Identifying needs: asking questions to determine exactly what it is that the customer wants and needs from you, and how you can serve him best

4. Presenting solutions: showing the prospect that your product or service is the ideal choice for him, all things considered, at this time

5. Answering objections: resolving any questions or concerns that the customer may have about your product or service

6. Closing the sale: asking the prospect to take action on your offer

7. Getting resales and referrals: creating "customers for life" who will buy from you again and recommend you to their friends and colleagues

Give yourself a grade on a scale from one to ten, with one being the lowest score and ten being the highest, in each of these seven key result areas.

## Start with Your Weakest Key Skill

Here is a discovery: Your weakest key result area sets the *height* of your sales and your earnings. You may be excellent at six out of the seven of these key result areas, but your weakness in the seventh area will determine how much you sell and earn overall.

The good news is that all sales skills are learnable. You can learn any skill you need to achieve any goal you have set for yourself. The most rapid improvement in your sales results will come from your identifying your weakest skill and working exclusively in that area until you have mastered it.

Ask yourself this question: "What one skill, if I developed and executed it in an excellent fashion, would have the greatest impact on my sales and my income?"

Whatever your answer is to that question, write down the development of that skill as a goal, make a plan, organize your plan by priority, and work on getting better in that area every single day. Read every morning on the subject. Listen to audio programs in your car. Attend seminars and workshops to learn how to master that key skill. This decision can have a greater (and faster) affect on your income than anything else you could do.

# Plan Your Work in Advance

Once you have clearly determined your sales, income, and activity goals, you can then plan your year, your month, your week, and, especially, every day in advance. Plan your upcoming week on the weekend before. Plan your upcoming day the evening before. Always work from a written plan of action.

Many top salespeople will take one or two hours, on either a Saturday or a Sunday, to plan the coming week. Some of them will plan the upcoming week on the previous Friday. The very act of planning gives you a tremendous sense of control over your work. It gives you a feeling of personal power. Prior planning increases your self-confidence and raises your self-esteem. And every minute in planning saves you ten minutes in execution, so you'll get much more done than someone who does not plan at all.

## The Acid Test of Prospecting

A good measure of how well you are doing in prospecting is to determine how far in advance you are booked for sales appointments and presentations. A good salesperson usually has his appointments for the following week all planned out by Friday of the previous week. If you ask where he is going to be the next week, he can tell you within one hour where he will be each day, from Monday to Friday.

Poor salespeople have no idea where they will be in the coming week. They have few appointments and no plans. Every day is a new adventure for them. They don't know how it is going to turn out. As a result, they work less than ninety minutes a day and spend most of their time around the office, or having lunch or coffee with their coworkers.

From now on, resolve to plan every day the day before, preferably at the end of the day, or in the evening. Make out a list of everything that you have to do the following day, and organize the list by time and priority before you turn out the lights.

Set a goal to structure your day with appointments thirty to sixty minutes apart. The Law of Forced Efficiency says that if you put tight time constraints on yourself for each appointment, you will cover everything of importance in the sales call within the time allotted.

## Plan Your Calls Geographically

One of the most important time management techniques for salespeople is to group calls in a specific geographic area. This allows you to reduce travel time and to increase the number of calls that you can make during the day. Keep reminding yourself that you have nothing to sell but your time, face-to-face with prospects and customers, and how you use your time determines your income.

Don't make the mistake of making your first appointment in the north end of town and your second appointment at the south end, and then spending half your day driving in between. Many poor salespeople organize their time this way. They are somehow able to convince themselves that they are actually working when they are traveling great distances between appointments.

## Close the Sale

One of the best time management techniques is to close the sale after the presentation so that you do not have to return to the prospect over and over. Give the prospect an opportunity to buy at the end of every sales conversation. Ask for the order, one way or another. Fully 50 percent of all sales calls end without the salesperson asking for the order once.

One of the very worst uses of time is for you to go through the laborious process of prospecting, getting appointments, making presentations, and answering objections, and then not closing the sale. For you to lose the sale because you cannot, or will not, ask a closing question wipes out all of the time you have invested up to now.

Study and become proficient with a variety of closing techniques or decision-making questions. A closing technique can be defined as a question that gets the prospect to commit to an action of some kind, or to comment one way or another on your product. For example, you can ask simple questions designed to elicit feedback from the prospect and that tell you how well you're doing.

Ask questions such as the following:

Does this make sense to you so far?

Do you have any questions, or concerns, that I haven't covered?

Do you like what I am showing you so far?

Is this the sort of thing you are looking for?

## Invite the Prospect to Buy

If it appears that the prospect likes what you have shown him and is interested in what you are selling, you can use the invitational close and ask, "Well, if you like it, why don't you give it a try?"

You can use the directive close, saying, "Well, then, if you have no further questions, the next step is. . . ." You go on and explain the plan of action, and wrap up the sale.

It is amazing how much time you can save in your sales career if you just muster up the courage to invite people to make a decision on your offering. In follow-up interviews with prospects, many of them have said that they would have bought if the salesperson had just asked them or invited them to buy.

It is sad that so many sales are lost every single day because the salesperson did not ask for the order. Developing a habit of asking for the order in a polite, courteous, and carefully preplanned way is a tremendous technique for improving your efficiency and productivity.

# Eliminating the Time Wasters in Selling

There are several time wasters in selling. Based on interviews with thousands of salespeople and sales managers, here are the ten major reasons why people waste their time and fail to realize their full potential for sales and income.

## Procrastination

Procrastination is the thief of time. It is usually accompanied by delaying tactics, such as finding all kinds of excuses for not getting out and getting going. Usually, procrastination is caused by a deep fear of rejection, or a fear of failure. This is often called *call reluctance.*

This kind of fear of rejection and disapproval, which leads to procrastination and delay, can only be overcome by confronting it everyday until it goes away. The most remarkable thing about your fears is that if you face them squarely, they diminish. But if you back away from them, or avoid the situation that you fear, your fears grow until they paralyze all productive action.

When I started selling, I was terrified of cold-calling and prospecting. But then I learned something that changed my career. I learned that "rejection is not personal." If people say that they are not interested in what you are selling, it is not aimed at you personally. It is merely an automatic response to a commercial offer in a competitive society. The person does not know you well enough to reject you personally. Once I learned that, I began calling on people, both door-to-door and office-to-office and by telephone. All my fears of rejection disappeared. Eventually, I reached a point where the negative reaction to my sales activities had no affect on me at all. This must be your goal as well.

## Incompletion of the Sale

Incomplete sales that require callbacks are a major time waster. These usually occur when the salesperson does not have everything he needs to make the sale. Sometimes because of poor preparation, salespeople do not have the proper price lists, the proper brochures, the correct inventory figures, or the necessary information to conclude the sale. Sometimes the salesperson lacks the ability to answer objections or to ask for the order. Making a sales call on a qualified prospect and then not being ready to conclude the sale is a tremendous waste of time. Often, when you call back on the prospect again, she has lost all interest.

## Poor Preparation

Poor preparation is usually evident when there are obvious inaccuracies and deficiencies in the presentation. Proper preparation, prior to a sales call, requires that you learn as much about the prospect as possible before you meet with him. There is nothing quite so insulting to a prospect as when a salesperson tries to sell him something without knowing anything about him.

## Ignorance

A salesperson usually demonstrates his ignorance with a lack of product knowledge. The salesperson has obviously not taken the time to study the sales literature to thoroughly understand the product or service that he is trying to sell. When the customer has questions about the product or service, the salesperson stumbles, bluffs, or tries to make up an answer. This not only undermines the credibility of the salesperson and the company, but it shakes the confidence of the salesperson as well.

### *Know What You Are Selling*

Some years ago, my wife and I went out looking for an expensive home in San Diego. We contacted several realtors to view homes for sale.

Having been a real estate agent and broker at one time, I know a lot about buying and selling real estate. As we would drive up to a house that was for sale for several hundred thousand dollars, I would ask the agent a series of questions about the house. I was always amazed to find out that very few of the realtors had even taken the time to read the Multiple Listing Service sheets to get the details on the house. Many of them had never been to the open houses on the homes they were showing for sale. They were attempting to sell a product where they would be earning several thousand dollars in commissions, and they often had no idea of the size of the house or any of its amenities. They had not earned the right to offer the product for sale because they had not taken the time to fully understand the product in the first place.

## Unconfirmed Appointments
Unconfirmed appointments lead to the situation where the salesperson arrives for an appointment that was made by phone, and he finds that the prospect is gone. The salesperson has now wasted the time he spent in prospecting, the time of preparation, and the time of travel. Why does this happen so often? The main reason is because of the fear of rejection. The salesperson is reluctant to phone and confirm the appointment for fear that the prospect will cancel it.

Here is a very simple method that has been effective for me and many other salespeople over the years. You call the office of the prospect before you leave. You ask the receptionist if the prospect is in. If the receptionist says "Yes," then you say, "Thank you very much. Please tell him that this is Brian Tracy calling, and that I will be there for my appointment on schedule." You then hang up the phone.

In this way you remind the prospect that you are coming, and you put the prospect under a sense of obligation to see you when you arrive. You stop wasting your time by going out to unconfirmed appointments.

## Poor Planning of Calls Geographically

One of the biggest time wasters in selling is traveling all over your sales territory and spending most of your time in traffic, rather than face-to-face with people who can (and will) buy within a reasonable period of time.

One simple way to cluster your calls geographically is to divide your territory into four parts. Discipline yourself to work in one quadrant of your territory each day or half day. If you call to make an appointment, tell the prospect that you will be visiting customers in his area at a specific time of the week. Would he be available to see you at that time?

It is interesting to note that the more structured and scheduled your time usage is as a salesperson, the more you are respected by your prospects and customers. The more that they feel that you have a tight schedule, the more they will adjust their schedule to accommodate meeting with you.

## Needless Perfectionism

This occurs when you insist that everything be perfectly in order before you go out and sell. It is another form of indecisiveness, and it is closely tied up with call reluctance. It is caused by fear of rejection and a fear of failure.

Whenever you find yourself studying and overstudying your materials, insisting that everything be exactly right before you pick up the phone or before you make a call, you must have the honesty to realize that you are dealing with fear.

As Emerson wrote, "Do the thing you fear, and the death of fear is certain." If you confront your fear, your fear will go away. The only real anecdote to fear and worry is purposeful action. If you get going and start moving forward, you will forget to be afraid.

## Distraction or Mind Wandering

These are subtle time wasters, but they are far too common. They result in not paying attention in a sales presentation. You do not hear the prospect fully, or you do not read between the lines to understand what the prospect is really saying. Many salespeople are guilty of mind wandering. They simply do not pay sufficient attention because they are preoccupied with their own thoughts. Unfortunately, the prospect picks up on this very quickly and soon loses all interest in doing business with you.

The way that you overcome the tendency to mind wander is to discipline yourself to face the prospect directly, lean forward, and watch him intently while he speaks. Imagine that your eyes are sunlamps and you want to give his face a tan. This approach will keep you focused more intensely on the prospect, and snap you out of the tendency toward distraction.

## Fatigue and Overwork

These are real killers in every area of work, and especially in selling. It is estimated that more than 50 percent of salespeople today are working in a state of fog. They are going to bed too late and not getting enough sleep. As a result, they go through the day tired, lacking the ability to fully concentrate on their work.

My rule is this: If you are going to sell five days of the week, you must go to bed early five days per week. Selling is a draining and demanding profession. It requires a tremendous amount of physical and emotional energy for someone to be effective at sales. You cannot afford to stay up late at night watching television, or socializing, if you're going to be sharp and alert the next day.

You can break the tendency to sleep too little and work too hard by disciplining yourself to go to bed by ten o'clock each night. Turn off the television, and resolve to get lots of rest. This practice will translate into more and better sales, higher income, and generate the money you need to take all the vacations you want.

### Lack of Ambition or Desire

There are many people who are just going through the motions at work. This is usually the result of having too few goals or no goals at all. Sometimes, people lack ambition or desire because they are selling the wrong product. They are trying to sell something that they don't like or believe in. Sometimes, lack of ambition or desire to succeed in sales is caused by not believing in your boss, or not believing in the company, or not getting along well with your coworkers.

Whatever the reason, if you are not positive and enthusiastic about your product or service, this could be an indication that you should be doing something else. If you don't like the people you are selling to, you are probably in the wrong business.

You cannot (for very long) force yourself to sell something that is wrong for you. It will simply make you tired and depressed, and you will never be successful at it.

## Use Your Time Well

Here are some valuable ideas you can use to help increase your sales effectiveness by using your time to its best advantage.

### Get to Bed Early

Early to bed, early to rise is the key to sales success. Get up and get going by 6:00 A.M. Get lots of sleep. Sometimes, the very best use of your time is to go to bed early and get a solid nine, ten, or even twelve hours of sleep so that you can bright-eyed and cheerful the next morning. It is difficult to be full of energy, excitement, and enthusiasm about your product or service when you're tired from not getting enough sleep.

### Start Your Day Right

Read thirty to sixty minutes of material related to sales, or motivation, to start your day. This is one of the most important habits you will ever develop. Many salespeople have told me that this technique of getting up each morning and reading for thirty to sixty minutes has changed the whole direction of their careers.

If you spent thirty to sixty minutes reading a book on sales each morning, over the course of a week you will probably read one whole book. If you read one book per week for the next year, and you don't even read on the weekends or holidays, you will read fifty books on sales over the next twelve months. If you keep this up over the next ten years, you will have read 500 books. The average salesperson never reads a book on sales in her life. Knowing that, do you think that if you read 500 books over the next ten years it would affect your income?

The fact is that you could probably become one of the best-informed, best-skilled, and highest-paid salespeople in America simply by reading thirty to sixty minutes on sales each morning. Each day, you can go out and apply something that you learned that morning. You never stop learning and growing.

## Start Work Early

Schedule your first appointment early. Get up, get out, and get going. Try to set your first appointment for 8:00 A.M. or even 7:30 A.M. Often, prospects who do not have time to see you in the daytime can meet with you at odd hours. Sometimes they work early or late or both. If you offer to meet them for breakfast, or to meet them in their office at 7:30 A.M., they can often fit you in.

## Focus on Prospecting

A tremendous way to increase your time and effectiveness is to spend 80 percent of your time prospecting, until you become so busy closing sales and servicing customers that you do not have time to prospect anymore.

Remember, sales success is in direct proportion to your ability to initiate new contacts. Sales success comes from being eager to call on customers.

When I was a sales representative leasing new office space, I would take the elevator to the top floor of an office building and then call on every office in the building as I worked my way down. Over the course of a month, I could make several hundred calls.

If you find yourself with time on your hands, sit down and make twenty or thirty phone calls. You will be amazed at the results you get, and how much better you will feel as a result.

## Work All the Time You Work

Spend your entire day working. Make every minute count. Work all the time you work. Remember, the average salesperson is only working 20 percent of the time. If you work 80 percent of the time, it could catapult you into the upper ranks of sales success. If, instead of working ninety minutes you worked six hours, you would quadruple your income.

Don't waste time. Don't sit around drinking coffee or reading the newspaper. If you must take coffee breaks, do it with prospects, or while you are on the move.

The average salesperson who takes two twenty-minute coffee breaks per day spends forty minutes a day unproductively. Forty minutes per day, multiplied by five days per week, equals 200 minutes per week. Two hundred minutes per week, multiplied by fifty weeks per year, is equal to 10,000 minutes, or the equivalent to 166 hours of productive time that the average person spends sitting around drinking coffee and wasting.

One hundred and sixty-six hours is equal to four forty-hour weeks, which is the equivalent of one month's income. If you want to give yourself a raise, the fastest way to do it is to work through your coffee breaks.

### Use Your Lunch Breaks Wisely

Don't waste lunchtime, either. Use your lunch hour to prepare for the afternoon appointments, or to exercise, or to do something that improves your productivity and performance.

If you use your lunchtime wisely, and you take one hour per

day for lunch, this will give you an additional five hours per week, or 250 hours per year. Two hundred and fifty hours per year is more than six forty-hour weeks, or more than one and one-half months of additional income. Just by using your coffee breaks and lunch breaks for productive activities, you will increase your sales and your income by 20 percent almost immediately.

### Listen and Learn

Listen to educational audio programs in your car. Turn your driving time into learning time. Turn your car into a university on wheels.

From the time you get into the car until the time you get out, your audio player should be working. Remember, the average salesperson spends 500 to 1,000 hours per year behind the wheel of his car, and sometimes much more. If you use that time to educate yourself, you can become one of the most knowledgeable and highest-paid salespeople in America, just by listening to audio programs.

### Use a Time Planner

Use a time planner of some kind, and write down every appointment and activity. Let your time planner be your control center for your sale activities. Use it as a tickler file to remind you when to get back to your prospects. Purchase a time planner that lets you store contacts and plan a month in advance, as well as a year in advance.

Once you have a time planner, use it religiously. Write down everything. Plan every single activity in advance. Keep accurate notes of every telephone conversation and presentation. The power is always on the side of the person with the best notes.

Start and end each day by reviewing the information that you record in your time planner. Use it to run your sales business from one place. Make your time planner into your mobile office.

## The Only Thing You Have to Sell

Remember, all that the salesperson has to sell is his time. And the only time you are working is when you are face-to-face with a prospect. Learn and practice these time management techniques over and over, until they become second nature. Good time management skills are the perfect vehicle to get you from where you are to where you want to be. More than anything else, they will ensure your success in sales.

*"New knowledge is of little value if it doesn't change us, make us better individuals, and help us to be more productive, happy, and useful."*

—HYRUM SMITH

## Action Exercises

1. Take charge of your sales career today; resolve to double the amount of time you spend face-to-face with prospects and customers.

2. Set clear sales and income goals for yourself, broken down by year, month, week, day, and hour.

3. Only do work that pays you the amount you want and need to earn every hour; delegate, defer, and eliminate everything else.

4. Plan the activities of prospecting, presenting, and following up that you will need to engage in to achieve your sales and income goals; discipline yourself to work on them all day, every day.

5. Prepare thoroughly for every sales call; do your homework on the prospect and have everything you need to make a successful sale.

6. Reduce traveling time by organizing your sales territory in advance; don't waste time driving all over the city to see people.

7. Work all the time you work; don't waste time in coffee breaks and lunches. Spend the time working instead.

# CHAPTER TWELVE

# The Philosophy of Time Management

*"It's good to have money and the things that money can buy, but it's good, too, to make sure that you haven't lost the things that money can't buy."*

—GEORGE HORACE LORIMER

To be fully rounded as a person, you need a philosophy of time management. You require a worldview that recognizes time as the one invaluable, indispensable, irreplaceable ingredient of a successful, happy, highly productive life. You need an attitude toward time as something more than the clock or the calendar.

How do you go about developing a philosophy of time management? First of all, you take the long view. Look as far into the future as you can. All truly successful people are those who have long time horizons.

Sociologist Dr. Edward Banfield from Harvard University wrote a groundbreaking book in 1965 called *The Unheavenly*

252

*City.* In it, he explains the results of his many years of research into the reasons for upward social and economic mobility in our society and other societies.

# The Best Predictor of Success

Banfield's research was devoted to uncovering the reasons for financial success and the predictors of social class in America. He wanted to know what behaviors would most likely lead to increases in wealth from one generation to another. As part of his work, he studied factors such as education, intelligence, family background, race, occupation, and personal attributes. He found that none of these were accurate predictors of upward social mobility.

There were many people who ranked high in one or more of these factors, but they still failed to move up during the course of their working lifetimes. Many of them actually experienced downward social mobility. They ended up earning less than their parents did at the same ages, and sometimes considerably less.

Banfield finally concluded that there was only one factor that could accurately predict whether you were going to move upward and onward financially and socially. He called it *time perspective.* He defined time perspective as the period of time that you take into consideration when making your day-to-day decisions and planning your life.

### Think Into the Future

Banfield found that successful people were those who had a long time perspective. They planned their lives in terms of five, ten, and even twenty years into the future. They evaluated and determined their choices and actions in the present in terms of how those choices might effect them in the distant future, and the consequences that might occur as a result of what they did right now.

It is traditional among the British upper classes to register their children at Oxford or Cambridge as soon as they are born, even though they won't be attending for eighteen to twenty years. They fill out the applications and go through the registration process for their children exactly as if they were going to attend in the next semester. This is an example of a long time perspective.

In America, many parents open a college savings account for their children as soon as they are born. They then add to this account regularly for many years to ensure that their children can get the very best education possible when they grow up. This is also an example of long time perspective.

## The Common Attitude of Achievement

This attitude of taking the long view seems to be common among most men and women who achieve a great deal in the course of their lifetimes. The longer your sense of time perspective, the more likely it is that you will do the sort of things, and make the kind of sacrifices in the short term, that will lead to greater success in the long term. Your thoughtfulness about time today will tend to increase your income and your social standing in the future.

The reverse is also true. As you move down the socioeconomic ladder, the time perspective at each level becomes shorter. When you arrive at the very bottom of the social pyramid, to the hopeless alcoholic or drug addict, you find a time perspective of less than an hour—the time it takes to get one drink or one shot. Often the time perspective of people at the bottom of society is only a few minutes. They do not think beyond the moment.

The average hourly worker has a time perspective of about two pay periods. The salaried worker has a time perspective of about two months. As you proceed up the socioeconomic ladder, the time perspective lengthens until you reach the most respected people in society, such as the family doctor.

## The Most Respected Profession

In every study that asks individuals who they consider to be the most respected people in society, the family doctor ranks at the top. More people look up to and respect the family doctor than any other professional in our society. Why? It is probably because we recognize that these people spent eight, ten, or even twelve years of study, internship, residency, and practice to reach the point where they can become our doctors.

The average doctor in America earns $132,000 per year. He will enjoy high earnings and higher social standing for his entire life. He will have complete job security. His children will have advantages not enjoyed by most other children. But the average doctor has spent almost twelve years of hard work and sacrifice preparing himself to earn that kind of money and achieve that level of social status. This is an example of long time perspective that most people recognize and admire.

## Long Time Perspective Predicts Social Class

Many immigrants arrive in America with no money and no language skills. They then go to work at menial jobs, doing whatever they can to support themselves. But even at low levels of income, they often save their money so that their children can get a good education and have a chance at the American dream. Even though they are poor, these are people with real class. They have long time perspective.

In a way, these people starting at the bottom have better characters than people who have had all the benefits of an American upbringing but who spend every single penny they can get their hands on with little thought for the future. Their willingness to sacrifice in the short term so they can have better futures demonstrates the qualities of vision, courage, self-discipline, and persistence. They have real *class*, even though they have little money.

You begin to move yourself upward in society the day you begin to take the long view in your own life. People who consistently save 10 percent of their income and put it away toward financial independence are virtually guaranteeing a higher quality of life for themselves and their children. They have long time perspective.

## Plan Your Life for the Long Term

Ask yourself, "What time period do I take into consideration when I set my goals and make important decisions for my life?" Your answer to this question largely shapes your entire future.

How far into the future do you look when you make decisions on how to allocate your time and your resources? There is a rule that says, "Long time perspective improves short-term decision making." The further ahead you look when contemplating a current decision, the better decisions you will make. Your long-term success will be determined by the quality of all the decisions you make in the short term. The cumulative result of good decisions is the assurance that your long-term goals will materialize exactly as you had planned.

Many years ago, I worked for a wealthy man who started with nothing and built a fortune worth more than $500 million in real estate. He taught me to think always of owning a piece of property for twenty years when I was considering buying it. He said that if you think about owning the property for twenty years, you will be much more alert to the strengths and weaknesses of the investment in the moment.

### Keep Your Eye on the Summit

The long view sharpens the short view. This is one of the most valuable pieces of advice I ever received. In your life, think as if you were on a long hike climbing a mountain. Stop regularly and look up at the summit, your eventual goal, and then adjust your footsteps to ensure that every step is still taking you in that direction.

One way of determining your priorities in the short term is

to analyze the future impact of present decisions. An important choice, or activity, is one that has a potential long-term impact on some part of your life. An action or decision that is unimportant is something that can have little or no effect on your life or future.

Reading a book, listening to an instructional audio program, or taking a course that teaches you something valuable are examples of activities with a *high* potential future impact on your career. On the other hand, watching television, reading the sports page, or taking a coffee break, no matter how well or how often you do them, will have no effect on your future. Remember, you are always free to choose.

## Your Choices Determine Your Future

You see examples of this confusion over time perspective all around you. On the same street living in two houses of similar value will be two different families. Each family earns approximately the same amount of money. But one family has a twenty-year time perspective and the other family has little or no time perspective at all.

Over the years, the family with long time perspective will carefully save, invest, and accumulate an estate that will eventually enable them to retire in comfort. The other family, earning the same amount of money, perhaps even doing the same kind of work, but lacking time perspective, will spend everything they make, and a little bit more besides. They will end their working days with little or no money put aside.

If you were told today that unless you made some dramatic changes in the way you earn and spend, you were going to be *penniless* when you reached retirement, how would that affect your attitude toward your money? What would you do differently in your work and financial life with such a possibility hanging over your head? Well, the truth is that unless you begin to do something different with your money today, that is very likely the way you will end up. Because of limited time perspective, 95 percent of people working today will end up either broke, dependent on pensions, or still working when they reach the age of 65. Don't let this happen to you.

## Develop Your Own Character

The practice of thinking with long time perspective not only requires character, but it also develops character in the person who does it. Character is always the result of practicing self-discipline. Developing the habit of taking the long view in decisions concerning health, wealth, relationships, and reputations requires self-discipline at a high level.

Character comes from thinking continually of living with each of your decisions for the long term. Economists and sociologists generally agree that the primary reason for economic failure and underachievement is the inability to *delay gratification*. This is the tendency to spend everything you make, and a little bit more, with little thought for the future. It is a lack of time perspective with a regard to money. It virtually guarantees that you will have financial problems throughout your life and end up unable to retire when you reach the age of 65.

Decide today to plan and act for the long term. Practice short-term pain for long-term gain. Be willing to pay the price of success in advance, in terms of hard work, sacrifice, and delayed gratification. Be prepared to sow before you reap, and often you will have to sow for a long time before you can bring in the harvest. Nowhere is this truer than in financial matters.

If you save and invest 10 percent of your income from the age of 21 to age 65, you will become a millionaire over the course of your working lifetime. Most self-made millionaires save 15 percent to 20 percent of their income and learn to live comfortably on the balance. You should resolve to do the same. Think long term. The quality of character that you will develop as a result of the self-discipline you impose on yourself to become financially independent will make you a truly exceptional human being.

## Think Short Term as Well as Long Term

If the first part of developing a philosophy of time management is to take the long view, the second part is to take the short view. Treat your time like your life. Measure out your time in minutes, rather than in hours or days.

In an article in *Fortune* magazine, several of the most successful and highest-paid executives in America were interviewed about their attitudes and practices toward time. Their average incomes were $1,380,000, and all of them had worked themselves up from entry-level positions in business and industry.

It turned out that all of these highly paid, top performers treated their time as a scarce resource. They saw it as an indispensable ingredient of achievement. They looked upon it as an essential tool of accomplishment. They allocated their time very carefully.

They were very jealous of their time. They did not spend it, give it away, or use it thoughtlessly. While average employees and junior managers thought in terms of days and weeks, they planned out their days in terms of minutes and fractions of hours.

It turns out that the smaller the unit of time in which you think when planning your day, the more successful you are likely to be. Unsuccessful people think in terms of whole days, or mornings and afternoons. Successful people think in terms of ten-minute blocks of time, like lawyers or accountants. They make every minute count.

## Time Is Your Most Valuable Resource

Because time is your scarcest resource, you must use your intelligence to preserve it in every way possible and to acquire more time whenever you can. Whenever possible, you should trade money for time. The money is replaceable, but the time is not.

This brings us back to David Ricardo's Law of Comparative

Advantage, which was discussed in Chapter 10. Whenever you can, you should hire people to do tasks of lower value so that you can create more time for yourself, your family, and your work.

If you aspire to earn $50,000 per year, which translates into about $25 per hour, you must never do work that does not pay $25 an hour or more. If you can hire someone for $5 or $6 an hour to mow your lawn or clean your house, you should pay the money willingly to free up your time for higher value activities.

Apply this same principle to your spouse. Many of the successful executives and entrepreneurs who come through our advanced coaching and mentoring program take the lessons home and change their spouse's lifestyle. They encourage them to hire housekeepers, gardeners, and personal assistants to do errands and go shopping. They "buy their freedom" so that they can enjoy a higher quality of life and spend more time with the family and in personal pursuits. The payoff for both parties is often extraordinary.

## Track Your Time Usage Carefully

Keep track of how efficiently you use your time. The more you think about how you are spending your minutes and hours, the better and more precise you will become at time management. Because most people do not monitor their time usage, they are not even aware of the amount of time they waste each hour.

Get a wristwatch with an alarm that beeps every fifteen minutes. Each time the alarm sounds, stop and observe yourself. Look at what you are doing at that moment. If possible, keep a time log and make a note of what you are doing each time the alarm rings. Ask yourself regularly, "Is what I am doing right now making the very best use of my time?"

All of life is the study of attention. The more attention you pay to the way you are using your time, the more efficient and productive you are likely to be. The more aware you are of the fleeting nature of time, the better you will use it.

## Spend Your Time Like Money

When you take the short view, you look upon every request for your time as taking away from the amount of time you have left on earth. Continually ask yourself, "How much of my life am I willing to donate or spend on this particular person, situation, or activity?

Your time is at least equal to your hourly rate. If your hourly rate is $25, that person is, in effect, asking you for a gift of $25 for an hour of your time. If someone asks you to donate your time to a particular cause or activity, you have to ask yourself, "How important is that cause or activity to me, and how much of my time and money am I willing to donate to it?"

If a person or activity is not important enough for you to open your wallet and peel off $20 bills to give to it, you must discipline yourself not to do it. Just say "No!"

# The Wrong Job Is a Major Time Waster

Chapter 7 talked about the major time wasters in the world of work, including personal and telephone interruptions, unexpected emergencies, drop-in visitors, and unplanned meetings. However, working at the *wrong job* is a bigger time waster than all of these put together.

Many people are working at jobs that they are not suited for or are not suitable for them. They would rather be doing something else, somewhere else, using different skills and abilities. The majority of working people, by their own admission, do not feel fully challenged by their current jobs. Getting into or staying at a job for which you are not ideally suited is one of the greatest wastes of time in life. It can rob you of some of your most productive years.

Here is a question for you: If you received $1 million in cash, tax free, would you continue to work at your current job?

To put it another way, if you were independently wealthy, is there anything that you would change about your job, your work, or your career? If you think you would quit, or change your job, if you had enough money, this is a good indicator that you are working at the wrong job *for you*. You may only be working at your current job because of your financial situation and your monthly bills and expenses.

## Do the Work You Love

Here is another question: Do you love what you are doing? Only a small percentage of people love what they do, and these people are always the happiest, the most satisfied, and usually, the highest paid in every field.

You can tell if you are spending your time and your life at the right job by examining your attitude toward your job and your future. Do you like what you are doing enough to want to be the very best at it? If the job is right for you, not only do you want to get better and better at that job, but you very much admire those people who are at the top of your field. If you find that you have no desire to excel in your field, this is a good sign that it's probably not the right job for you.

Would you like to continue doing your job for the next twenty years? Do you find your job challenging and fulfilling? Can you hardly wait to get to work on Monday morning, and do you hate to leave on Friday evening? All successful people can answer "yes" to these questions. Unsuccessful people invariably answer "no."

## There Are No Limits

There are more than 100,000 different jobs available in our economy today. There are an endless number of jobs that you could do successfully, and make a good living doing them. You never have to feel stuck in a particular position, company, or industry. There is never a job shortage for good people.

One of your primary responsibilities to yourself is to select the kind of work that you enjoy and are best suited to do. It is to find a job where you can use your natural talents and abilities at a high level. Your duty to yourself is to work at something that gives you joy and satisfaction. You must find a job that brings out the very best in you, and that inspires you to want to become excellent at what you're doing.

## The Past Is a "Sunk Cost"

In accounting, a sunk cost is an amount of money that has been spent in the past and has no further value. It may be a piece of equipment that is broken and irreparable, obsolete, or completely useless. It could be advertising dollars just spent last year. The money spent on these items is gone forever. It can never be retrieved.

One of the first rules with regard to a sunk cost is that you never spend additional money to retrieve or extract some value out of it. You write it off as a loss and focus on the future. You get on with the rest of your business life.

In your career, you have sunk costs as well. These are jobs that may have taken weeks, months, or even years to learn, from which you gained considerable experience, but which are no longer of value in today's market. You may have a sunk cost in college education or in courses of instruction and training that you have taken to develop knowledge and skills that are no longer of any use. Much of what you have done in the past in your career is a sunk cost of some kind. It has no current or future value.

One of the worst wastes of time is for you to attempt to recover a sunk cost. Many people take a university degree in a subject that turns out to have no market value when they leave school. They spend months, and even years, plodding from door to door, trying to find someone to hire them and pay them a salary for knowledge acquired that has no economic value. Sooner or later, they realize that they took the wrong courses or learned the wrong skills. Now, they have no choice but to learn new skills that have a value in the marketplace.

## Be Prepared to Cut Your Losses

One of the reasons for massive time wastage, and failure in life, is the inability or unwillingness to cut your losses. Instead, you should continually remind yourself: It doesn't matter where you're coming from; all that really matters is where you're going.

A major time waster is an investment in your ego. You make a decision, or a commitment of time, money, or emotion, that is not successful. Then, because of your ego, you are unwilling to admit that you made a mistake, that you were wrong, and that your decision has turned out to be in error. You then invest an enormous amount of time, emotion, and often money to cover up the fact that you made a mistake. You justify and rationalize, refuse to face the facts, and you often make yourself physically ill.

Learn to take control of your ego, rather than letting your ego take control of you. Accept that you are not perfect. Most things you try in life won't succeed the first time in any case. Just say the words, "I made a mistake." Admit that you made a poor choice. Admit that, if you had to do it over again, you would do it very differently. The unwillingness to admit error keeps people locked in unhappy and unsatisfying situations year after year.

Once you have admitted a mistake, you no longer need to explain or justify yourself. You can then get on with the rest of your life. You can make new decisions and choose new directions. You can focus your special talents and abilities on doing things that can have a great future for you.

## Take Your Whole Life Into Consideration

Put your current life, your past investments, and your sunk costs in your education and career into perspective. Ask this question: How long do I intend to live? Asking and answering this question immediately lengthens your time perspective.

Most people have never decided upon exactly how long they intend to live. They say, "I am going to live to be a hundred." But they are really not serious because they have no definite plans to get to that age.

The average life expectancy today is age 76 for men and age 79 for women. This means that half of the population will die after they reach those ages, and half of the population will die before reaching them. Because you are reading this book, you are probably better educated, more intelligent about your health habits, earn a higher income, and much more likely to beat the averages. Therefore, it is not unreasonable to assume that you will live to age 90 or older.

The formula that insurance companies use to predict your age is to take two-thirds of the number of years between your current age and 100, and then add that to your current age. This will estimate your average life expectancy for actuarial and insurance purposes. If you are age 40, then $2/3 \times (100 - 40) = 40$. Therefore, your calculated age or life expectancy is 80 years. The big companies write insurance policies based on these projections all day long, and they are seldom wrong.

## Add Ten Years to Your Life

Many people are still stuck in the twentieth-century paradigm of retiring at age 65. This age for retirement was set in 1935, when Social Security and old-age pensions were first introduced. At that time, the life expectancy of the average working American was 62 years. Most people worked jobs requiring physical labor in those days, making and moving things and objects. By the time working people reached age 62 or 65, they would be like worn-out pieces of machinery. The average life expectancy was approximately 2.7 years after retirement.

Today, however, everything has changed. Most people are knowledge workers. They work with their minds, rather than with their muscles. They become sharper and smarter with age and experience. They get older and better. Simultaneously, an explosion of invention, innovation, and discovery in medicine and medical procedures has boosted the life expectancy of people in the industrialized world by almost thirty years in the last century alone.

What this means, in the simplest terms, is that the equivalent of age 65 for retirement in 1935 is age 75 for retirement in the twenty-first century. When you reach age 60 or 65, you will still be at the top of your game. You will be sharp and alert and possessed of all your faculties. You will be bright, creative, and enjoy high levels of physical, mental, and emotional energy. There is no way that you will want to retire to a rocking chair and just laze around for twenty or twenty-five years.

From this day forward, think of yourself working productively to the age of 75. Of course, once you become financially independent, you will not work because you have to, but because you *want* to. You will work at different jobs, doing different things that allow you to specialize in those tasks and activities that you most enjoy. But it is not likely that you will ever retire. Even if you do, you will have ten extra years of active work before you stop.

## Most of Your Life Lies Ahead

From the perspective of your current job, and the sunk costs of the past, what would you really like to do with your life in the coming years? Look forward and imagine that you have several decades of productive work life ahead of you. If you could work at any job at all, what would it be? If you could work in any industry, or in any part of the country, performing any particular function, and you were free to choose, what would you choose for yourself? All these options are open to you today.

Here's a wonderful story I read in the newspaper recently. It was about a woman who had come from a limited family background and only finished high school. Her first job was as a nurse's aide. But she was both ambitious and determined. By working hard and studying evenings and weekends, she eventually became a registered nurse. She took additional courses, and she was promoted. Eventually, she became a head nurse in her hospital. Meanwhile, she married and had two children.

When she was forty years old, it dawned on her that she could be a doctor, if she put her mind to it. Her exposure to other doctors had convinced her that they were no smarter than she was. She sat down with her family and told them of her dream. Her husband and teenage children supported her completely. From that day forward, they took care of all the family work responsibilities so that she could return to school, complete the necessary courses, and become a doctor.

At age 48, she graduated with honors with a degree in pediatric medicine. By the time she was age 50, she was established in a medical practice working with children. She was deriving more joy and satisfaction out of her life and work than she ever thought possible.

## Think About Your Future

Today, it is not uncommon to see men and women going back to college or university in their forties and fifties. They spend several years earning advanced degrees and then settle in to practice their specialty for the next ten to twenty years. This is possible for you, as well.

No matter what you have done, or failed to do, in the past, your future can be unlimited. You can decide, right now, that you are going to go to work on yourself and prepare yourself to do the kind of job that you love to do. You are going to do work that fills you with the greatest joy and satisfaction possible. You then set it as a goal, make a plan, and start to work. You do something every day to increase your knowledge and upgrade your skills, which moves you faster toward doing the work that you were meant to do in the field that is ideal for you.

Sometimes, people complain that it may take several years to achieve the level of knowledge and skill that will allow them to do what they love to do. But, as I said earlier, "The time is going to pass anyway!" Five years from now, you will be five years older. Ten years from now, you will be ten years older. If there is something that you would really like to do that requires years of advance preparation, the best time to get started is right now. The time is going to pass anyway.

Because of the dynamic nature of the job market, the average person in America will have ten major full-time jobs lasting two years or more, and as many as four or five different careers over the course of her working lifetime. Look at your current job and ask yourself if this is what you would like to do for the rest of your life. If it is not, then sit down and decide what it is that you would like to do, and what you would have to do to get into that position.

Working in the wrong job wastes not only your time, but your life. Working at the right job for you is one of the very best ways of living a long life of happiness and fulfillment. It is a way of ensuring that you get the greatest possible value out of your time and your life.

## Perhaps the Greatest Time Waster of All

Perhaps the greatest time waster of all in life is getting into and staying in the wrong relationship. It is absolutely amazing how many people get married early in life, or begin living with someone in their twenties, and then stay in a situation where they are unhappy year after year. They don't stop to think that these years are gone forever. They can never be recaptured.

What is the purpose of a relationship? The simplest answer is so you'll be *happier* than you would be if you were not in that relationship at all. This is so obvious that it is overlooked by many people.

Every human act is aimed at improving your life in some way, at increasing your level of happiness beyond what it might have been if you had not taken that act or made that decision. The choice of a relationship is, therefore, one of the most important choices that you make in life. The choice of the right relationship can have more of an impact on your happiness than any other choice you make. The choice of a wrong relationship can do more to destroy your hopes and dreams than any other choice.

## Be Honest with Yourself
Apply the zero-based thinking question: If I had not gotten into this relationship or marriage, knowing what I know now, would I get into it again today if I had to do it over? Asking and answering this question is one of the hardest yet most important things you will ever do.

If you find that you are unhappier inside the relationship than you would be outside the relationship, you owe it to yourself to seriously consider making some changes. Think about how long you are going to live. If you are unhappy in your relationship today, are you prepared to live with this level of unhappiness and dissatisfaction for the rest of your life?

## People Don't Change
There is a basic rule in human relationships. It is that "people don't change." Both you and every person you meet are products of their entire lives. Starting in infancy and early childhood, people are exposed to influences that shape their behaviors. By the late teens, their values and their personalities are largely fixed. If you ever attend a ten, twenty, or thirty-year high school reunion, you will be amazed to see that, aside from the signs of aging, the people you grew up with are very much the same decades later.

People don't change. You should never hang your hopes for happiness on the possibility that someone is going to change and become a different person. You have not changed in your entire life. It is not realistic to expect that others might change, even if they want to, or if they promise to. In fact, not only do people not change, but under pressure, they go from bad to worse. They become even more of what they already are.

## Evaluate Your Options

If you decide that you would not get into this relationship again, knowing what you now know, your next question is: How do I get out of this situation, and how fast?

Remember, your main goal in life is to achieve your own happiness and to fulfill your potential as a human being. Anything that stands in the way of your becoming the very best person you can possibly be needs to be carefully examined and, if necessary, changed.

One of the most popular plays ever written and performed is *Cyrano de Bergerac* by Edmond Rostand. Toward the end of the play, Cyrano is asked why he has been so intensely individualistic his whole life, not caring about the opinions and criticisms of others. He replies with these words: "At an early age, I decided that in life I would choose the line of least resistance, and please at *least myself* in all things."

This is a profound observation. Throughout our lives, because of the desire for approval and the fear of rejection, we bend our personalities and adjust our behaviors so that others will like us and approve of us. We constantly think about what we need to do to be liked and accepted. If we are not careful, we can lose our own personalities and become preoccupied with pleasing other people.

## Please at Least Yourself

But this kind of behavior is a dead end. The likes and dislikes of others change continuously, and often momentarily. It is not possible for you to ever do, be, or say all of the right things necessary to get people to like, respect, and accept you. No matter how hard you try to conform to their wishes, you will always make mistakes, trigger their disapproval, and end up feeling foolish.

The key to happiness is to "please at least yourself in all things." In this way, you can be sure that at least *one person* is happy with what you do and the way things turn out. Since you can never predict what will please others, please at least yourself.

One of the marks of the "fully functioning person," as defined by psychologist Carl Rogers, is that he is not unduly influenced by the opinions of others. A fully mature, fully functioning adult takes the likes, dislikes, and the opinions of others into consideration, but then makes his own decisions and goes his own way. If others do not like or approve of his course of action, he ignores it and carries on regardless.

The key is for you not to worry about what people think of you. The fact is that people are not really thinking about you at all. Most people are so preoccupied with their own problems and concerns that they don't have time to think about the lives or actions of others. Set your own sails. Play your own game. Determine your own destiny. Do whatever seems to you to be the right thing to do at the moment. Please yourself. Ignore the rest.

## Your Time and Your Life Are Precious

Be selfish with your time. Remember, your time is your life, and this life is not a rehearsal for something else. Say "no" to requests for your time that don't move you toward your own goals and personal aspirations. When you say "no," people will often express a little disappointment or even try to make you feel guilty. Nonetheless, you should stick to your guns. Their shallow disapproval will only last for a few seconds, and then they will be off to ask someone else to donate their time or money. And you will be free.

In developing a philosophy of time management, treat your time like money. Allocate your time at your hourly rate. Use this hourly rate as a measuring tool for everything you do.

Concentrate your efforts on high-value tasks—tasks that can pay you what you want to earn. If you want to earn $25 per hour, continually ask yourself, "Is what I am doing right now the sort of work that pays $25 an hour or more?" If it is not, discipline yourself to stop doing it. Discipline yourself to only do work that pays what you really want to earn.

## What Makes You Special

You are your most valuable asset. The part of you that makes you distinct and unique is your mind. It is your ability to think and act. Throughout your life, you should work at upgrading the quality of your thinking and improving your skills for doing the most important things you do in your work and in your life.

Invest regularly in self-improvement and in personal and professional development. Continually look for ways to increase the value of your contribution to the people who depend on you. Dedicate yourself to lifelong learning. The development of your expertise and skills through hard work and study can do more to multiply your value, and your earning ability, than almost anything else you can do.

Personal and professional development is an extremely high-value use of your time. The future impact of self-study can be immeasurable. By developing an additional skill at the right time, you can often catapult your career to much higher levels. You can jump ahead five years by becoming extremely good at a key skill that is very much in demand at the moment.

## See Yourself as a Role Model

In developing your philosophy of time and life management, see yourself as a role model for others. Discipline yourself to set a positive example of personal efficiency for your staff, your co-workers, and your boss, as well as your family and children.

Imagine that others are looking up to you as a model of personal efficiency. Imagine that you are the one who is setting the standards for time management and personal effectiveness in your organization. In everything you do, act as if you are being carefully observed by others. This will force you to be far more disciplined and controlled in your daily actions than if you thought that no one was watching.

## Keep Your Life in Balance

Perhaps the most important part of both the psychology and philosophy of time management is your willingness and ability to keep your life in balance. Use your increased efficiency and productivity to create more time that you can spend with the people you care about the most.

The major sources of life's joys are loving relationships with other people. The great aim of *Time Power* is to enable you to get more happiness and joy with the people you care about the most. Keep your life in balance by regularly asking yourself, "How would I spend my time if I only had six months left to live?"

Once you have decided how you would spend your last six months on earth, you can then ask yourself, "How would I spend my time if I only had six *weeks* left to live?"

How you would spend your time if you only had *six days* to live? Or *six hours*? Finally what would you do, who would you want to talk to, and what would you want to say if you found that you only had *sixty minutes* left to live?

If you only had a short time to live, the only thing you would think about would be the most important people in your life. If you only had a short time left to live, there is nothing that would be more important to you than to reach out and communicate with them in some way. Whatever you would do if you only had a short time left, be sure to include those words and activities into your daily life. You never know.

## Think About Your Values

To keep your life in balance, continually review your values and what is most important to you. You will always feel the happiest, and enjoy the highest levels of self-esteem, when your goals and day-to-day activities are congruent with your values. When what you are doing on the outside is perfectly aligned with the very best person you could possibly be on the inside, you will always feel better than at any other time.

Define and determine your ideal lifestyle. If you were financially independent and you could organize your life in any way you wanted, what would you want to do differently from today? Imagine creating your perfect calendar, week by week, and month by month. If you could design your year from January 1 to December 31, how would you want to spend each day and each week? Where would you like to go? What sort of vacations would you like to take with your family? If your life were ideal, what time would you go to bed and what time would you rise? If you were completely free to choose, what changes would you make in your lifestyle starting today?

The greater clarity you have regarding your ideal lifestyle, the easier it is for you to make the decisions in the short term that will ensure that you create that lifestyle sometime in the future. Clarity is everything.

## Four Ways to Change Your Life

There are only four ways that you can change your life. First, you can do *more* of some things, the things that are working well for you. Second, you can do *less* of other things, those things that are not working in your work and personal life. Third, you can *start* doing something that you are not doing today. And fourth, you can *stop* something altogether.

In bringing your life into better balance, the first questions you ask are, "What should I be doing more of—or less of—to improve the quality of my life?" Almost invariably, you will decide that you need to work more efficiently so that you can spend more time, face to face, with people you care about the most.

Then ask yourself, "What should I start doing that I am not doing today, if I want to improve the quality of my life?" Finally, you should ask, "What should I stop doing altogether, if I want to have more time to do more of the things that are most impor-tant to my life and goals?''

Sit down with your spouse and children and ask them, "What would you like me to do more of, or less of? What would you like me to start doing, or stop doing?" They will give you ideas and opinions that can have a profound effect on the quality of your family relationships.

## Divide Your Life Into Two Parts

Divide your life into two main parts, work and family. Prioritize almost all other activities as secondary to these two primary con-cerns. Instead of doing your work, plus a whole series of other activities, and then giving your family the crumbs that are left over, put your family and your relationships in the center of your life. Organize your work and all your other activities around them.

When you work, work all the time you work. Don't waste time. Don't chat with coworkers or sit around drinking coffee and reading the newspaper. Don't surf the Internet. Don't take long lunches and coffee breaks. Don't start late and finish early. When you work, work! Keep repeating to yourself, "Back to work! Back to work! Back to work!"

When you are with your family, be there 100 percent of the time. Do not read the newspaper, channel surf the television, talk on the phone, or play with your computer. Instead, spend more time face to face with the most important people in your life.

## Time Is the Measure of Value

The quality of a relationship is largely determined by the amount of time you invest in that relationship. You can only increase the value of a relationship to you, and the value of yourself in that relationship, by spending more time with that person. This is as true at work and with customers as it is with your spouse and your children. The more time you invest in them, the deeper and richer will be the quality of your relationship. There is no substitute for time.

## Your Highest Goal

Peace of mind is the greatest human good, and the goal of all human activity. You should select peace of mind as your highest goal and organize your entire life around it. It is only possible when your life is perfectly in balance. You experience peace when you are doing what you were meant to do, with the people with whom you were meant to do it. You experience peace of mind when you are able to feel that your whole life is under your control and consistent with your own values and goals.

To achieve greater peace of mind, listen to your intuition. Trust your inner voice. The more you listen to the "still, small voice" within, the better and more accurate guidance you will receive. As you follow the guidance of this inner voice and this higher power, you will be directed and prompted to do and say the right things in the right way at the right time. Men and women begin to become great when they begin to trust their inner voices.

## Two Types of Time

Work and family require two different types of time. Work requires *quality* time. This is where you set priorities and discipline yourself to focus on the most valuable use of your time. Work is aimed at achieving concrete, measurable results for yourself and other people.

Relationships, however, require *quantity* time. They require long, unbroken periods of time, in thirty-, sixty-, and ninety-minute chunks, or even longer, where you allow ample space for the relationship to unfold and develop. You cannot rush an important relationship. There is no such thing as an efficient family life.

To get the most done at work, you must set clear goals and objectives, organize clear priorities, overcome procrastination, work on your most valuable tasks, and press forward to completion and closure.

To get the very most out of your family and relationships, you must create large periods of unhurried time, where the most pleasurable and enjoyable moments can occur unbidden and unexpectedly.

## Take Care of Yourself
Keep your life in balance by investing time in physical fitness, whether it is walking, running, swimming, or playing golf. Every joint in your body should be exercised and engaged every day. Every muscle should be flexed and stretched every day. You should engage in aerobic exercise three times a week to maintain maximum levels of physical fitness and to perform at your best.

If ever you feel that you are too busy to exercise, it means that your life is out of balance. Whenever you feel that you are on a treadmill that you cannot get off because you have too much to do, it means that you are approaching the breaking point. Whenever you feel that you cannot stop, nature is telling you that you must stop as soon as possible.

During the working day, take frequent breaks to stretch, go for a walk, and change your position. Going for a walk during the day will do more to ensure that you are alert and productive in the afternoon than almost any other activity.

## Maintain High Levels of Mental Energy
In Texas they say, "It is not the size of the dog in the fight, but the size of the fight in the dog." In keeping your life in balance, a paraphrase of this statement would be, "It is not the number of hours you put in, but the quality of thoughtfulness and alertness that you put into those hours."

Decisions that you make, like going to bed early and getting a good night's sleep, have an inordinate impact on the quality of your day. When you are fully rested, you produce higher-quality work than when you are tired because you have not slept enough. When you are fully rested, you make better decisions, which lead to better results. When you are tired, you often make poor decisions, which lead to mistakes and misunderstandings that have to be dealt with or remedied, often at great cost. Fatigue is an enormous time waster.

## Eat Well for High Energy

What you eat, and when you eat, can have a major impact on your levels of energy. When you eat a high-quality breakfast and lunch, you will be brighter and more alert throughout the day. You will be sharper and have more energy. You will be more creative and confident. You will make better decisions and get better results when you are properly nourished. The practice of eating lightly, and avoiding sugars, salts, and fatty foods, will ensure that you have more brain energy, and are more effective, than if you consume foods that are not particularly good for you.

## Teach Your Children Time Power

Make good time management a part of your family life. Teach your children good work habits by helping them with their homework and insisting that it be done promptly, before they do anything else. In more than 8,000 studies of men and women who became high achievers early in life, one of the consistent factors disclosed was that their parents were concerned about and involved in their homework. The more children think that their parents care about them completing homework on time, the more committed the children become to doing good schoolwork. This habit of doing good work, and getting it done promptly, then extends into adult life.

## Take Time Off to Rest and Relax

In keeping your life in balance, relaxing is often the most valuable use of your time. Sometimes, the most important thing you can do is *nothing*. Take at least one or two days off from work each week, and resolve to do nothing work-related on those days. Take the time to smell the roses.

Go for a walk with your spouse, your children, or your friends. Take time to sit back, to think, reflect, and adjust your goals and priorities. Make sure that your daily activities are consistent with your deepest convictions. Be sure that your goals and priorities are congruent with your values.

Take time regularly to think about what is really important to you, and to make sure that the outer aspects of your life are consistent and harmonious with the inner aspects.

## You Can Only Manage Yourself

Finally, in developing your philosophy of time management, continually remind yourself that you cannot manage time. You can only manage yourself. Time management is life management. Time management requires self-control, self-mastery, and self-discipline. Time management behaviors and disciplines are skills that you can learn through practice and repetition. Eventually, your ability to manage yourself and your life will become automatic and easy.

Time management is a lifestyle that must be practiced every hour, every day, all the days of your life. It is the one habit, the one discipline that is essential to everything else you want to achieve. With excellent time management skills and practices, there are no limits.

*"Life is not easy for any of us. But what of that? We must have perseverance and, above all, confidence in ourselves. We must believe that we are gifted for something, and that this something, at whatever cost, must be attained."*
—MARIE CURIE

## Action Exercises

1. Think long term; project forward five and ten years and design your perfect life in every respect. What does it look like?

2. Make a detailed plan today to achieve financial independence by a specific time in the future. How much will you need?

3. Do what you love to do; determine the kind of work that would make you the happiest, then organize your life to do it in an excellent fashion. What is it?

4. Examine your relationships; make sure that you would be happy where you are for the rest of your life. If not, what changes are you going to make?

5. Take excellent care of your physical health; eat, exercise, rest, and behave in such a way that you live to be age 90 or older. What changes should you make in your lifestyle?

6. Change your life by doing more, less, starting, or stopping things in your life to improve your results, and increase your overall satisfaction. What changes are you going to make immediately?

7. Keep your life in balance by placing your family at the center of every decision and organizing everything around them. What could you do, or stop doing, immediately to improve the quality of your family life?

# Index

# About the Author

Brian Tracy is one of America's top business speakers, a best-selling author, and one of the leading consultants and trainers on personal and professional development in the world today. He has started, built, managed, or turned around twenty-two different businesses in diverse industries. Brian addresses 250,000 people each year on subjects ranging from Personal Success and Leadership to Managerial Effectiveness, Creativity, and Sales. He has written more than thirty books, including *Focal Point* (AMACOM), *Maximum Achievement*, and *The 100 Absolutely Unbreakable Laws of Business Success*, and has produced more than 300 audio and video learning programs. Much of his work has been translated into other languages and is being used in thirty-five countries.

Brian has consulted with more than 500 companies—IBM, McDonnell Douglas, and The Million Dollar Round Table among them—and has trained more than 2,000,000 people personally. His ideas are proven, practical, and fast-acting. His readers and seminar participants learn a series of techniques and strategies that they can use immediately to get better results in their lives and careers.

# Focal Point Advanced Coaching and Mentoring Program

This intensive one-year program is ideal for ambitious, successful men and women who want to achieve better results and greater balance in their lives.

If you are already earning more than $100,000 per year, and if you have a large degree of control over your time, in four full days with Brian Tracy in San Diego—one day every three months—you will learn how to double your productivity and income and double your time off with your family at the same time.

Every ninety days, you work with Brian Tracy and an elite group of successful entrepreneurs, self-employed professionals, and top sales-people for an entire day. During this time together, you form a "master-mind alliance" from which you gain ideas and insights that you can apply immediately to your work and personal life.

The Focal Point Advanced Coaching and Mentoring Program is based on four areas of effectiveness: **Clarification, Simplification, Maximization, and Multiplication.** You learn a series of methods and strategies to incorporate these principles into everything you do.

**Clarification**: You learn how to develop absolute clarity about who you really are and what you really want in each of seven key areas of life. You determine your values, vision, mission, purpose, and goals for yourself, your family, and your work.

**Simplification**: You learn how to dramatically simplify your life, getting rid of all the little tasks and activities that contribute little to the achievement of your real goals of high income, excellent family relationships, superb health and fitness, and financial independence. You learn how to streamline, delegate, outsource, minimize, and eliminate all those activities that are of little value.

**Maximization**: You learn how to get the very most out of yourself by implementing the best time and personal management tools and techniques. You learn how to get more done in less time, how to increase your income rapidly, and how to have even more time for your personal life.

**Multiplication**: You learn how to leverage your special strengths to accomplish vastly more than you could by relying on your own efforts and resources. You learn how to use other people's money, other people's efforts, other people's ideas, and other people's customers and contacts to increase your personal productivity and earn more money.

Brian Tracy gives the Focal Point Advanced Coaching and Mentoring Program personally four times each year in San Diego. Each session includes complete pre-work, detailed exercises and instruction, all materials, plus meals and refreshments during the day. At the end of each session, you emerge with a complete blueprint for the next ninety days.

If you are interested in attending this program, visit our Web site at www.briantracy.com, or phone our Vice President, Victor Risling, at 1-800-542-4252 (ext. 17) to request an application form or more information. We look forward to hearing from you.